CATHERINE PHIPPS

MODERN PRESSURE COOKING

The Comprehensive Guide
to Stovetop and Electric Cookers,
with over 200 Recipes

Photography by Andrew Hayes-Watkins

Hardie Grant

QUADRILLE

INTRODUCTION

Pressure cookers have been around for a long time. It is over 340 years since Denis Papin first presented his 'steam digester', an ingenious invention that created a pressurized build up of steam inside a weighted, sealed vessel. There have been many manifestations since and they have fallen in and out of fashion, no more so than in the last 70–80 years. When I first started writing about them over a decade ago, persuading people away from outdated negative preconceptions was often difficult but in the interim years my job has become easier. This is in part due to familiarity – some of our most prominent chefs have talked about them being a 'secret weapon' in their professional kitchens, they have started to appear regularly on TV shows such as *MasterChef* and certain brands of electric pressure cookers have become so popular they have achieved cult status. I am hopeful that at last the UK has started to catch up with the rest of the world when it comes to understanding their value – that it is becoming fairly well accepted that a modern pressure cooker is a safe, efficient and easy-to-use piece of equipment – and that the food cooked within is a pleasure to eat.

WHY MODERN PRESSURE COOKING?

For me, the joy of pressure cooking is the fact that I am able to cook properly from scratch, but in a fast, convenient and sustainable way. This feels increasingly important when addressing some of the challenges of modern living we all face and cooking can be just one more thing we have to do on a difficult day when we are time-pressed, stressed and over-tired. Most of us are worried about climate change and are trying to navigate our way through the endless debates on how to be sustainable, and food is often at the centre of these debates. We know that

a diet high in ultra-processed foods is really bad for us and that we should be cooking much more than many of us do. I believe that being a modern cook paradoxically involves winding the clock back to a time before eating ultra-processed food was the norm and cooking properly again – but with the added benefit of a much wider range of ingredients to work with and more mod cons to make us more efficient. We need to be mindful of what we cook but also how we cook it. I would struggle to do this to the extent I do without the help of a pressure cooker. A pressure cooker helps you in the kitchen by saving you time (cutting off around 70% of the cooking time), making certain processes easier, reducing your fuel bill by a quite staggering amount, as well as being much greener as your consumption will be so much lower. It will also reduce your water consumption considerably. In short, it is a very sustainable option in the kitchen. This is in addition to the benefits in terms of flavour and nutrition. Meat will be tender, flavours will intensify, vegetables will keep their colour and vitality as well as maintaining a higher nutritional value than their conventionally cooked counterparts. There is no compromise on flavour as the flavour will be better.

HOW TO GET THE MOST OUT OF YOUR PRESSURE COOKER AND THIS BOOK

In a novel by one of my favourite writers, Joan Aiken, the resilient and practical heroine reaches for her pressure cooker and says in an aside that she never goes far without one. This is me. I am writing this from a coastal holiday cottage. The weather is typical English summer holiday weather – changeable, frequently wet and grey. We often return from a day's outing, uncomfortably damp, if not sodden, needing comfort and warmth from the food we eat, which is why I bring the pressure cooker. It means I can quickly whip up fast soups, pastas and rice dishes without resorting to processed food. But lest you think pressure cookers are a cold-weather tool, for comfort food only, let me catch you up with those in hotter climates who understand that they are indispensable because shorter cooking times mean cooler kitchens. In warmer weather they are put to good use preparing eggs, meat for cold cuts, potatoes, pulses and grains for salads, lightly steaming vegetables. If we're lucky enough to be able to get good seafood, we can use them for a seafood boil too. I know people who take them camping (it makes sense as you will conserve gas or wood), they are beloved in boating communities where fuel and water are always at a premium and they are necessary if you want to cook anything at a high altitude.

This book is aimed at people who want to cook. I feel it is important to say this right from the start; a pressure cooker isn't a replacement for the hands-on mechanics of cooking, it just speeds up part of the process. Therefore, while there are a lot of one-pot recipes and even a few dishes where you can put minimally prepped ingredients into the cooker and that is all you need to do, the majority of the recipes do require some preparation on your part prior to pressure cooking. To really get the most out of them you need to think about how they might help you at times when you might not have considered using them. For example, let's take a traditional roast dinner. Even if you are roasting the meat in your oven (and you can do it in the pressure cooker if you want to, see page 56), the pressure cooker can help you with other elements. You can par-boil the potatoes and parsnips in the

pressure cooker, you can cook the sides (greens, numerous other vegetables) in moments, you may have made the stock for your gravy in it...and even if you aren't saving a massive amount of time and fuel with this, every little helps and quickly adds up. I also find timings easier when I don't have to factor in boiling water to cook vegetables, for example. It is all geared up to helping you be much more efficient in the kitchen.

I have deliberately included a lot of classic, favourite recipes in this book, mainly to showcase as many different ingredients and styles of pressure-cooker-friendly dishes as I can; look to the variations in the recipes for examples of how to tweak them, they are all designed to be flexible within the parameters of timings and in some cases, ratios. This should quickly give you the confidence to experiment and convert your own recipes or other conventional recipes to pressure cooking. The main issues you will contend with are how much liquid to use – conventional recipes need considerably more – and whether ingredients have similar cooking times, plus how to get around it when they don't; by following a few recipes you will soon get to grips with both of these things.

I hope you will be inspired by the many ways in which you can use your pressure cooker and that the recipes will give you the confidence to use it to its full potential. I am constantly learning, considering every dish I might cook conventionally with the question, 'Will this work in the pressure cooker?' If you have this mindset – if you approach using your pressure cooker as not just a souped-up version of a saucepan or stockpot, but something that can also sauté, braise and even bake and roast – you will get so much more out of it.

HOW DO PRESSURE COOKERS WORK?

A pressure cooker is simply a saucepan with a specially adapted lid. This lid has a rubber gasket (a circular seal that fits snugly within the inner rim of the pressure cooker) and which expands as the pressure cooker heats up and creates a tight seal. The lid is also weighted. The combination of the seal and the weight ensures that the steam builds up inside the pressure cooker, which in turn increases the heat beyond boiling point to up to around 119–121°C (246–249°F). This means that on average you can reduce cooking times by around 70%, depending on how the cooker is weighted – the more weight, the more pressure and the higher the temperature. And as some of the cooking time takes place off the heat when the pressure cooker is dropping pressure (so still cooking at above boiling point), this 70% saving in time translates to more savings on fuel consumption.

Most modern pressure cookers will work at two different pressures – low pressure, which is very useful for cooking delicate foods, such as fish and eggs, and high pressure for just about everything else. The measurement of weight is usually defined by its PSI – pound per square inch in the US, but commonly used in the UK as well, and kilopascals for everywhere using metric measurements (kPa). To be able to follow the timings I've given in this book, you need a pressure cooker that has a PSI of 12–15PSI/90–103kPa.

However, like ovens, all pressure cookers do vary from one another, so you may occasionally find the timings are on the fast side. I have deliberately chosen a faster time rather than slower on the basis that it is much better to initially under- rather than over-cook your food.

WHICH PRESSURE COOKER?

I am assuming that most of the people tempted to buy this book will already have a pressure cooker of some sort, but if you don't and you are browsing because you are thinking of buying one (hooray!), there are a few things to consider when deciding which sort to buy. The good news is that pressure cookers have changed dramatically in the last 20–30 years. Modern designs have more safety features, mainly involving extra safety valves for releasing steam so pressure cannot build up beyond what is safe. As long as you follow the instructions on how to use your pressure cooker safely, you can use it without fear of incident. The other main feature of modern pressure cookers is that the vessels are completely sealed when cooking at high pressure. Old-fashioned pressure cookers will normally either have a small but constant amount of steam leaving the pressure cooker or will let it out at intervals. Modern pressure cookers will not do this – when they are cooking at pressure, they will be virtually silent and as they do not let out steam, they won't let out any flavour either. This makes them much more efficient in terms of how much water you use – a modern pressure cooker needs much, much less to operate effectively.

ELECTRIC OR STOVETOP?

This is the first decision you will need to make. There are pros and cons to both, so while it generally comes down to personal preference here are a few pointers to help:

Space: Do you have space to keep an electric pressure cooker on your countertop? If you keep it in a cupboard, the chances are you won't use it nearly as much as you could. If you don't, then a stovetop is a more practical solution.

Functionality: Stovetops are made for pressure cooking and to a certain extent conventional cooking – if you keep them on your stovetop, you can use them as an extra saucepan or sauté pan if not cooking at pressure. Electric pressure cookers are multifunction cookers – they can work as a slow cooker, yogurt maker, they can be set to time and have a keep warm function. Some of the more recent models have air fryers built into the lid – useful for browning dishes such as gratins or pot roasts you have pressure cooked.

Efficiency: Twelve years ago, when I was writing my first pressure cooker book, I put a modern stovetop over an electric pressure cooker every time. However, these days there is now very little in it – it used to take longer to cook certain foods in an electric pressure cooker, these days, this is rarely the case. My only issue with electric pressure cookers is that sometimes when fast releasing they can take much longer than a stovetop to drop pressure – plus you can't put them under the cold tap.

Portability: Think about when you are likely to use your pressure cooker and what for. Does it need to be portable? I take mine on self-catering holidays (I would take them camping if I liked camping).

Power Source: An electric pressure cooker, or a stovetop using an electric, preferably induction, heat source is a much greener option than a stovetop using gas or oil, especially if you are on a green tariff with energy from renewables. If using induction, make sure the pressure cooker is induction friendly (most are). Stovetops also work well with range cookers such as Agas, as the shorter cooking times help keep the lids down.

OTHER GENERAL CONSIDERATIONS

Size: For most small families, a 4.5-litre (4 or 5-quart) pressure cooker is a reasonable size. All the recipes in this book will work in a pressure cooker of this size although certain things will be a snug fit – for example a large chicken or a deep 20cm (8in) cake tin. It will also put limitations on how much stock you can make at any one time. If you really want to make the most out of pressure cooking, including batch cooking and stock making, a 6-litre (6 or 8-quart) version makes more sense. I use different sizes for different dishes, and since writing my first book have come to really love some of the sauté-pan-sized pressure cookers available. The main advantages to these are that they take less time to come up to high pressure – especially useful when cooking greens – and as they are shallow, they are great for serving directly at table. However, I would never rely on one of these alone because they are limiting. The ideal combination for me is one of these and a larger capacity 6-litre version. Some pressure cooker manufacturers do deals that will give you two different-sized pressure cooker bases with one lid, which gives you the best versatility – and if you find you are wanting to use them both at the same time, you can always buy an extra lid.

When considering size, look also at dimensions. Consider what you will be using your pressure cooker for. Do you need a wide surface area for browning? Are you likely to want to use your pressure cooker for cakes and desserts? If so, wider is better as you will need it to hold a 20cm (8in) dish or tin with space around the sides.

HOW TO USE YOUR PRESSURE COOKER SAFELY

If you don't read anything else in this introduction, please, please read this section. This will give you a step-by-step guide on how to use your pressure cooker, and while much of it refers to safety features on a stovetop, most still applies to electric pressure cookers too. If you are using pressure cookers for the first time, this may seem a lot to take in at once, but you will be amazed how quickly it will all become second nature.

I have said that today's modern pressure cookers are safe to use, but this comes with a huge caveat – you must treat them with respect, as you would any other piece of kitchen equipment – like, for example, a sharp kitchen knife, a pressure cooker can be dangerous if we are careless. So please, in order for your pressure cooker to work at optimum efficiency and safety, please pay attention to the following:

1 Start the cooking process. This will often involve some kind of browning or sautéing, although in the case of some soups, and cooking batches of beans, this will not be the case. Use the pressure cooker to brown as normal – if using an electric pressure cooker you will usually have more than one setting for this function, so be guided by the recipe in terms of whether you need it low (gentle sauté) or high (browning).

2 If sautéing or browning first, it is very, very important to deglaze. The reason for this is that if using a stovetop, the base can burn and inhibit the pressure cooker from coming up to pressure, and in an electric cooker it will trigger a burn alarm.

3 Add the right amount of liquid. Liquid is necessary to create steam. How much you need is dependent on what you are cooking (how much liquid it gives out during the cooking process) and the size of the pressure cooker (you need less for a smaller cooker as you need less steam to create pressure). Please be guided by the recipes in this book, rather than your instruction manuals (which tend to add too much) until you are comfortable.

4 Lock the lid in place. All pressure cookers have slightly different mechanisms for this. Some involve setting the right pressure – it is very important to do this because if you forget, the cooker will not come up to pressure and your food will burn.

5 Bring the pot up to high pressure. For stovetops, you should set over a high heat and bring it up to pressure as quickly as possible. After years of troubleshooting for people, I have found that this is the most common mistake made. It feels counter-intuitive to say that doing this on a low heat, slowly, will result in burning, but it will. As soon as pressure is reached, the risk of burning stops. So set over your fastest ring, the highest setting on your induction, the hot plate of your Aga.

YOU MUST NOT LEAVE YOUR PRESSURE COOKER UNATTENDED WHILE IT IS COMING UP TO PRESSURE. This is very important. If you wander off and leave your pressure cooker on a high heat, once it has reached high pressure it will continue to create steam and the steam will have nowhere to go. This is how explosions used to happen, back in the days when pressure cookers weren't blessed with a multitude of safety features. Steam would build and might eventually create enough pressure to force the lid off. Today, if you forget about the pressure cooker, the steam will be released safely, but as with conventional cooking, you run the risk of the cooker boiling dry and burning. There is a clear advantage to having an electric pressure cooker if you are prone to inattention – it does everything automatically for you.

6 Maintain high pressure. As soon as your cooker reaches high pressure, it will need less heat from your heat source to maintain it. At this point you can turn the heat down or move to a smaller ring. It will take a little trial and error before you work out exactly how much heat your pressure cooker needs to maintain the pressure so keep an eye on it to start with – if it drops pressure you will need to return it to a higher heat. Once you are sure that you have the right heat to maintain the pressure, you can set your timer and leave the cooker to its own devices. It does not need the same attention. As before, you will not need to do this with an electric pressure cooker as it will automatically adjust to maintain the pressure.

7 Releasing pressure. The recipes in this book are very specific about how pressure should be released. It's important to pay attention to which method to use as it will impact on how the food cooks.

• Natural pressure release: This simply involves removing your pressure cooker from the heat and leaving it to drop pressure on its own. The contents of the cooker will continue to cook off the heat during this period (for much of it the temperature will still be above boiling point) and this has been factored in to all the timings in this book. The benefits of this are especially evident with meat dishes, as this will give the meat time to relax and stay tender. It also means that any steam will condense back into the sealed cooker and no flavour or moisture will be lost.

• Natural pressure release with manual release: There are a few recipes and methods in this book that will tell you to leave your cooker to drop pressure naturally for a certain period of time, then release the rest manually. There are several reasons for this: sometimes the contents needs to settle before you release the pressure (this is especially relevant to starchy dishes); sometimes it will be because it impacts on the timings/how the food cooks. If using an electric pressure cooker, you can set it to time the length of the natural pressure release before manually releasing the rest; with a stovetop you will need to time it yourself.

• Manual pressure release: There are a couple of ways to do this. With all types of pressure cooker it will involve a pressure release mechanism – you should see your user manual for details, but it will normally be a sliding mechanism, a dial or depressing a pressure gauge. This will release a jet of steam that you need to keep away from, so keep your head well back and protect your hands and forearms with oven gloves. If using a stovetop, you can also put it under a running cold tap. This is faster and safer, and especially useful if you need to fast pressure release with anything starchy as it will make sure starchy steam and water won't spit out, but I try to avoid it because it involves using water unnecessarily.

Some recipes may call for you to gradually release the pressure manually – this will mainly be because the contents inside the pressure cooker are starchy, and you don't want starchy liquid spitting up through the safety vents. How easy this is to do depends largely on your pressure cooker – some will allow you to slightly open the vent and will then drop pressure quietly on their own; others will need you to do this in short bursts.

8 Some recipes will involve some simmering after pressure release, mainly to reduce liquid. You can add other ingredients at this stage. I often add greens at this point and return the pressure cooker to high pressure after I have added them. Be guided by individual recipes on when this will work as certain dishes, particularly those that are thick and starchy such as dals, will burn if you attempt to return them to pressure.

You can also put your pressure cooker under a hot grill if you are careful. Triple wrap the handles in foil in order to do this.

9 After you have finished using your pressure cooker, make sure the lid is cleaned properly, especially if you have cooked anything starchy. Check all of the safety mechanisms to make sure they aren't blocked and wash the rubber gasket thoroughly.

USEFUL EQUIPMENT

A timer: Most pressure cooker timings are very specific; the shorter the cooking time, the more precise you need to be. Kitchen timers are therefore essential.

A probe thermometer: Not essential, but very useful if you are cooking chickens or large pieces of meat and want to be absolutely sure that they are cooked to a safe temperature.

Trivets and steamer baskets: Most pressure cookers will come with at least one trivet, for elevating cake tins, dishes etc. I have a collection of different depths, useful as it means I can sit a deeper cake tin lower in the cooker, for example. You can also use an upturned steamer basket, and for those dishes that do not need to be elevated above the water level, you can simply fold up a piece of tea towel or an old napkin to put in the base instead – it will stop your dishes from rattling around.

Foil and baking paper (and how to replace them): We are all trying to reduce our consumption of non-reusable items, so I do try to keep foil and baking paper use to a minimum; see below for an alternative to baking paper. One foil item that is indispensable, is a foil sling or handle – this is a long piece of foil that is folded over until it is 4 sheets thick. You can then use it as a handle by placing any receptacle in the centre of it and using it to lower in and out of the pressure cooker. This is particularly useful if the space between a cake tin and the sides of the pressure cooker is tight. Simply fold the edges down to fit inside, then unroll when you want to remove and lift out. You can reuse this again and again. Alternatively, you could make a fabric one, preferably double thickness and hemmed.

Teflon-coated fabric: In order to turn my pressure cooker into a non-stick vessel, I use Teflon-coated fabric a lot – it is heavier than non-stick paper so will sit happily in the base without moving around and can be reused endlessly – I have some that is almost 20 years old. It comes in various thicknesses and the thinner version can be cut to various sizes to cover dishes and ramekins.

QUICK AND
SIMPLE SOUPS

There are a lot of very robust full-meal soups and stews dotted throughout this book, but this chapter is devoted to the really fast fixes – the sort of thing I might make first thing in the morning to fill the children's Thermoses before school, or consider making for myself during the working day. It's also the quickest route to comfort food I know – a bowl of creamy, buttery homemade tomato soup (see page 14) is perfect when all you want is something uncomplicated and really easy to eat.

Many of these soups are really good as receptacles for leftovers or a few random vegetables that need using up. They are also really useful for eking out more expensive ingredients that can be used in very small quantities to flavour or garnish. Therefore, don't be surprised by the number of recipes that call for flexibility. As long as you pay attention to the quantities and ratios, especially in respect of liquid, you can swap, mix and match to your heart's content.

This is the one chapter where I use a style of cooking that is barely cooking at all – which basically involves putting all the ingredients into a pressure cooker with very little prep and even without initial sautéing. I was dubious about the merits of this – I always saw sautéing as something essential to flavour. However, I am no longer convinced, when it comes to pressure cooking at least, because caramelization naturally takes place during pressure cooking because of the higher temperature. In fact, the main reason I sauté these days is to allow the vegetables to give off a little liquid and perhaps collapse down a bit, not really necessary when making soup.

There is good pedigree with this method, and I don't mean all the grubbily titled 'dump and go' recipes you find on the internet, but with a Marcella Hazan method for tomato sauce that I have been making for years, in which tomatoes are simmered with a whole onion and lots of butter. It works like a dream.

BUTTERY TOMATO SOUP

SERVES 4

2 x 400g (14oz) cans chopped tomatoes

2 celery sticks, roughly chopped

1 large onion, halved

2 carrots, roughly chopped

1 small sweet potato or 200g (7oz) piece butternut squash, unpeeled and roughly chopped

4 garlic cloves, peeled

A pinch of ground cinnamon

1 litre (35fl oz) vegetable or chicken stock or water

2 large sprigs of basil

50g (1¾oz) butter

A pinch of sugar (optional)

Sea salt and freshly ground black pepper

This is a very simple, if counter-intuitive, recipe, based on the famous Marcella Hazan tomato sauce. The addition of butter gives the soup a texture and flavour as comforting as the classic canned variety – but it has more depth, is definitely better for you and is not remotely laborious to make.

You can make it with water instead of stock if you like and vary the vegetables – try to at least use celery, onion and carrot, but apart from that, most root vegetables, squashes or bulbs such as fennel will work.

This could not be simpler. Put everything in the pressure cooker, season well with salt and pepper, then bring up to pressure. Cook at high pressure for 10 minutes, then leave to drop pressure naturally. Taste and add a pinch of sugar for extra sweetness, if you like. Fish out the basil sprigs, then purée. Push through a sieve for an ultra smooth texture if you feel it is necessary.

VARIATIONS

Tomato and Red Lentil Soup
This is the version I do when everyone in the house is feeling a bit coldy and sorry for themselves: add 30g (1oz) well-rinsed split red lentils, 10g (¼oz) piece ginger and an (optional) red pepper, roughly chopped. Include 1 teaspoon each of ground turmeric, cumin and coriander in the spicing. Replace the basil with 1 small bunch of coriander (cilantro) if you like, cooking the stems with the soup and adding the leaves just before puréeing.

Vegan Tomato and Coconut Soup
Replace the butter and 300ml (10½fl oz) of the vegetable stock or water with coconut milk. This will work with either the main or lentil version.

SPICED PUMPKIN AND LENTIL SOUP

SERVES 4

1 large onion, halved or quartered

1 celery stick, cut into 3 pieces

1 large carrot, cut into large chunks, unpeeled

1 large piece butternut squash, sweet potato or pumpkin, cut into large chunks (unpeeled)

100g (3½oz) split red or yellow lentils

15g (½oz) piece ginger, roughly chopped (don't bother peeling)

4 garlic cloves, peeled

10g (¼oz) piece fresh turmeric, sliced (don't bother peeling), or 1 tsp ground turmeric

1 tbsp curry powder of your choice

2 tbsp coriander (cilantro) leaves and stems

800ml (28fl oz) vegetable or chicken stock or water

25g (1oz) butter, ghee or coconut oil

Sea salt and freshly ground black pepper

This soup is another one to vary depending on what you have in the fridge. It might have sweet potato or butternut squash or pumpkin, onion or shallots, or curry powder or a collection of spices – you get the picture. But whatever you do, it will be warming. You will notice I don't bother peeling squash or sweet potatoes – as long as it is clean and relatively blemish-free, the skin can be eaten and just adds fibre. If you are worried that your blender won't deal with this adequately or you don't want to push it through a sieve at the end, you can always peel them.

Put everything in the pressure cooker and season with salt and plenty of black pepper. Close the lid, bring up to high pressure and cook at high pressure for 5 minutes. Leave to drop pressure naturally, then blitz using a jug or hand blender. You can pass the soup through a sieve if you like.

VARIATION

Jerusalem Artichoke, Mushroom and Lentil Soup
This is a different kind of warming – robust and satisfying on cold winter days. Replace the butternut squash with 250g (9oz) peeled and chopped Jerusalem artichokes and 150g (5½oz) chopped mushrooms. Dice the vegetables instead of roughly chopping them and increase the stock to 1 litre (35fl oz). You could add diced bacon to this to enhance the smokiness of the artichokes, or to keep it vegetarian, add 1 teaspoon of dulse flakes. Blending optional.

POTATO AND WHITE CABBAGE SOUP

SERVES 4

1 large potato, peeled and cut into large chunks

Around 200g (7oz) white cabbage, roughly chopped

1 onion or leek, roughly chopped

1 garlic clove

800ml (28fl oz) vegetable, chicken or even smoked ham stock

15g (½oz) butter

100ml (3½fl oz) whole milk or single (light) cream

Sea salt and freshly ground black pepper

TO SERVE

1 small bunch of flat-leaf parsley, chervil or dill, finely chopped

A few rashers of bacon, fried until crisp and crumbled (optional)

The basic recipe here is wonderful – creamy and soothing. But you can vary the flavour by replacing the potato with celeriac (celery root) or Jerusalem artichokes or even turn it into cream of chicken (see Variation, below). Using a smoked ham stock adds an extra dimension and is especially good with a garnish of crisp bacon or ham.

Put the potato, cabbage, onion or leek and garlic in the pressure cooker and season with plenty of salt and pepper. Add the stock and butter and stir. Close the lid and bring up to high pressure. Cook for 5 minutes and allow to drop pressure naturally. Add the milk or cream and purée using a jug or hand blender. Sprinkle with the herbs and bacon, if using, before serving.

VARIATION

Cream of Chicken Soup
Replace the cabbage with an extra leek and 100g (3½oz) cooked chicken. Use chicken stock. Add 50g (1¾oz) finely chopped chicken after blitzing to provide a little texture.

1-MINUTE GREEN SOUP

1 tbsp olive oil

15g (½oz) butter

1 onion or leek, finely chopped

100g (3½oz) greens of your choice, stems chopped separately if applicable (green cabbage, kale or chard work well)

2 garlic cloves, finely chopped

200g (7oz) broccoli, cut into florets

750ml (26fl oz) vegetable or chicken stock

Zest and juice of 1 lemon or lime

Sea salt and freshly ground black pepper

OPTIONAL EXTRA

Large handfuls of herbs of your choice, chopped (mint, flat-leaf parsley, chervil, dill, fennel are especially good)

The beauty of cooking greens this quickly in the pressure cooker is that they remain a fresh and vibrant green. You can pretty much get away with using any type of greens – not just leaves but asparagus, courgettes (zucchini), peas or beans too. Just be careful about collards or any of the woodier kales that might be better destemmed.

Heat the olive oil and butter in your pressure cooker. Add the onion or leek and any stems from the greens and sauté for 5 minutes just to start the softening process. Add the garlic, broccoli and leaves and pour over the stock. Season with salt and pepper and add the lemon zest.

Close the lid and bring up to high pressure. Lower the heat to maintain pressure and cook for 1 minute only, then fast release. Purée using a jug or stick blender until smooth. If using the herbs, add at this point and whizz again until the soup is flecked with green. Taste and add the lemon juice a little at a time, tasting until the balance is right.

VARIATIONS

Broccoli and Cheese Soup
Add 1 tablespoon of wholegrain mustard when you stir in the garlic and broccoli. Don't add the lemon zest or juice. Add 100g (3½oz) mature cheese after blending, along with 50ml (1¾fl oz) double (heavy) cream.

Cauliflower Cheese Soup
Replace the greens and broccoli with a small cauliflower and proceed as for the Broccoli and Cheese Soup variation (above).

Spiced
Add 15g (½oz) finely chopped ginger with the garlic along with ½ teaspoon of ground turmeric and a pinch of ground cinnamon. Add a handful of mint and coriander (cilantro) leaves with the broccoli and kale.

SPICED LENTIL SOUP WITH GREENS

SERVES 4

2 tbsp olive oil

1 onion, very finely chopped

1 carrot, finely diced (optional)

2 garlic cloves, finely chopped

½ tsp ground cinnamon

½ tsp ground cardamom

½ tsp ground allspice

¼ tsp ground cloves

A large pinch of saffron, ground with a pinch of sea salt (optional)

A piece of pared lemon zest

200g (7oz) brown, green or red lentils, well rinsed

8 blocks of chopped frozen spinach or 100g (3½oz) chard or kale, finely chopped

1 litre (35fl oz) vegetable or chicken stock or water

Sea salt and freshly ground black pepper

This is one of those soups with which you can travel the world, as it will take on all kinds of flavours. I love the combination below, but might instead use a tablespoon of ras el hanout, or a favourite curry powder or even a paste – try harissa.

I love the convenience of storecupboard and/or freezer soups and this one will work with frozen spinach, or you can finely chop any robust greens, such as chard or kale.

Brown or green lentils will give a little more texture and an earthier flavour, red will collapse completely. Use one or the other or even better, a combination of them both.

Heat the oil in your pressure cooker. Add the onion and carrot, if using, and sauté on a high heat for 5 minutes until the onion starts to take on some colour. Stir in the garlic, spices, lemon zest and lentils and stir to combine. Season with salt and pepper.

If using the blocks of spinach, drop on top; stir in any other greens. Pour over the stock. Bring up to high pressure and cook for 2 minutes if using red lentils or 5 minutes if using brown or green lentils, then allow to drop pressure naturally. Remove the lemon zest before serving.

VARIATION

Lentil and Herb Soup
This makes a really good base for a very herby soup, utilizing those generous bunches of herbs we can find in good international supermarkets. Separate the stems from the leaves. Tie the long stems loosely together and add to the soup for flavour along with the lentils. After the soup has cooked, remove the bundle. Finely chop the leaves and stir in.

KALE AND CHORIZO SOUP

SERVES 4

200g (7oz) cooking chorizo (picante or dulce – it's up to you)

2 red onions, cut into wedges

400g (14oz) waxy or floury potatoes, sliced

50ml (1¾fl oz) red wine, port or sherry (optional)

2 bay leaves

800ml (28fl oz) chicken, ham or vegetable stock or water

150g (5½oz) cavolo nero or similar, coarsely shredded

Sea salt and freshly ground black pepper

One of the best and simplest of chunky soups, based on a caldo verde. The flavours are also good with pasta, almost like a pared down minestrone – see the Variation, below.

Choose the type of potato you use according to the texture of soup you prefer. Floury potatoes will break down a little and thicken the soup, waxy will keep their shape and will not give out so much starch so the soup will remain brothy.

Add the chorizo to your pressure cooker and fry, stirring for 2–3 minutes until browned on both sides and rendering out plenty of ochre-coloured oil. Add the onion and potatoes and stir until coated in the oil. Pour in the red wine, port or sherry if using (port or sherry adds a pleasant sweetness) and wait for most of it to bubble off, then add the bay leaves and stock. Season with salt and pepper and pile the cavolo nero on top.

Bring up to high pressure and cook for 2 minutes. Allow to drop pressure naturally.

VARIATIONS

You could double carb this and add a handful of short pasta, broken noodles or some cooked beans. You won't have to adjust the cooking time – 2 minutes at high pressure, plus the natural release, gives it plenty of time to cook.

Chestnuts work really well with all the flavours in this soup. Replace 100g (3½oz) of the potatoes with 100g (3½oz) cooked chestnuts and add 50g (1¾oz) chopped tomatoes too.

SMOKED HADDOCK CHOWDER

SERVES 4

300g (10½oz) smoked haddock

2 bay leaves

A few black peppercorns

100ml (3½fl oz) white wine (optional)

25g (1oz) butter

1 onion, finely chopped

1 celery stick, finely chopped

400g (14oz) root vegetables (floury potato, celeriac/celery root, sweet potato), diced

2 leeks, finely sliced

100g (3½oz) sweetcorn (optional)

75ml (2½fl oz) single (light) cream or whole milk

Sea salt and freshly ground black pepper

OPTIONAL EXTRAS

100g (3½oz) cooked prawns (shrimp)

A few cooked clams, mussels or cockles

TO GARNISH

A few chopped chives, finely chopped chervil, curly or flat-leaf parsley or dill

While it is possible to pressure cook milk in certain circumstances, I don't recommend it in soups as it can curdle. Therefore this method – that you can use to adapt any of your favourite chowder recipes – involves adding the dairy element after the initial high-pressure cooking.

Put the smoked haddock, bay leaves and peppercorns in your pressure cooker and cover with 400ml (14fl oz) water and the wine, if using, or simply 500ml (17fl oz) water. Bring up to low pressure and immediately remove from the heat. Leave to drop pressure. Remove the fish to a plate and strain the liquid into a jug. When the fish is cool enough to handle, remove any bones and skin and roughly flake.

Melt the butter in your pressure cooker and add the onion and celery. Stir for a few minutes until the onion is looking translucent, then stir in the root vegetables and leeks. Stir for a few minutes until everything is glossy with butter, then add the sweetcorn, if using, and pour over the reserved cooking liquor. Season with a little salt and pepper. Bring up to high pressure and cook for 3 minutes, then fast release.

Stir in the cream or milk and return the fish, plus any additional seafood to the cooker. Stir to combine and heat through for another minute or two. Serve garnished with the herbs.

VARIATION

Bacon and Clam Chowder
Start the recipe by sautéing 100g (3½oz) bacon lardons with the onion and celery. Add a bay leaf to the soup before pressure cooking. After cooking at pressure, stir in the drained contents of a can of clams along with the cream and make sure it is piping hot before serving. Replace the water in the recipe with fish stock if possible.

SPICED LAMB AND LENTIL SOUP

SERVES 4

1 tbsp coconut oil, ghee or olive oil

300g (10½oz) lamb or goat neck fillet, leg or shoulder, finely diced and trimmed of fat

1 large onion, finely diced

250g (9oz) carrots, finely diced

250g (9oz) swede (rutabaga), finely diced

2 turnips, finely diced

2 celery sticks, diced

3 garlic cloves, crushed or grated

25g (1oz) piece ginger, grated

1 tbsp medium curry powder

1 litre (35fl oz) lamb or chicken stock

50g (1¾oz) split red lentils, well rinsed

50g (1¾oz) green or brown lentils, well rinsed

25g (1oz) basmati rice, well rinsed

1 red pepper, diced

2 small eating apples, peeled, cored and diced (optional)

Sea salt

TO SERVE

1 small bunch of coriander (cilantro) leaves

1 tbsp mango chutney (optional)

VARIATION

This can be made with just vegetables or with chicken, or – in true Boxing Day spirit – with any leftover meat. Either way, you can cook everything all at once instead of in two stages. Simply stir all the ingredients together, add the stock and cook at high pressure for 3 minutes before leaving it to drop pressure naturally.

This is a chunky version of mulligatawny. It has a retro feel, slightly reminiscent of a turkey Boxing Day curry because of the apple, but it is none the worse for that.

Heat the oil or ghee in your pressure cooker. Add the lamb, vegetables, garlic, ginger and curry powder and stir thoroughly until everything is well coated. Add the stock and season well with salt. Close the lid and bring up to high pressure. Cook for 3 minutes, then remove from the heat and leave to drop pressure naturally.

Add the lentils, rice, red pepper and apples, if using. Stir thoroughly, fix on the lid and bring up to high pressure again. This time cook for 2 minutes and again, leave to drop pressure naturally.

Serve with a garnish of coriander (cilantro) leaves and the mango chutney, if you like.

SUMMER VEGETABLE SOUP

SERVES 4

1 tbsp olive oil

1 onion, finely chopped

½ fennel bulb, finely diced
(fronds reserved)

2 garlic cloves, finely chopped

50g (1¾oz) fregola or other
short pasta or large couscous
(maftoul)

100ml (3½fl oz) white wine

750ml (26fl oz) chicken or
vegetable stock

A bouquet garni of: 1 stem each
parsley, basil, oregano, tarragon,
plus 1 strip pared lemon zest

2 ripe tomatoes, finely diced or
puréed

2 slender leeks, finely sliced into
rounds

3 small courgettes (zucchini),
finely sliced

150g (5½oz) broad (fava) beans,
blanched and peeled

100g (3½oz) fine green beans,
trimmed, or runner (string)
beans, shredded

2 little gems, cut into wedges

TO SERVE

Pesto

OR

A handful of basil leaves

Leaves from 1 sprig of tarragon

Juice of ½ lemon

2 tbsp olive oil

Sea salt and freshly ground
black pepper

This soup is proof that delicate flavours do not suffer from pressure cooking. It is also all about using what you have available – the sort of soup made up from a walk around the vegetable garden or farmers' market. You could use peas instead of broad (fava) beans or any type of lettuce in place of the little gems for example. I love delicate fregola or maftoul couscous in this but you could use diced new potatoes, a handful of rice or just omit the carb element completely.

Heat the olive oil in your pressure cooker. Add the onion and fennel and sauté on a high heat for a few minutes until they have taken on a very little colour. Turn down the heat and add the garlic. Stir for a minute or two, then stir in the fregola, short pasta or maftoul.

Add the white wine. Bring to the boil and allow to boil off, then pour in the stock. Tuck in the bouquet garni. Close the lid and bring up to high pressure. Adjust your heat setting to maintain the high pressure and cook for 3 minutes. Remove from the heat and fast release the pressure.

Stir in the tomatoes, then add the leeks. Push the leeks just under the surface of the liquid, then pile the courgettes (zucchini), broad (fava) beans, green beans and little gems on top. Close the lid again, then bring up to pressure. Immediately remove from the heat, time for 1 minute only, then fast release.

Remove the bouquet garni and and stir very gently. Serve with either pesto, or purée the basil, tarragon, lemon juice and olive oil together with seasoning for a quick herb oil.

COCONUT BROTH WITH PORK AND PRAWN BALLS

SERVES 4

FOR THE MEATBALLS

350g (12oz) minced (ground) pork

150g (5½oz) minced (ground) raw prawns (shrimp)

30g (1oz) coriander (cilantro) including stems, finely chopped

Zest of 1 lime

2 green chillies, finely chopped

1 egg

30g (1oz) plain (all-purpose) flour

Sea salt and freshly ground black pepper

FOR THE BROTH

2 lemongrass stalks

A piece of lime zest

6 garlic cloves

25g (1oz) ginger, roughly chopped

1 tsp coconut oil

Heads and shells from the prawns/shrimp (optional)

500ml (17fl oz) fish, chicken or vegetable stock (not too herbal)

2 tbsp fish sauce

1 tsp palm sugar or light soft brown sugar

Juice of 1 lime

400ml (14fl oz) coconut milk

1 Chinese (napa) cabbage or other greens, cut into wedges

TO SERVE

1 portion sticky rice (see page 183)

A couple of spring onions (scallions), green garlic, wild garlic or garlic chives

A handful of mint and coriander (cilantro) leaves

Hot sauce, chilli flakes or sliced chillies

There is something very comforting about soft, steamed meatballs in a bowl of soup. These steam incredibly quickly, but won't suffer at all if you cook them for longer, which gives you a lot of flexibility about adding other vegetables. I like to keep it simple and just throw in some greens and serve with a little rice.

First make the meatballs. Put all the ingredients in a bowl, along with plenty of salt and pepper, and mix thoroughly. The mixture will feel quite wet to start with – mix until it starts to feel firmer, then cover and put in the fridge to chill and to let the flavours meld a bit. Leave for as long as you can – at least 1 hour, or overnight if possible.

Next make the broth. Put the lemongrass, lime zest, garlic and ginger into a small food processor and pulse to a very rough purée – you can just finely chop everything if you prefer. If using the prawn (shrimp) carcasses, heat the coconut oil in your pressure cooker and add the carcasses. Fry for a minute or two until they have turned pink and start to smell sweet and toasted. Add the paste and stir for another minute or two, then pour in the stock. Bring up to high pressure and cook for 1 minute, then remove from the heat and allow to drop pressure naturally.

Strain the broth and return to the pressure cooker, discarding all the solids. Add the fish sauce, sugar and lime juice, along with the coconut milk. Put on a low heat so any solids in the coconut milk can dissolve. Taste for seasoning – add salt and pepper and a little more fish sauce if necessary.

Form the pork mixture into meatballs, around 30g (1oz) each. Add these to the pressure cooker and lay any greens on top. Bring up to high pressure and cook for 1 minute. Allow to drop pressure naturally.

Serve with sticky rice and with as many of the garnishes as you like.

FRENCH ONION SOUP

SERVES 4

15g (½oz) butter

1 tsp plain (all-purpose) flour

1 portion caramelized onions (see page 331)

100ml (3½fl oz) white wine

750ml (26fl oz) beef, chicken or vegetable stock

1 large sprig of thyme

2 bay leaves

Sea salt and freshly ground black pepper

FOR THE TOASTS

4 slices of decent sourdough

1 garlic clove, cut in half

125g (4½oz) Gruyère, grated

This is probably the most involved recipe in this chapter. There are a lot of pressure cooker recipes around for French Onion Soup that are very quick, but sadly none of them gets a proper caramelization on the onions. So while they are onion soups, they are not French onion soups. This one uses the caramelized onions on page 331 as a base. If you want to do a quicker version, see the Variation.

A time- AND space-saving tip: make a double portion of the caramelized onions and freeze half of them. Then when you want to make French Onion Soup again, take them out and proceed as below. The onions take up much less space in your freezer than portions of soup would and you can then cook them in the soup from frozen, just adding an extra minute to the cooking time.

Melt the butter in your pressure cooker. When it is foaming, add the flour and stir to combine into a roux. Add the caramelized onions, then add the wine. Allow the wine to boil off, then add the stock, thyme and bay leaves. Season with salt and pepper. Bring up to high pressure and cook for 2 minutes, then leave to drop pressure naturally.

Meanwhile, rub the slices of bread with the garlic clove, then sprinkle with the Gruyère. Put under a hot grill until the cheese bubbles and starts to brown, then put into bowls. Ladle the soup over and serve.

VARIATION

Simple Onion Soup
Use 700g (1lb 9oz) sliced onions. Double the amount of butter. Add the onions to the butter and flour mix and cook just for 3–4 minutes until they are starting to release liquid, then proceed as above, but cook for 4 minutes not 2.

SOLYANKA SOUP

SERVES 4

2 tbsp olive oil or butter

1 large onion, finely chopped

1 large carrot, finely diced

2 celery sticks, finely diced

100g (3½oz) smoked bacon lardons and/or 100g (3½oz) chorizo or kielbasa (optional)

200g (7oz) chicken, diced (optional)

1 beetroot, peeled and diced (optional)

2 bay leaves

6 allspice berries, crushed

100g (3½oz) tomato purée

½ red or green cabbage

1.2 litres (40fl oz) chicken, ham or vegetable stock

2 large gherkins, finely sliced

Sea salt and freshly ground black pepper

TO GARNISH (OPTIONAL)

200g (7oz) cooked kasha (buckwheat – see page 201) or other grains

Sour cream

50g (1¾oz) pitted black olives, finely sliced/chopped

50g (1¾oz) capers, rinsed and roughly chopped

A small handful of dill and coriander (cilantro) sprigs, torn or chopped

This is my version of the Russian classic. It became part of my repertoire after I first tried it because it is such a good, fast storecupboard-based soup, which can also mop up any leftovers, usually the province of minestrone. It doesn't have any grains in it, but if you have any cooked, you could easily add some at the end – add to bowls then ladle over the soup. Kasha (buckwheat) works really well with this, so does wild, black or brown rice.

For the gherkins, those that have been brined are better than those in vinegar, but either will work.

Add your choice of fat or oil to the pressure cooker. When it is hot, add the onion, carrot, celery, bacon and/ or the sausage, chicken and beetroot, if using. Stir until the meat has browned, then add the bay leaves, allspice berries and tomato purée. Stir to coat, then stir in the cabbage.

Add the stock and gherkins and season with salt and pepper. Give a quick stir, then close the lid. Bring up to high pressure and cook for 5 minutes at high pressure. Remove from the heat and leave to drop pressure naturally.

Serve with all or any of the garnishes at the table.

KIMCHI SOUP

SERVES 4

1 tbsp olive or groundnut oil

1 onion, finely chopped

200g (7oz) diced lean or belly pork, depending how fatty you want it

1 tsp sugar or honey

4 garlic cloves, finely chopped

25g (1oz) piece ginger, finely chopped (optional)

300g (10½oz) kimchi, roughly chopped

1 litre (35fl oz) vegetable or chicken stock or water

2 tbsp light soy sauce

Sea salt and freshly ground black pepper

TO SERVE

4 spring onions (scallions), halved and shredded lengthways

1 small bunch of coriander (cilantro), pulled into small sprigs

Sesame oil or crispy chilli oil

This soup is a good example of how to make a small amount of meat go a long way, as it is here mainly for flavour. If you want to make it more about the meat, you can double the quantity; conversely, you can dispense with it altogether and replace with vegetables, see the Variations below.

A word of warning – this soup has the potential to be really fiery, depending on the kimchi you use. If your kimchi is particularly hot, you can reduce the amount and add more greens at the end (see the Variations).

Heat the oil in your pressure cooker and add the onion and pork. Cook on a high heat, stirring regularly until the pork is browned on all sides, then stir in the sugar or honey along with the garlic and ginger, if using. Cook for a further minute, then add the kimchi.

Pour in the stock or water and season with salt and pepper. Close the lid. Bring up to pressure and cook for 15 minutes. Remove from the heat and leave to drop pressure naturally.

Add the soy sauce and taste for seasoning. Serve with spring onions (scallions), coriander (cilantro) and a drizzle of sesame or chilli oil.

VARIATIONS

Greens
Any greens can be added to this soup. When the pressure has finished dropping, you can place any roughly chopped Chinese greens or small florets of broccoli/sprouting broccoli on top and bring up to high pressure again. Release pressure immediately for perfectly cooked greens.

To make vegetarian
You can replace the pork with mushrooms or aubergine (eggplant). Sauté 300g (10½oz) halved/thickly sliced mushrooms or 1 large diced aubergine with the onion. Soak 10g (¼oz) dried shiitake mushrooms in water, finely chop and add along with the stock. Cook for 3 minutes at high pressure instead of 15.

Ribs
If you have leftovers from making the ribs on page 83, use around 100–150g (3½–5½oz) cooked meat in place of the pork. Reduce the cooking time to 3 minutes at high pressure.

CHEESE, GARLIC AND NOODLE SOUP

SERVES 4

1 portion of cheese stock
(see page 327)

½ head of garlic

50g (1¾oz) short (broken) egg
noodles

OPTIONAL EXTRAS

Any vegetables you fancy

Grated cheese, to garnish

Handful of wilted wild garlic
leaves, to garnish

This is one of the best uses for the cheese stock recipe on page 327. The garlic poaches to a creamy finish in the time it takes the noodles to cook and can be mashed back into the soup. When it's in season, wilting in some wild garlic at the end really rounds the soup off nicely. Add other vegetables as well if you like; I love the simplicity of a soup that is essentially three ingredients.

For this soup I usually use the short (broken) egg noodles found in the Jewish or Eastern European section of the supermarket, which take no time at all to cook. If you use regular pasta or anything thicker, you may need to cook for a little longer, but err on the side of caution and try this timing first.

Put the stock in your pressure cooker. Separate the garlic cloves from one another and leave all but one unpeeled. Put the unpeeled cloves and the noodles in the pressure cooker. Bring up to high pressure and cook for 1 minute, then fast release.

Remove the garlic from the pressure cooker. Squeeze the flesh from the skins and mash. Return to the pressure cooker. Finely chop the remaining garlic clove and add to the pressure cooker. Simmer for another minute or two just to take the raw edge off the garlic. Serve garnished with cheese and a few wilted wild garlic leaves if you have them.

SAVOURY
EGG DISHES

I often get quizzical looks when talking about cooking eggs in the pressure cooker. Eggs are the ultimate ingredient for quick and easy meals – it takes no time at all to fry or scramble, or to make an omelette, so what purpose could a pressure cooker usefully serve?

There are advantages to using the pressure cooker for a variety of egg-based dishes. First of all, they will steam (as opposed to boil) eggs brilliantly so you will save time and water. You can steam eggs alongside other ingredients to save even more time – see the recipes for Salad Niçoise (page 46) and Kedgeree (page 47) for examples of how this can work. They can be baked – whether in individual ramekins for a quick lunch or dropped into vegetables for a Shakshuka (see page 44), when you've already used the pressure cooker to make the base sauce.

They make short work of anything using a custard base – no endless stirring in a bain-marie, just a short cooking time and a quick whisk at the end. This has transformed how I make custards for everything from ice cream to fruit curds, and it is especially useful in summer if you want to make a rich ice cream but don't relish standing over a hot stove for ages. Look to the desserts and baking and basics chapters in this book for recipes for a number of very adaptable recipes.

There are one or two egg dishes I don't use my pressure cooker for, but this is purely a personal taste thing. Firstly, poached eggs. To make these in the pressure cooker you need to use the silicone cups as opposed to floating the eggs in water and I don't think the resulting texture is right. Secondly, frittata and tortillas. These take longer to make in the pressure cooker than making conventionally. The pressure cooker can be useful for cooking ingredients before you add them to this sort of omelette – par-cooked potatoes (see page 271), caramelized onions (see page 331) or 'roast' or steamed vegetables (see the vegetable chapter) are all good examples, but I don't think the longer time it takes is made up for by the slightly lighter texture. If an electric pressure cooker is your only cooking source, you may want to try – in which case, either line or generously butter a dish, add beaten eggs and any vegetables, cheese etc., and cook at high pressure for 10 minutes, then allow to drop pressure naturally.

HOW TO BOIL EGGS IN THE PRESSURE COOKER

Why boil eggs in the pressure cooker? Well, first of all, you aren't really boiling them, you're steaming them. You need a fraction of the amount of water, you don't need to boil the water first, which saves you a lot of time and, finally, they will be much, much easier to peel, because the pressure helps separate the inner membrane from the egg white – this is especially useful if your egg is very fresh or you want perfectly peeled eggs for devilled eggs or Scotch eggs.

I have seen all kinds of formulae for steaming eggs floating around but I have found it is one of those things that is very variable as it is dependent on your pressure cooker, your eggs (size and freshness) and even the time of year. This method works for me. The key thing to remember is that you are cooking at low pressure, not high. My timings are for room temperature eggs as this is how the majority of people (including me) store them. If you have fridge-cold eggs, you will need to add ½–1 minute depending on their size.

Put 2cm (¾in) water in the base of your pressure cooker and place the steamer basket on top of a trivet. Balance the eggs on top of a bottle top, pointed side up if you want the egg yolks perfectly centred in the egg (particularly good if making devilled or Scotch eggs), otherwise you can leave them loose. Bring up to low pressure and cook for 3 minutes for a soft-boiled egg, 3½ minutes for a mollet egg and 4–5 minutes for a hard-boiled egg. Fast release and immediately plunge the eggs into cold water to stop them cooking.

TO MAKE TAMAGO EGGS FOR RAMEN

Steam your eggs under low pressure as described above for mollet eggs – 3½ minutes. Plunge into ice-cold water, then peel. Put 100ml (3½fl oz) each of light soy sauce, mirin and chicken stock in a saucepan with 10g (¼oz) sliced ginger and 25g (1oz) caster (superfine) sugar. Stir on a low heat until the sugar is dissolved, then pour over the eggs. Leave to cool, then marinate in the fridge for at least 12 hours. You could also use the marinade from making char siu (see page 79).

BAKED OR SHIRRED EGGS

PER PERSON

Butter, for greasing

2–3 cherry tomatoes, finely chopped

1 tbsp capers

A little lemon zest

1 tbsp chopped herbs (oregano, thyme or chervil are good)

1–2 eggs

1 tbsp double (heavy) cream

Sea salt and freshly ground black pepper

Also known as eggs en cocotte, this is the type of thing I love eating for lunch, but used to not do because it involved either switching on the oven – something I try to avoid as much as possible – or steaming for too long over water.

This is a very simple, adaptable recipe. You can add meat, cheese, chopped tomatoes, sautéed spinach or mushrooms, anything you like. But I really love the two simple options I give you here.

For each person, butter a ramekin. Put the chopped tomatoes in the base of the ramekin and season. Add half the capers and herbs along with a little lemon zest. Break in the eggs, season again and add the double (heavy) cream. Top with the remaining capers, herbs and a little more lemon zest.

Cover the top of the ramekin with foil (make sure you don't cover the sides). Put 2–3cm (¾–1¼in) of water in the base of your pressure cooker. Top with the trivet and the steamer basket. Place the ramekin(s) in the steamer basket and close the lid. Bring up to low pressure and cook for 4 minutes. Fast release the pressure and serve immediately.

VARIATION

This is almost a version of Turkish eggs. Butter your ramekin(s) and rub with a cut garlic clove. Add the egg(s). Heat 1 tablespoon of olive oil and 1 tablespoon of butter in a small frying pan (skillet) and add 1 crushed garlic clove and ½ teaspoon of Aleppo pepper. Pour this over the eggs. Bake as above. Squeeze with lemon or lime juice and serve with Greek yogurt.

BOILED EGGS WITH ASPARAGUS SPEARS

PER PERSON

1–2 eggs

4 fat asparagus spears

1 tbsp olive oil or butter

Sea salt and freshly ground black pepper

There are two ways of doing this: you can make it in one pot, by boiling the eggs and steaming the asparagus together – the asparagus will be al dente – or you can cook them separately, but still in the pressure cooker, keeping the asparagus warm while the eggs cook.

Method 1: Place the eggs in the cooker as described in the method for soft-boiled eggs on page 38. Put the asparagus spears on a piece of foil, season well and dot with butter. Loosely close up the parcel and place on top of the eggs. Cook as above, then fast release and plunge the eggs into cold water just for 30 seconds before serving.

Method 2: Alternatively, cook the asparagus first. Heat the olive oil or butter in the base of your pressure cooker. When really hot, add the asparagus spears and cook for 2 minutes on one side, then 1 minute on the other until starting to brown. Bring up to high pressure and release pressure immediately. Remove from the pressure cooker and keep warm while you boil the eggs using the method on page 38.

SAVOURY BREAD PUDDING

SERVES 4

3 eggs

150ml (5½fl oz) whole milk

1 tsp chilli flakes

200g (7oz) robust bread, diced

100g (3½oz) Cheddar or similar hard cheese, grated

15g (½oz) butter, plus extra for greasing

1 onion, finely chopped

4 rashers of smoked or unsmoked bacon, diced

Sea salt and freshly ground black pepper

This is an old-fashioned, eggy brunch dish that is great for using up stale bread. You can add anything to it – fried mushrooms, sausage meat, cherry tomatoes...the children's author Hilary McKay tells me she makes a vegetarian version with walnuts, which I like with a blue cheese. This elevates it from comfort to luxurious and needs a decent tomato salad or some bitter leaves to go alongside it.

Put the eggs into a large bowl and whisk in the milk. Season with salt and pepper and add the chilli flakes. Stir in the bread, making sure it is all covered in the egg and milk mixture, then stir in the cheese.

Melt the butter in a frying pan (skillet) and add the onion and bacon. Fry on a high heat until the onions start to brown around the edges, then stir into the bread mixture.

Butter an ovenproof dish and pile the bread mixture into it, squashing it down evenly. Cover with buttered baking paper. Put 2cm (¾in) water in the base of your pressure cooker, add the trivet and place the dish on top. Close the lid and bring up to high pressure.

Cook at high pressure for 10 minutes, then remove from the heat. Preheat your grill if you want to brown the pudding. Leave the pressure cooker to drop pressure naturally, then remove the paper from the dish and brown under the grill if you like – this isn't strictly necessary as it will have browned on the base.

VARIATIONS

Use blue cheese in place of the Cheddar. Omit the bacon and add 40g (1½oz) walnuts to the onions just for 30 seconds or so to lightly toast. Stir in sprigs of finely chopped flat-leaf parsley, chervil or tarragon.

Add ½ portion of the caramelized onions (see page 331) with the bacon and onion.

SAVOURY CUSTARDS

SERVES 4

3–4 eggs, depending on size

400ml (14fl oz) dashi (instant or see recipe on page 329) or any savoury stock

1 tbsp light soy sauce

1 tsp mirin

2 spring onions (scallions), finely sliced

Sea salt

These are very soft set and silky in texture, thanks to the high proportion of liquid to egg. You can make them firmer by reducing the liquid – basically, the more you reduce the liquid, the firmer they will be – at one end of the scale think of a smooth savoury crème caramel and at the other a much eggier custard tart. The type of liquid also makes a difference. The recipe below uses stock, which makes the finished dish much lighter. Replace with milk, cream or add an extra step to melt in cheese and it will be altogether richer.

This recipe is based on chawanmushi – the Japanese version, which I really love. The ratio should be roughly 1:3 egg to liquid. One of my absolute favourite things to do though is to make it with half cream, half garlic stock, perhaps with a few coriander (cilantro) leaves on top.

Cut 4 rounds of baking paper, using your chosen ramekin or cup as a template. Lightly oil 4 ramekins or Japanese teacups. Beat the eggs until smooth, making sure you don't let them froth up. Mix the dashi or alternative with the soy sauce and mirin. Season with a little salt. Pour the stock mixture over the eggs, again, taking care not to let it foam, then pour through a sieve to make sure it is completely smooth. Divide between the ramekins and sprinkle with the spring onions (scallions).

Cover the ramekins with the rounds of baking paper – they will sit on top of the custard.

Put 2cm (¾in) just-boiled water in the base of your pressure cooker and insert an upturned steamer basket. Add the ramekins. Bring up to high pressure and cook for 5 minutes. Fast release the pressure.

VARIATIONS

Add texture: All kinds of things can be added to these custards – a handful of enoki mushrooms, cooked shrimp, a little raw chicken diced and tossed in soy sauce, a few spinach leaves.

Vary the liquid: To make a creamier version of these, you can substitute half the liquid with cream. If you want to add cheese, it is important to melt the cheese very gently in the liquid first, stirring carefully on a very gentle heat so the cheese doesn't separate. 50g (1¾oz) should be enough, or you could use the cheese stock on page 327.

SHAKSHUKA

SERVES 4

1 tbsp olive oil

2 red onions, sliced into wedges

2 peppers (any colour), cut into strips

3 garlic cloves, finely chopped

1 tsp cumin seeds

½ tsp caraway seeds

½ tsp fennel seeds

½ tsp ground turmeric

¼ tsp ground cinnamon

1 small bunch of flat-leaf parsley, stems and leaves separated, finely chopped

1 x 400g (14oz) can chopped tomatoes or fresh equivalent

4 eggs

200g (7oz) feta, cut into cubes (optional)

Sea salt and freshly ground black pepper

TO SERVE

Chilli flakes

Finely chopped flat-leaf parsley, mint or coriander (cilantro), or a combination of all three

Toast or flatbreads

This has become a brunch classic and is one of those dishes that can be varied enormously. I sometimes add fennel along with the onions and peppers, or start by frying some merguez sausages – these are very thin and will cook in the same time, so there is no need to alter the timings.

The feta replaces the more usual yogurt, and under pressure it softens to a mellow creaminess.

Heat the olive oil in your pressure cooker and add the red onions and peppers. Sauté on a high heat for a couple of minutes just to get them started, then stir in the garlic, spices, parsley stems and tomatoes. Season with salt and pepper and add 100ml (3½fl oz) water.

Close the lid and bring up to pressure. Cook for 3 minutes, then fast release. Make 4 wells in the sauce and add an egg to each, then drop in the cubes of feta, if using. Close the lid and bring up to high pressure again, then remove from the heat and leave for 30 seconds. Fast release the remaining pressure.

Sprinkle with parsley, mint or coriander (cilantro) and serve immediately with chilli flakes and toast or flatbreads, if you like.

SALAD NIÇOISE

SERVES 4

150g (5½oz) baby new or salad potatoes, halved or sliced if large

3 garlic cloves, unpeeled

4 medium eggs

200g (7oz) green beans, trimmed

FOR THE SALAD

8 cherry tomatoes, halved

1 shallot, thinly sliced

12 black olives, pitted

1 tbsp capers, rinsed

A selection of salad leaves

A few basil leaves

A small can or jar of tuna, roughly flaked or a few anchovies, roughly chopped (optional)

FOR THE DRESSING

2 tbsp olive oil

1 tbsp red wine vinegar

1 tsp Dijon mustard

1 small garlic clove, crushed

4 anchovies, finely chopped

I have included plenty of salads in this book, mainly because I like them, but also because they often showcase how pressure cookers can be used effectively for composite dishes – as they will cook the separate components at once, which saves massively on time, fuel and water. The best example is probably this classic salad niçoise. The new potatoes and eggs cook together and the beans cook on top – so all three cooked elements are ready at the same time and just need plunging into iced water to chill down quickly after they have finished cooking. I have added garlic to the pot too, as I prefer the slightly subdued, creamier flavour of poached garlic in a salad dressing.

Put the potatoes and garlic cloves in the bottom of your pressure cooker and add around 100ml (3½fl oz) water. Add the trivet and steamer basket and arrange the eggs on top. Add the green beans – you have two options here – for slightly crisp, al dente beans, wrap them lightly in foil, preferably in a shallow layer (ie, not in a fat bunch); for slightly softer beans, leave them unwrapped next to, but not touching, the eggs.

Close the lid of your pressure cooker and bring it up to high pressure. Time for 3 minutes and fast release. Remove the eggs immediately and plunge into cold water. Remove the parcel of beans and drain the potatoes. Leave both to cool naturally so they are still slightly warm or room temperature for the salad. When the eggs are cool enough to handle, peel and cut into quarters.

Squeeze the flesh out of the garlic skins and mix with all the dressing ingredients and 1 tablespoon of water. Leave to stand for a few minutes, then taste and adjust the acidity and/or salt levels as necessary.

Toss all the salad ingredients together with the cooked potatoes, eggs, beans and the dressing and serve.

KEDGEREE

SERVES 4

250g (9oz) smoked haddock

150g (5½oz) green beans, trimmed and halved (optional)

15g (½oz) butter, plus extra for greasing

1 tbsp olive oil

1 onion, finely chopped

4 cardamom pods, lightly crushed but left whole

1 small piece cinnamon stick

1 tbsp mild curry powder

2 green chillies, left whole but pierced with a knife point

250g (9oz) basmati rice, well rinsed

200g (7oz) peas (optional)

325ml (11fl oz) cold water or stock

2–4 eggs

Sea salt and freshly ground black pepper

TO SERVE (OPTIONAL)

150g (5½oz) Greek yogurt

2 tbsp hot mango chutney

A few sprigs of coriander (cilantro)

A few green chillies, sliced

A breakfast or brunch classic that I used to have much more as lunch or evening meal because it always seemed too much trouble to make first thing in the morning. But this method really does make things simple. Everything in one pot, with no having to cook fish and eggs separately, so not only is it faster, but you are saving fuel and lots of water too.

I like this with green beans, which is not traditional – you could replace them with peas, which can be cooked alongside the rice, or a few frozen cubes of spinach. Alternatively, creamed spinach or other greens are good to serve alongside.

First, prepare the fish and green beans for steaming. Butter a piece of foil and wrap the haddock in it. Wrap the beans loosely in another piece of foil.

Heat the olive oil and butter in your pressure cooker. When the butter has melted, add the onion, spices, curry powder and chillies. Stir for a couple of minutes until aromatic, then add the rice and peas, if using. Stir so the rice is well coated with the spices, then pour over the water or stock. Season with salt and pepper.

Put the trivet in the pressure cooker and balance the haddock and bean parcels on top – you can use the steamer basket if you prefer. Tuck the eggs on top.

Close the lid and bring up to high pressure. Cook for 3 minutes at high pressure, then remove from the heat. Leave to drop pressure naturally for 5 minutes, then release the rest manually. Remove the eggs and fish, put a tea towel over the top of the pressure cooker and place the lid on top – this will help the rice dry out while you attend to the fish and the eggs.

Flake the fish, removing any skin and bones, then gently stir through the rice. Transfer to a serving dish if you like. Peel the eggs, cut into quarters and arrange over the rice.

Mix the yogurt and mango chutney together, if using, then serve on the side of the kedgeree with the sprigs of coriander (cilantro) and green chillies.

SPICED POTATO AND SPINACH WITH EGGS

SERVES 4

1 tbsp coconut oil or ghee

½ tsp mustard seeds

½ tsp cumin seeds

1 tbsp medium curry powder

4 medium-boiled eggs (see page 38), peeled

1 onion, finely sliced

4 garlic cloves, finely chopped (optional)

15g (½oz) piece ginger, grated

400g (14oz) potatoes, diced (skin on)

750g (1lb 10oz) frozen spinach (don't worry about defrosting)

1 small bunch of coriander (cilantro), stems and leaves separated, finely chopped

Juice of ½ lemon

100ml (3½fl oz) double (heavy) cream

100g (3½oz) cheese, such as Cheddar, grated (optional)

Sea salt and freshly ground black pepper

This is a hybrid of a curry and comforting bake, which makes a really good brunch dish. It comes courtesy of my mother-in-law.

Heat the coconut oil or ghee in your pressure cooker. Add the mustard and cumin seeds and when they start to pop add the curry powder. Stir for a minute. Add the whole eggs and fry for a minute, rolling around the cooker so they are well coated in the spices. Remove from the pressure cooker and cut in half.

Add the onion, garlic and ginger and cook for 2 minutes. Add the potatoes, then drop the spinach on top along with the coriander (cilantro) stems. Season with salt and pepper and add 50ml (1¾fl oz) water to the pressure cooker. Close the lid, bring up to high pressure and cook for 3 minutes. Fast release.

Stir to break up the spinach, then add most of the coriander leaves and the lemon juice. Stir in the cream, then return the eggs to the cooker and set over a low heat. Sprinkle with cheese, if using, and either put the lid on the pressure cooker loosely, just to create an ambient temperature to melt the cheese, or transfer to an ovenproof pot and put under a hot grill if you would prefer the cheese browned. You can also use your air-fryer attachment if you have one.

VARIATIONS

Use fresh greens such as chard or kale in exactly the same way as the frozen spinach.

Turn this into a tomato dish. Replace the spinach with a 400g (14oz) can of chopped tomatoes and increase the cooking time for the potatoes by 1 minute.

MEAT

A major advantage to pressure cooking is the fact that it is one of the most sustainable ways to cook; your fuel consumption is reduced and if you are using an induction hob or an electric pressure cooker run on renewable sources of electricity, so much the better. Highlighting this may sit strangely with a rather large chapter on meat when we are repeatedly led to believe that a modern, mindful, sustainable way to eat is to avoid red meat and dairy because of their negative impact on our planet.

My opinion on meat consumption, for what it's worth, is this: we need to understand the difference in environmental impact between industrialized, feed-lot livestock, fed mainly a diet of soy or grain usually grown at the expense of biodiversity and soil health, and the livestock that are grass fed and part of an extensive, regenerative closed system. And we then need to take responsibility for the meat we eat – find out its provenance and ask the questions of our butchers or supermarkets. You will find that in the UK, at least, meat from livestock raised in this way is not as rare as you might think. Of course, it can be more expensive, but using a pressure cooker can help mitigate this for you – it will help you make the most of cheaper (often more flavoursome) cuts without having to spend a small fortune and long hours tenderizing them in the oven. You can also eat more nose to tail – look for example at the lamb breast recipe on page 74 and the oxtail one on page 54.

Pressure cooking helps me efficiently cook the meat I do buy; for example, cooking a large piece of meat can take a fraction of the time (see the roast beef recipe on page 56), or you can cook them alongside the vegetables too. A favourite in my house all year round is haggis with crushed carrots and swede (rutabaga). Simply wrap the haggis in foil, place on top of diced carrot and swede in the steamer basket and cook at pressure for 15 minutes. Also, if you cook a large amount but control portion sizes, there should be plenty of leftovers – the pressure cooker will then help you eke them out, supplemented by grains, beans and pulses – for example, making a classic ragù, chilli or cottage pie filling with leftover beef, which can be bulked out with lentils or beans.

The one-pot nature of pressure cooking can also help you move away from the tradition of meat and two veg. I frequently use very small amounts of meat – whether leftover or trimmings or cured – to flavour large pots of beans and pulses, or grains. This way of eating, which harks back to good household economy, is the modern way to eat; meat is nutritionally dense and full of flavour – you don't need a lot of it to supplement all the nutrients you will get from upping your wholefood and vegetable content.

BEEF, BARLEY AND SPLIT PEA SOUP

SERVES 4–6

1 tbsp olive oil or 15g (½oz) dripping

300g (10½oz) beef ox cheeks or stewing steak, diced

1 large onion, finely diced

2 carrots, diced

3 celery sticks, diced

2 turnips, peeled and diced

100g (3½oz) pearl barley

50g (1¾oz) green split peas

100ml (3½fl oz) beer or wine

1 litre (35fl oz) beef, chicken or vegetable stock

100g (3½oz) fresh or canned tomatoes, thoroughly chopped

A bouqet garni of 1 sprig of thyme and 1 sprig of rosemary (optional)

½ green cabbage, shredded, or 1 bunch of kale, shredded

2 leeks, cut into rounds

Sea salt and freshly ground black pepper

TO SERVE

Very finely chopped parsley and/or rosemary (optional)

Mustard of your choice

This is a proper hearty beef stew, based very loosely on a Scotch broth, which might also use lamb, mutton or goat, so please don't feel confined by the beef, use whatever you like. What I would urge, though, is that you use a relatively lean cut with connective tissue. This will dissolve into the soup to provide texture without being unpleasantly fatty. The fattier cuts, such as oxtail or short ribs, could also be used, but you need twice the amount, and you will have to strain and skim the soup of excessive fat, which can be a bit of a faff.

The beauty of stews like this is that while they are wonderful as they are, they provide a neutral enough base for doctoring at the table or adding to during a second outing. Hot sauces, oils or chilli flakes are the obvious choice, but you are limited only by the contents of your cupboard. One of my favourites to add to stews is a sprinkling of gremolata – a combination of finely chopped citrus zest, garlic and herbs.

Heat the oil or dripping in your pressure cooker and when it is hot, add the beef. Brown on all sides, then remove from the pan. Add the vegetables, sauté for 5 minutes on a high heat to take on a little colour, then stir in the pearl barley and the split peas.

Add the beef back to the cooker and season with plenty of salt and pepper. Pour in the beer or wine and bring to the boil. Allow most of it to boil off, then add the stock, the tomatoes and the bouquet garni, if using. Close the lid, bring up to high pressure and reduce the heat to maintain the pressure.

Cook on high pressure for 25 minutes, then remove from the heat and leave to drop pressure naturally. Make sure the base of your pressure cooker is still clean (ie, stir to make sure nothing is sticking), then put the greens and leeks on top of the soup and bring the cooker up to high pressure again. Immediately remove from the heat and leave to release pressure naturally for 5 minutes, before releasing the rest of the pressure quickly.

Serve with herbs, if using, and plenty of mustard.

OXTAIL, SHORT RIB OR OX CHEEK PEPPER SOUP

SERVES 4-6

1.5kg (3lb 5oz) oxtail, 1kg (2lb 4oz) short ribs or 750g (1lb 10oz) ox cheeks

1 tsp plain (all-purpose) flour

1 tsp garlic powder

1 tsp mustard powder

1 tbsp ground black pepper

25g (1oz) butter

1 tsp light soft brown sugar

1 onion, roughly chopped

2 carrots, roughly chopped

2 celery sticks, roughly chopped

4 garlic cloves, finely chopped

250ml (9fl oz) pale ale or similar

A bouquet garni of 2 sprigs of thyme, 3 bay leaves, 1–2 Scotch bonnets, 1 tsp allspice berries, 3 cloves, ½ tsp aniseed (optional)

Beef or chicken stock, to cover

200g (7oz) canned chopped tomatoes

Sea salt and freshly ground black pepper

TO SERVE

A little Madeira or port (optional)

If using oxtail, this recipe works best in a 6-litre (210-fl oz) pressure cooker although it will fit into a 4.5-litre (156-fl oz) version. This recipe contains flour and also has sugar at the beginning, which may send off alarm signals to electric-pressure cooker users. If you deglaze thoroughly, this will not be a problem, but if you are worried, sear the meat in a pan and deglaze before transferring it and the deglazing liquid to your electric pressure cooker.

This is one of those soups that is always better the next day. It should always be skimmed and the fat is really worth keeping for frying, sautéing and roasting. You can leave the meat whole and turn it into a casserole if you prefer – it's common to add broad (fava) beans or butter (lima) beans, but potatoes or dumplings also work really well.

Season the meat with salt and pepper. Mix the flour with the garlic and mustard powders and black pepper and toss the meat in this mixture, patting off any excess. Put the butter and sugar in your pressure cooker and melt gently together. Turn up the heat a little and add the oxtail, short ribs or ox cheeks. Sear briefly on all sides and remove from the cooker. Add the vegetables and garlic and sauté for 2–3 minutes, just so they can take on the flavour of the butter and sugar, then pour in the beer. Make sure you deglaze the base of the cooker thoroughly, then return the meat to the cooker. Add the bouquet garni, season with salt and pepper, and pour in enough stock to completely cover the meat. Add the tomatoes.

Bring up to high pressure and cook for 45 minutes. Slow release. Strain the soup, then take out the meat and the bouquet garni and push the vegetables through a sieve back into the liquid. Leave the liquid to cool down, preferably transferring to a fridge to set the fat on top. This will make it much easier to remove. Remove most of the fat and keep as dripping. When the meat is cool enough to handle, pull off all the meat, discarding the bone and fat, then return to the liquid. Reheat and serve with a little Madeira or port poured in if you like.

POT-ROAST BRISKET

SERVES 6–8

1 large piece of brisket, around 1–1.5kg (2lb 4oz–3lb 5oz)

2 tbsp olive oil

1 large onion, finely chopped

1 large carrot, finely diced

2 celery sticks, finely diced

250ml (9fl oz) red wine

250ml (9fl oz) beef stock

1 large sprig of thyme

2 bay leaves

Sea salt and freshly ground black pepper

FOR THE RUB

1 tsp mustard powder

1 tsp garlic powder

1 tsp onion salt

1 tsp ground black pepper

TO FINISH

1 tbsp Dijon mustard

TO MAKE ONE POT

A selection of potatoes and root vegetables

VARIATION

Salt Beef/Corned Beef
For each 1kg (2lb 4oz) of meat you will need 1 litre (35fl oz) of water, 120g (4¼oz) table salt, 75g (2½oz) light soft brown sugar, 7.5g (⅙oz) Prague Powder (optional) and any whole spices you like (cinnamon, bay, mace, allspice, peppercorns, mustard seeds, cloves). Heat to dissolve the sugar and salt then cool. Put meat and liquid in a large bag or container and cure for 10 days in the fridge, turning daily. Then strain and cook as above.

I have kept this recipe fairly plain, because it is a blueprint recipe that can be adapted in many ways. It is great if you want a very tender, almost melting pot-roast that just needs teasing apart with a fork. It will accommodate all kinds of flavours, and will also work well pulled, in a chilli, or smothered in a sticky barbecue sauce. You can reduce the cooking time to keep the meat firmer so it is excellent for slicing – and best of all as far as I am concerned – you can cook a salted or corned brisket in the same way, which is exactly what you need for salt beef sandwiches.

There is a lot of liquid left in this recipe, deliberately so, as it makes excellent stock for gravy.

Mix the rub ingredients together with 1 teaspoon of salt and coat the brisket in it. Heat the olive oil in your pressure cooker and quickly sear the brisket on all sides. Remove and set aside. Add the vegetables and sauté for several minutes, then season with salt and pepper. Pour in the red wine and allow it to come up to the boil, then stir to make sure you have thoroughly deglazed the pan. Add the stock and herbs, then return the beef to the pan.

Bring up to high pressure and cook for 1 hour for a tender, but sliceable brisket, up to 1½ hours if you would like it softer and falling apart.

What you do next is up to you. To serve as a pot roast, slice thickly. Make a gravy by whisking in the mustard (the mustard will help thicken it), and strain, pushing through as much of the vegetable matter as possible – alternatively, don't bother straining and serve with the diced vegetables.

To turn it into a one pot, remove the brisket from the cooker and keep warm. Add a selection of root vegetables, including potatoes. Bring up to high pressure and cook for 5 minutes, then remove from the heat and fast release.

ROAST BEEF WITH ONION GRAVY

SERVES 4–6

FOR THE BEEF

500–750g (1lb 2oz–1lb 9oz) joint of silverside, topside or sirloin

2 tbsp olive oil

FOR THE GRAVY

1 large onion, finely sliced

2 garlic cloves, crushed

100ml (3½fl oz) red wine

150ml (5fl oz) beef stock

1 sprig of thyme

2 tbsp bone marrow (optional)

1 tbsp soft butter or beef dripping (optional)

1 tbsp plain (all-purpose) flour (optional)

Sea salt and freshly ground black pepper

I usually use this method for fairly small pieces of meat – between 500g–1kg (1lb 2oz–1lb 10oz) in weight and around 10cm (4in) thick – a piece of topside, silverside or sirloin works best. Don't use a cut with a lot of connective tissue or the sort of cut that needs long, slow cooking – for that, make a pot roast (see page 55). My favourite thing to do with this is a French Dip – very thinly sliced beef, French bread, plenty of mustard and the gravy for dipping.

Take the beef out of the fridge 1 hour before you want to cook it to come up to room temperature. Sprinkle it with salt. Heat the olive oil in your pressure cooker, then sear the beef on all sides – take your time as you want a good crust. Remove the beef and set aside.

Add the onion to the pressure cooker and brown on a high heat. Stir constantly and scrape up any brown bits from the beef that might be found on the base. When the onion has softened a little and is brown around the edges, add the garlic and stir for another minute. Pour in the wine and bring to the boil. Cook for another 2 minutes, then add the beef stock, thyme, bone marrow, if using, and plenty of seasoning.

Put a trivet in the pressure cooker and place a steamer basket on top. Put the beef on the steamer basket. Close the lid and bring up to high pressure. Cook for 3–5 minutes, depending on how you like it cooked; 3 minutes will give you rare, 5 minutes will give you medium for the size specified – add an extra minute of cooking time for every additional 500g (1lb 2oz). Leave to drop pressure naturally. Check the internal temperature – for rare meat this should read 52°C (126°F).

Put the meat on a board or plate and wrap loosely in foil. Leave to rest for at least 15 minutes. Pour any juices from the meat into the gravy. Simmer to reduce. If you want it much thicker, mix the butter or dripping and flour together to make a beurre manié. Whisk a little of this at a time into the gravy until you are happy.

BEEF OR VENISON CASSEROLE

SERVES 4-6

1 tbsp olive oil

100g (3½oz) smoked bacon lardons or pancetta

750g (1lb 10oz) beef or venison, diced

2 tsp plain (all-purpose) flour

½ tsp mustard powder

1 onion, sliced

2 carrots, cut on the diagonal

2 celery sticks, cut into chunks

150ml (5fl oz) red wine or beer

1 head of garlic, broken up but unpeeled

A bouquet garni of 2 bay leaves, 1 sprig of thyme, 1 sprig of rosemary and 1 tsp crushed juniper berries (if using venison)

150ml (5fl oz) well-flavoured beef stock or jus

Sea salt and freshly ground black pepper

TO THICKEN (OPTIONAL)

1 tbsp plain (all-purpose) flour

1 tbsp butter

TO SERVE

Chopped parsley

One of the most useful things about pressure cooking is that less frequently gives you more. In rich red wine casseroles, for example, you need much less alcohol than you would in a conventional recipe because all the liquid stays in the sealed cooker and intensifies the flavour at the same time. This recipe is a good example of this.

The recipe as written is a good blueprint for any meat/alcohol casserole, so you can vary all aspects of it if you just keep the liquid levels the same. To make it more of a standout dish, see the bourguignon variation (following page).

The use of flour is usually frowned upon when using a pressure cooker as it is starchy and can cause burning or stop your pressure cooker from coming up to pressure. However, if you make sure you deglaze the cooker properly, this won't happen.

This is good served with dauphinois (see page 273) or potato and celeriac purée (see page 271 for method). Any leftovers can be shredded and added to pasta and cooked as in the Variation on page 167.

Heat the olive oil in your pressure cooker. Add the bacon or pancetta and sauté until crisp and brown. Remove. Toss the beef or venison in the flour and mustard powder and season well with salt and pepper. Sear in the pressure cooker until brown on all sides. Remove.

Add the onion, carrot and celery to the pressure cooker and sauté for a few minutes until just starting to take on some colour. Pour in the red wine or beer, then stir, making sure you deglaze the base of the cooker properly – this is especially important if you are using an electric pressure cooker as anything stuck to the base can set off the burn alarm.

Add the garlic, bouquet garni and beef stock or jus. Return the beef or venison to the cooker. Season again, then close the lid and bring up to high pressure. Cook for 20 minutes. Remove from the heat and allow to drop pressure naturally. Remove the garlic cloves and squeeze

Beef or Venison Casserole *continued*

out their flesh. Return these to the casserole along with the bacon lardons and stir on a low heat for a couple of minutes. Serve with a sprinkling of parsley.

If you want to thicken the casserole at all, use a little beurre manié – mash the flour with the butter and whisk into the casserole a little at a time until thicker.

VARIATIONS

To turn this into a ragù
Cut the onion, celery and carrots into smaller dice or use 4 tablespoons of the sofrito on page 330. Replace the beef stock with a 400g (14oz) can of chopped tomatoes. Add a couple of chopped anchovies at the beginning, if you like. Pull apart the meat after cooking.

To add leeks
Cook before you make the rest of the casserole. Melt 15g (½oz) butter in your pressure cooker and add 3 thickly sliced leeks. Bring up to pressure and fast release immediately. Remove and add back to warm through when the casserole has cooked.

To turn into a bourguignon
Before you start, make the roast shallots on page 264. Add these to the casserole after cooking and heat through.

To use in a suet pudding
You can use virtually all of the casseroles and curries in this chapter and the poultry one to make a suet pudding. To turn this beef casserole into a steak and kidney pudding, follow the instructions for the suet pudding on page 312. Use ½ portion of this casserole, straining off two thirds of the liquid for gravy. Fry 150g (5½oz) quartered kidneys and add these too. Cook for 45 minutes at high pressure and serve turned out with the reheated gravy.

SPICED BEEF IN COCONUT

SERVES 4-6

1–2 tbsp coconut oil

800g (1lb 12oz) stewing steak, chuck steak, ox cheeks or shin, cut into large pieces

1 large cinnamon stick

6 cloves

3 star anise

1 tsp cardamom pods

50g (1¾oz) fresh coconut, grated, or 25g (1oz) desiccated, (shredded) soaked in a little water

1 tbsp palm sugar or light soft brown sugar

150ml (5fl oz) coconut cream

2 tbsp fish sauce

1 tbsp tamarind paste

8 lime leaves

Sea salt and freshly ground black pepper

FOR THE PASTE

3 lemongrass stalks, white core only

2 fresh red chillies

½ tsp chilli flakes or powder (heat up to you)

6 garlic cloves, peeled

25g (1oz) piece ginger, peeled

15g (½oz) piece galangal, peeled (optional)

15g (½oz) fresh turmeric or 1 tsp ground turmeric

½ tsp black peppercorns

TO SERVE

Rice or rotis

Coriander (cilantro) and/or laksa leaves

Red or green chillies, sliced (optional)

Flavourwise, this dish is based on a rendang; however, cooking any cuts of meat in a pressure cooker will always result in much more liquid than you would expect from what is essentially quite a dry curry. To get the balance between savoury meat, coconut and spicing right, you do need to add the coconut milk, which will result in a lot of gravy. So you have three options. You can strain off most of the gravy and use it in something else – it is wonderful with rice or noodles and just some greens added to it. You can leave it to simmer uncovered to reduce – an option I don't go for because if you do, you will lose some of the time saved by cooking this way in the first place. Finally, you can just accept that it isn't going to be a dry curry and serve in the gravy. I usually go for the first option as that pretty much gives me two meals.

Put all the paste ingredients in a small food processor or blender with a generous pinch of salt and a splash of water. Process, stopping to scrape down the sides regularly, until you have a bright orange paste – you may have to add a little more water if it is resistant. Set aside.

Heat half the coconut oil in your pressure cooker. Season the steak with salt and pepper and sear on all sides. Remove from the pressure cooker. Add the whole spices and fry for a minute or two, then pour in the paste, the coconut and the sugar. Fry for several minutes, scraping up any brown bits from the bottom of the pressure cooker as you do so.

Return the meat to the cooker and stir to coat with the paste. Add all the remaining ingredients, then close the lid and bring up to high pressure. Cook at high pressure for 30 minutes, then slow release.

Serve, or for a drier curry, ladle off most of the liquid to use in a separate dish and simmer what is left for a few more minutes to thicken and concentrate.

Serve with rice or rotis, plenty of coriander (cilantro) or laksa leaves and sliced chillies, if you like.

BEEF GOULASH

SERVES 4

2 tbsp olive oil or dripping

2 green peppers (or 1 red and 1 green), cut into strips

4 garlic cloves, finely chopped or grated

750g (1lb 10oz) braising or stewing steak, diced

1 onion, finely chopped

½–1 tsp caraway seeds

1 tsp plain (all-purpose) flour

1 tsp hot paprika

1 tbsp sweet smoked paprika

75ml (2½fl oz) red wine

100g (3½oz) canned or fresh tomatoes

75ml (2½fl oz) beef stock or water

2 bay leaves

A squeeze of lemon juice

150ml (5fl oz) sour cream

One tricky thing about working out timings with the pressure cooker when converting favourite recipes is reconciling the length of time it takes to cook certain ingredients together. So, in this dish the beef would usually take over 2 hours to cook before you add the peppers to cook for another 30 minutes or so. Peppers soften very quickly in the pressure cooker and if you aren't careful, will disintegrate and flood your goulash with too much liquid so they should not be added for the duration. Cooking them first and then adding back at the end will help flavour the meat from the outset while making sure you have the right texture.

I'm not sure about the aesthetics of this, but the flavours work really well with the red kidney bean and beetroot dish on page 212. You will probably want carbs to soak up the sauce too – try the crushed potatoes on page 271 or perhaps some buttered noodles.

Heat half the olive oil or dripping in your pressure cooker. Add the peppers and sauté on a high heat until they start to take on a little colour around the edges. Add half the garlic. Close the lid and bring up to high pressure, then immediately remove from the heat. Leave for 2 minutes, then release the rest of the pressure. Remove from the pressure cooker and set aside.

Heat the remaining olive oil or dripping in the pressure cooker and add the beef. Sear on all sides, then remove. Add the onion and stir until the pan is deglazed. Add the remaining garlic and caraway seeds to the cooker and stir for another minute, then return the beef to the cooker. Sprinkle over the flour, hot and sweet paprika and stir.

Pour over the wine and allow to bubble up and evaporate. Add the tomatoes, stock or water and bay leaves. Make sure the base of the cooker is completely deglazed to avoid burning. Close the lid, bring up to high pressure and cook for 20 minutes. Allow to drop pressure naturally.

Add the peppers to the pressure cooker and simmer very gently to heat them through. Add a squeeze of lemon juice and serve with the sour cream on the side.

QUICK CHILLI CON CARNE

SERVES 4

2 tbsp olive oil

1 large onion, finely diced

1 red pepper, diced

1 green pepper, diced

400g (14oz) minced (ground) beef

200g (7oz) minced (ground) pork

4 garlic cloves, crushed or grated

4 tbsp coriander (cilantro) stems, finely chopped

1 tbsp chipotle paste

2 tbsp dried oregano

1 tbsp ground cumin

2 tsp ground coriander

1 tsp ground cinnamon

½ tsp allspice

200ml (7fl oz) whole milk

1 x 400g (14oz) can chopped tomatoes

250g (9oz) cooked kidney, black or pinto beans (see page 212)

100ml (3½fl oz) beef stock or water

10g (¼oz) dark chocolate (optional)

Sea salt

I'm not sure how many households eat this on a very regular basis but I'm betting it is a fair few. This is my favourite recipe – one that has served me well at my son's school Christmas Fair for several years.

Heat the olive oil in your pressure cooker. Add the onion, peppers and meat and sauté on a high heat until the meat is browned. Add the garlic, coriander (cilantro), chipotle paste, oregano and spices, then season well with salt. Pour in the milk.

Bring to the boil, and simmer until the milk has almost completely evaporated, stirring regularly – this really helps tenderize the meat. Add the tomatoes, beans and stock. Close the lid and bring up to high pressure. Cook for 5 minutes, then release pressure naturally.

Stir in the chocolate, if using, and leave on a very low heat for a few minutes.

LEFTOVERS

For very easy, lazy burritos, take a half portion of this chilli and put in the pressure cooker with 100g (3½oz) well-rinsed long-grain rice and 150ml (5fl oz) water and, if you like, 50g (1¾oz) frozen sweetcorn. Season and bring up to pressure. Cook for 3 minutes, then allow to drop pressure naturally. Pile into tortillas with any additions you like – salsa, guacamole, sour cream, lots of coriander (cilantro) and grated cheese.

CARNITAS

SERVES 8

1kg (2lb 4oz) pork or lamb shoulder, trimmed of fat and cut into large chunks, or 1 kg (2lb 4oz) brisket or bavette, cut into large chunks along the grain

1 tbsp olive or vegetable oil

1 onion, thickly sliced

Juice of 1 large orange

Sea salt

FOR THE RUB

1 tsp dried oregano

1 tsp dried thyme

1 tsp ground cumin

1 tsp mustard powder

1 tsp garlic powder

½ tsp allspice

½ tsp ground cinnamon

1 tbsp light soft brown sugar

Yet another recipe that is very adaptable. I use pork, beef or lamb for this recipe, just making sure that the cut is one that has long strands of meat, ideal for shredding. So pork or lamb shoulder, beef brisket, even bavette.

Mix all the rub ingredients together and add 1 teaspoon of salt. Rub all over the meat and leave to stand for 30 minutes.

Heat the oil in your pressure cooker and fry the onion on a high heat until browned. Push to one side and brown the meat on all sides. Pour in the orange juice and make sure you thoroughly deglaze the pan. Close the lid and bring up to high pressure. Cook depending on the cut of meat. For brisket, pork or lamb shoulder, cook for 45 minutes; for bavette, cook for 20 minutes. Release pressure naturally. Slice or shred the meat depending on how you want to serve it. Reduce any cooking liquid to a syrupy consistency and drizzle over.

VARIATION

Pressure-cooker Tamales
These steam so quickly in the pressure cooker. A very quick recipe when you have some carnitas you can use as filling. Take 75g (2½oz) butter or lard and cream it until soft and aerated. Mix 225g (8oz) masa harina with 2 teaspoons of baking powder and 1 teaspoon of salt. Beat into the butter or lard, then gradually pour in 150ml (5fl oz) tepid water. Knead until soft – I always think the texture is a bit like Play-Doh. Soak corn husks (or baking paper – no need to soak – if you don't have any) in warm water for 15 minutes until pliable. To assemble, take 1–2 heaped tablespoons of the dough and spread over the centre of a corn husk, leaving a wide border for folding. Put some of the carnitas and maybe a bit of grated cheese in the middle with some coriander (cilantro), then fold over into a parcel, making sure they aren't too tight as they will expand a bit. Pile into the steamer basket of your pressure cooker and steam at high pressure for 15 minutes, then allow to drop pressure naturally.

LAMB MEATBALL CURRY

SERVES 4

FOR THE MEATBALLS

1 small onion, finely chopped

2 green chillies, roughly chopped

4 garlic cloves, roughly chopped

1 tbsp tomato purée

1 small bunch of coriander (cilantro) leaves, finely chopped

2 tsp curry powder or garam masala

400g (14oz) minced (ground) lamb

1 tbsp olive oil

Sea salt and freshly ground black pepper

FOR THE SAUCE

1 tbsp olive oil

1 large onion, finely chopped

4 garlic cloves, finely chopped or grated

15g (½oz) piece ginger, finely grated

100g (3½oz) minced (ground) lamb (optional)

1 tsp Kashmiri chilli powder

1 tbsp medium curry powder

50g (1¾oz) split red lentils, well rinsed

1 x 400g (14oz) can chopped tomatoes

1 tbsp tamarind paste

½ tsp caster (superfine) sugar

250ml (9fl oz) lamb, chicken or vegetable stock

TO SERVE

Green chillies, sliced

Coriander (cilantro), chopped

Rice or flatbreads

These meatballs are based on a classic kofte kebab – minced (ground) meat that is usually moulded around a skewer or torpedo-shaped. I have left them round as that is the easiest way to cook them, but they will work with whichever shape you go with.

The lamb mince in the sauce is optional, but it does add an extra layer of savouriness. It also provides a very quick and easy sauce that you can serve without the meatballs and just stir into any type of grain or eat over potatoes for a simple, economical meal.

First, make the meatballs. Put all the ingredients (apart from the oil) in a food processor with a generous amount of salt and pulse until well broken down. Remove from the food processor and mould into 12 meatballs.

Heat the oil in your pressure cooker (or a frying pan/ skillet) and add the meatballs. Fry for 2 minutes on each side, then remove.

Next, make the sauce. Heat the olive oil in your pressure cooker and add the onion. Sauté for a few minutes, then add the garlic, ginger and lamb mince, if using. Stir until the lamb has lightly browned, then stir in the spices and lentils. Add the tomatoes, tamarind paste and sugar, then pour in the stock. Season with salt and pepper.

Arrange the meatballs over the sauce, then close the lid and bring up to high pressure. Cook for 7 minutes, then allow to drop pressure naturally. Serve with green chillies, coriander (cilantro) and either rice or flatbreads.

MEATLOAF

SERVES 4

1 tbsp olive oil, plus extra for greasing

1 onion, finely chopped

100g (3½oz) smoked bacon, finely chopped (optional)

2 garlic cloves, finely chopped

50ml (1¾fl oz) whole milk (optional)

50g (1¾oz) fresh breadcrumbs

500g (1lb 2oz) minced (ground) beef or pork

1 tbsp fresh oregano, finely chopped, or 1 tsp dried

1 egg, beaten

100g (3½oz) Cheddar or similar hard cheese, sliced

Sea salt and freshly ground black pepper

FOR THE GLAZE

2 tbsp tomato ketchup

1 tbsp tomato purée

2 tsp maple syrup

½ tsp chilli powder of your choice

VARIATIONS

Make a haslet/apple layer by using Lincolnshire sausage meat and putting a layer of Cheddar, butter-fried apple slices and sage leaves in the middle. Or use the lamb meatball mix and put a layer of mango chutney and coriander (cilantro) through the middle. These are best cooked, chilled and sliced for spectacular sandwiches.

This is a basic meatloaf recipe that you can play around with as much as you like, as long as you keep the basic quantities the same. It is adapted from Josceline Dimbleby's classic *Marvellous Meals with Mince*.

I really like meatloaf hot or cold as a very cheap alternative to sliced meat in sandwiches. Try it with a really good pickle or chutney.

Heat the olive oil in a frying pan (skillet). Add the onion and bacon, if using, and sauté on a medium–high heat until the bacon is crisp and the onion is lightly golden. Add the garlic and cook for another couple of minutes, then remove from the heat and leave to cool. Meanwhile, if using the milk, mix with the breadcrumbs and leave the breadcrumbs to swell.

Put the minced meat into a bowl and add the onion and bacon, along with the breadcrumbs, herbs and the egg. Season with plenty of salt and pepper, then mix together thoroughly using your hands to knead the mixture until it feels quite firm.

Divide the mixture in half. Lightly grease a large piece of foil with oil or butter. Place half of the mixture over it and form into a flat loaf, then top with the cheese, making sure you leave a border. Top with the remaining meatloaf mixture, making sure you seal the cheese in seamlessly.

Mix the tomato ketchup, purée and maple syrup together with the chilli powder and plenty of seasoning. Brush this all over the loaf. Put 2cm (¾in) water in the base of your pressure cooker, add the trivet and a steamer basket and lift in the meatloaf, using the sides of the foil as handles. Close the lid and bring up to high pressure. Cook for 15 minutes and natural release. To brown, put under a hot grill for a few minutes or use your air-fryer attachment if you like.

SLOW-ROAST LAMB

SERVES 4–6 WITH LEFTOVERS

2 tbsp olive oil

½ shoulder or leg of lamb, bone in

1 fennel bulb, cut into wedges

3 sprigs of rosemary

1 sprig of thyme

2 sprigs of oregano

3 pieces pared lemon zest

1 head garlic, cut in half crossways

150ml (5fl oz) white wine

Sea salt and freshly ground black pepper

This is one of those lamb dishes that is usually roasted in the oven for at least 4–5 hours, and is unbelievably tender when it is cooked – the bone should pull out easily and the meat should fall apart. It works equally well with shoulder or leg.

Heat the olive oil in your pressure cooker, or if you prefer, in a large, heavy frying pan (skillet). Add the lamb, skin-side down, and sear until well browned. You should see a reasonable amount of fat render out during this process. If you have done this in your pressure cooker, remove the meat from the cooker and strain off most of the fat. Return to the pressure cooker and add the fennel bulb, 2 of the sprigs of rosemary, the rest of the herbs, 2 pieces of lemon zest and the garlic. Pour over the wine and season with salt and pepper.

Close the lid and bring up to high pressure. Reduce the heat to maintain pressure, then cook for 1 hour. Remove from the heat and allow to drop pressure naturally.

If you want to crisp up the skin, you can at this point put it under a medium–hot grill for a few minutes, otherwise transfer it to a warm serving plate and wrap well with foil. Strain the contents of the pressure cooker and push through a sieve – fennel, squished garlic cloves and everything – you will end up with a creamy gravy. Leave to cool a little so the fat settles on top and spoon most of this off. Reheat the gravy, adding the reserved sprig of rosemary and lemon zest and any juices from the resting meat. Serve the gravy with the meat, which should be tender enough to pull apart with a couple of forks.

VARIATION

This is a good template for all kinds of slow-roast dishes, including this spicier lamb raan. Make a marinade with 100g (3½oz) yogurt, 2 tablespoons of lemon juice, 15g (½oz) grated ginger and 2 tablespoons of the spice mix on page 126. Leave the lamb to marinate for at least 1 hour, or overnight if you like. Add 1 teaspoon each of coriander seeds and cardamom pods and a small piece of cinnamon stick to the pot and replace the fennel with onion and the herbs with 2 bay leaves. Use water and an optional 100g (3½oz) canned tomatoes in place of the wine.

QUICK LAMB OR GOAT CURRY

SERVES 4

600g (1lb 5oz) diced lamb

FOR THE MARINADE

100g (3½oz) yogurt

Juice of 1 lemon

1 tsp ground turmeric

1 tsp medium chilli powder

1 tsp ground cumin

2 tsp ground coriander

Sea salt and freshly ground black pepper

FOR THE CURRY

1 tbsp coconut or vegetable oil or ghee

1 large onion, finely sliced

15g (½oz) piece ginger, grated

4 garlic cloves, finely chopped

4 black cardamom pods

3cm (1¼in) piece cinnamon stick

1 tbsp tomato purée

200g (7oz) canned chopped tomatoes

250g (9oz) peas (optional)

TO SERVE

Coriander (cilantro) leaves

Green chillies, sliced

This is based very loosely on a handi – a simple tomato curry that can also be made with chicken. The yogurt marinade is not essential but does help with the overall texture and the sauce's characteristic savouriness. The peas are also optional – if you want them very soft and sweet, cook them along with the lamb; if you want to retain their greenness and bounce, add afterwards and heat through for a few minutes.

This curry doesn't need any extra liquid, but as it is tomato-based you will need to take care with possible scorching. If you are using an electric pressure cooker, using a ceramic insert will help; alternatively if you are worried, add a splash of water and make sure the base of the cooker is completely deglazed.

Put the marinade ingredients into a bowl and add 1 teaspoon of salt and lots of black pepper. Add the lamb and mix so the lamb is thoroughly coated. Cover and leave to stand for at least an hour – you can leave overnight if you like.

Heat the oil or ghee in your pressure cooker. Add the onion and sauté on a medium–high heat until softening and starting to brown a little, then add the ginger and garlic. Cook for another couple of minutes. Alternatively, stir in 4 tablespoons of onion, garlic and ginger paste (see page 329). Add the whole spices and lamb and stir to coat the lamb in the onion mix. Stir in the tomato purée, then pour in the tomatoes. Season again with salt and pepper. Add the peas at this stage if you want them soft and sweet.

Bring up to high pressure and cook for 15 minutes. Allow to drop pressure naturally. If you haven't already added the peas, do so now and allow to warm through for a few minutes.

Serve with coriander (cilantro) leaves and sliced green chillies for extra heat.

LAMB SHANKS WITH FLAGEOLET BEANS

SERVES 4–6

1 tbsp olive oil

2 large or 4 small lamb shanks

1 onion, finely diced

1 large carrot, finely diced

1 celery stick, finely diced

2 sprigs of rosemary

2 sprigs of parsley

1 sprig of thyme

1 piece of pared lemon zest

200ml (7fl oz) red or white wine

2 tomatoes, finely chopped or puréed

250g (9oz) dried unsoaked flageolet beans

1 head of garlic, cut in half

500ml (17fl oz) lamb, chicken or vegetable stock or water

Sea salt and freshly ground black pepper

There are several different cuts of lamb you could use for this dish, but the reason I choose lamb shanks is that they are reasonably lean. This means that they will not give out a huge amount of fat, compared with, say, neck fillet or diced shoulder. This is important in this dish as the beans make it hard to skim the fat.

If you have made a large batch of sofrito for the freezer, you could use a portion of it for this recipe in place of the onion, carrot and celery (see page 330).

Heat the olive oil in your pressure cooker and add the lamb shanks. Brown on all sides, then remove from the pressure cooker. Add the onion, carrot and celery and sauté on a medium–high heat for a few minutes, stirring to lift up any brown residue left from the lamb. When the vegetables look as though they are starting to brown around the edges, add the herbs and lemon zest to the cooker, then pour over the wine. Bring to the boil and allow to bubble for a minute.

Stir in the tomatoes, then return the lamb shanks to the cooker. Pour the beans around the lamb and tuck in the head of garlic. Add the stock or water and season with salt and pepper.

Close the lid and bring up to high pressure. Cook for 30 minutes, then remove from the heat and leave to drop pressure naturally. Remove the shanks from the pressure cooker and – if using 2 large rather than 4 small – break up the meat into large chunks. Return to the pressure cooker and heat through. Serve with a generous side of greens.

VARIATION

Ham Hock with White Beans
A ham hock – or a small joint of gammon – will work very well in this recipe with a little adjustment. First, check if it needs soaking. You can do a quick soak in the pressure cooker by covering with cold water, bringing up to high pressure and immediately fast releasing. Discard the water, rinse the ham and the inside of the cooker free of any starch that may have coated them and proceed as above, replacing the flageolet with white beans.

BRAISED LAMB WITH APRICOTS AND ROSEMARY

SERVES 4

1 tbsp olive oil

1 red large onion, finely sliced

600g (1lb 5oz) lamb neck fillet or shoulder, trimmed and thickly sliced

3 garlic cloves, finely chopped

A large pinch of saffron, soaked in a little warm water

½ tsp ground cinnamon

1 tsp ground ginger

1 sprig of rosemary or summer or winter savory

100g (3½oz) dried apricots

A few sprigs of flat-leaf parsley or mint, roughly torn

Sea salt and freshly ground black pepper

TO SERVE

150g (5½oz) couscous

15g (½oz) slice of butter

Juice of 1 orange

A few drops of orange blossom water (optional)

25g (1oz) toasted almonds

This is based on a classic tagine, but I've added a herbal element with the rosemary; the combination of flavours reminds me of the way my mother used to roast lamb or goat when I was a child.

This is best served with a pile of herby, buttery couscous, but you could also turn it into a one-pot meal – see the Variations for details.

Heat the olive oil in the pressure cooker. Add the onion and sauté on a high heat until it starts to brown around the edges. Add the lamb and the garlic and cook until the lamb has taken on some colour. Stir in the spices and rosemary and season with plenty of salt and pepper.

Add 150ml (5fl oz) water to the cooker along with half the apricots. Close the lid and bring up to high pressure. Cook for 10 minutes, then release pressure naturally. Add the remaining apricots to the cooker and return to high pressure. Cook for another 5 minutes and again, leave to drop pressure naturally. Serve garnished with a little parsley or mint.

Put the couscous in a bowl with the butter. Measure the orange juice and make up with hot water to 175ml (5½fl oz). Add a few drops of orange blossom water if you like. Pour over the couscous and leave to stand until all the water has absorbed. Fluff up and garnish with the almonds.

VARIATIONS

Use quince in place of the apricots. Lamb and quince is a lovely combination, but quince will disintegrate in the time it takes to cook the lamb, so using 1 large or 2 small quince, follow the recipe on page 296; add a few of these cooked wedges to the pressure cooker when you cook the lamb, which should be cooked at high pressure for 15 minutes. Add the rest of the quince once the lamb has cooked completely and heat through for a couple of minutes.

To turn into a one-pot with less meat: reduce the amount of lamb by half and cook at high pressure for 15 minutes. Add 250g (9oz) root vegetables or squash, 250g (9oz) cooked chickpeas (garbanzo beans) and 1 sliced red pepper with the second batch of apricots. Bring up to high pressure for 2 minutes and natural release again.

LAMB BREAST SALAD

SERVES 4

FOR THE LAMB BREAST

1 lamb breast

2 tbsp olive oil

1 large sprig of rosemary leaves

4 garlic cloves, sliced

2 pieces of pared lemon zest

100ml (3½fl oz) red wine

25ml (1fl oz) red wine vinegar

Sea salt and freshly ground black pepper

FOR THE SALAD

150g (5½oz) cooked spelt, farro or buckwheat (see page 182)

100g (3½oz) spinach, rocket (arugula) or watercress (or a combination)

½ red onion, finely chopped and soaked in salted water for 30 minutes

Zest of 1 lemon or ½ orange, finely chopped

2 garlic cloves, finely chopped

1 large bunch of flat-leaf parsley, finely chopped

1 small bunch of mint leaves, chopped

FOR THE DRESSING

1 tbsp olive oil

1 tbsp lemon or orange juice

1 tsp sherry vinegar

A pinch of ground cinnamon

This is an example of how the pressure cooker can make the most out of those trickier cuts of meat, without it necessarily having to be winter comfort food. Lamb breast is just about the cheapest cut of lamb you can get; it is very fatty, but has a really good flavour. I gave it a rolled 'porchetta'-style treatment in my first pressure cooker book, but here I wanted something lighter and simpler. This recipe will also work well with lamb ribs.

I've served it with what is essentially a gremolata with a grain stirred through it. This will work with any grain you have as long as it has a bit of bite – spelt or farro, buckwheat, freekeh, brown rice – see page 182 for timings. Alternatively, instead of making this into a salad, simply serve the lamb breast and skimmed cooking liquor alongside any mash or gratin.

First cut the lamb breast into 4 large pieces – you should be able to just get them into your pressure cooker in a single layer. Season with salt and pepper. Heat 1 tablespoon of the olive oil and sear the lamb breast, skin-side down, until well browned. Remove and strain off any excess fat.

Add the rosemary leaves, garlic and lemon zest to the cooker, then pour in the red wine and red wine vinegar. Lay the lamb breast pieces on top, skin-side up, and close the lid. Bring up to high pressure and cook for 30 minutes. Allow to drop pressure naturally. Remove the lamb breast from the pressure cooker, and, while still warm, cut up into strips or shred, discarding any large pieces of fat that have not rendered. Decant the cooking liquor into a small pot and wait for the fat to settle on top. Skim off the fat and reheat the liquor to serve with the lamb as a gravy or reserve to use as a well-flavoured stock in other dishes.

If turning into a salad, whisk the salad dressing ingredients together and season with salt and pepper. Heat the remaining olive oil in a frying pan (skillet) and crisp up the lamb breast a little, then toss with all the remaining salad ingredients and dressing.

SPICED SHEPHERD'S PIE

SERVES 4-6

400g (14oz) minced (ground) lamb

1 tbsp coconut oil

1 onion, finely chopped

300g (10½oz) mixed root vegetables (carrot, swede/rutabaga, celeriac/celery root, sweet potato, turnip), finely diced

4 garlic cloves, grated or crushed

25g (1oz) piece ginger, grated

4 tbsp coriander (cilantro) stems, finely chopped

1 tbsp curry powder or spice mix (see page 123)

75g (2½oz) brown or green lentils or chana dal

100g (3½oz) canned chopped tomatoes

1 tbsp Pickapeppa sauce or 1 tsp Worcestershire sauce

100g (3½oz) coconut cream (optional)

250ml (9fl oz) chicken stock or water

Sea salt and freshly ground black pepper

FOR THE TOPPING

750g (1lb 10oz) floury potatoes, left whole and unpeeled

1 tbsp olive oil

1 onion, finely chopped

2 garlic cloves, finely chopped

12 fresh curry leaves

½ tsp mustard, cumin or nigella seeds

25g (1oz) butter

4 mild–medium green chillies, finely chopped

1 small bunch of coriander (cilantro), chopped

100g (3½oz) hard cheese, such as Cheddar, coarsely grated (optional)

This is one of the very few recipes in this book for which I will turn on the oven, but you can avoid it if you keep the filling hot while you make the potato topping and simply put it under the grill to brown the cheese. Alternatively, you can serve it as a ragù with mash.

You can speed things up in other ways too. It is perfectly possible to cook the potatoes in the steamer basket while you cook the lamb and lentils. I choose not to do this because I don't want all the flavours of the filling infusing the potatoes. You can also speed up the cooking of the potatoes by cooking them in the base of the pressure cooker rather than steaming them – this will be much faster (around 4 minutes) – and makes perfectly good mashed potatoes. I just really like the dry, fluffiness you get from cooking them as below.

First, make the filling. If your lamb is very fatty and you would like to remove some of it, put it in a frying pan (skillet) and fry until browned and a lot of fat has rendered out. Strain it and set aside.

Heat the oil in your pressure cooker and add the onion and root vegetables. Sauté until they start to brown around the edges, then stir in the garlic, ginger, coriander (cilantro) stems and curry powder. Cook for a couple of minutes, then add the mince and lentils. Season with plenty of salt and pepper. Pour in the canned tomatoes, Pickapeppa or Worcestershire sauce, the coconut cream, if using, and the chicken stock or water. Close the lid and bring up to high pressure. Cook for 10 minutes, then allow to drop pressure naturally. You should have quite a thick ragù. Transfer to an ovenproof dish.

Wash out your pressure cooker and add water. Put the potatoes in the steamer basket and steam at high pressure. Smallish potatoes up to 100g (3½oz) will take around 10 minutes, large baking potatoes will take up to 25 minutes. Release pressure quickly, then when the potatoes are cool enough to handle, peel off their skins. Break up and mash, preferably by pushing through a ricer.

Spiced Shepherd's Pie *continued*

Preheat your oven to 200°C (400°F/Gas 6). Heat the olive oil in a pan and add the onion. Sauté until soft, then add the garlic, curry leaves and spice seeds. When the curry leaves have stopped crackling, add the butter. When it has melted, stir in the mashed potatoes, green chillies and coriander.

Spread the mash over the filling, then rough up with a fork. Sprinkle over the cheese, if using. Bake for around 30 minutes until the cheese has melted and is starting to brown.

VARIATIONS

Of course this is adaptable to make a cottage or shepherd's pie. Take out the ginger and spices, replace the coconut cream with red wine and add a bouquet garni of bay, thyme and parsley. Make a straightforward mash – you might want to stir in some wholegrain mustard and chopped parsley.

To make this vegetarian: Replace the lamb with 1 diced aubergine (eggplant) and 150g (5½oz) chopped chestnut mushrooms. Cook down with the root vegetables.

To vary the topping: Use half sweet potatoes or celeriac (celery root) with the potatoes.

CHAR SIU

SERVES 8

4 thick-cut pork shoulder steaks or 1 piece of belly pork with the rind removed (around 750g/1lb 10oz)

100ml (3½fl oz) light soy sauce

50ml (1¾fl oz) hoisin sauce

50ml (1¾fl oz) mirin

2 tbsp rice vinegar

2 tsp chilli bean paste (optional)

2 tbsp light soft brown sugar

4 garlic cloves, crushed

15g (½oz) piece ginger, grated

2 star anise

There are so many ways to make this dish, but this is a really simple one. Instead of marinating for several hours, or overnight, the pork is cooked in the sauce, then left in the cooking liquid to cool and store, to be sliced as you need it. I freeze portions of it, still in the sauce, for quick meals.

Poke the meat all over with a skewer. Put in the pressure cooker with the remaining ingredients and add just enough water to cover the meat. Bring up to high pressure and cook for 15 minutes. Leave to drop pressure naturally.

Remove the meat and the cooking liquid from the pressure cooker and leave to cool, then chill. When you want to use the meat, slice quite thinly and fry in vegetable oil, using some of the cooking liquid to baste the meat and caramelize around it as it cooks.

Serve with greens and steamed rice, or drop into ramen (page 175), or use leftovers in the rice dish on page 192.

VARIATION

You can also make chasu pork in a similar way. Use a piece of rolled, tied pork belly – this time with the skin on. Put in the same sauce, but add just 250ml (9fl oz) water – it will need much more to completely cover and you don't want to dilute the flavours any more. Cook at high pressure for 1 hour with natural release – the pork should be completely tender after this time. Leave to cool in the liquid, then wrap the meat up in clingfilm (plastric wrap), reserving the liquid for something else, then chill for several hours before using. Thinly slice before using in ramen, lightly frying again first.

PORK AND GREENS WITH ORANGE AND CHILLI

SERVES 4-6

1 tbsp groundnut oil

1 kg (2lb 4oz) pork osso buco or ribs or 750g (1lb 10oz) pork shoulder or belly pork, diced

1 onion, thickly sliced

5 garlic cloves, grated or crushed

30g (1oz) piece ginger, grated

1 star anise

1 tsp Chinese 5 spice

1 tbsp tomato purée

1–3 tsp hot chilli paste or sauce, according to taste

2 tbsp dark soy sauce

Juice of 2 oranges

1 bunch of coriander (cilantro), stems and leaves separated

400g (14oz) greens, such as broccoli, sprouting broccoli, pak choi (bok choy)

Sea salt and freshly ground black pepper

TO SERVE

Black rice (see page 198)

Sesame oil or chilli oil

Spring onions (scallions), shredded

This is a fiery, showstopper of a casserole, especially if served with the intense-looking black rice. It's a bit of a Peruvian and Chinese fusion in terms of flavour and quite soupy, so I serve it over the rice in bowls. If you have one pressure cooker, cook the rice first – it will reheat when you pour over the hot pan juices. You can add any greens to this – I like regular or sprouting broccoli.

You can use most cuts of pork for this casserole. On the bone will give the most flavour, but diced pork shoulder or even belly pork will work really well, just make sure you brown them very well and be prepared to skim for fat at the end.

Heat the oil in your pressure cooker and add the meat. Sear on all sides to get some good colour, then remove from the cooker. Add the onion, garlic and ginger. Fry for a minute or two, then stir in spices, tomato purée and chilli paste or sauce.

Return the pork to the cooker and turn over to coat with the spices, then add the soy sauce, orange juice and coriander (cilantro) stems. Season with salt and pepper.

Close the lid and bring up to high pressure. Cook for 30 minutes, then remove from the heat and allow to drop pressure naturally. Remove the meat and keep warm. If the contents of the pot are looking very fatty, skim. Place the greens on top, bring up to high pressure and then remove from the heat and fast release.

Serve spooned over the rice with plenty of the broth. Drizzle with sesame or chilli oil and sprinkle with the coriander leaves and shredded spring onions (scallions).

KOREAN-STYLE BRAISED PORK RIBS

SERVES 4–6

2 tbsp neutral-tasting oil, such as groundnut, grapeseed or sunflower

1 kg (2lb 4oz) meaty pork ribs

1 large onion, very finely chopped

4 garlic cloves, grated

25g (1oz) piece ginger, grated

1–4 tbsp gochujang paste (according to taste)

50ml (1¾fl oz) light soy sauce

50ml (1¾fl oz) mirin

25ml (1fl oz) rice wine vinegar

1 tbsp light soft brown sugar or honey

Sea salt and freshly ground black pepper

TO GARNISH

Sesame seeds

Spring onions (scallions), shredded

Coriander (cilantro) leaves (optional)

This is a dish that requires thick, meaty ribs – the sort that would normally be braised slowly for 7 hours or more – not the skinny ends. If you can only get skinny ribs, reduce the cooking time by 10 minutes. The flavour is based around gochujang, the Korean hot red pepper paste, which can give fire and sweetness and a deep red colour to anything you add it to. The cooking time is, frankly, miraculous, with several hours being reduced to 30–45 minutes.

If you have leftovers, use in the soup on page 32, or shred off some of the meat as an option for the Basic Fried Rice on page 192.

Heat 1 tablespoon of the oil in either a frying pan (skillet) or your pressure cooker. Season the ribs with salt and pepper and brown quickly on the meatiest sides. Remove from the pressure cooker if that's where you have browned them, then add the remaining oil. Add the onion and sauté on a high heat until it starts to brown around the edges. Add the garlic and ginger and cook for a further couple of minutes.

Stir in the gochujang paste; 1 tablespoon will give you a fairly gentle heat, 3–4 tablespoons will give it proper fire. Pour in the soy sauce, mirin, rice wine vinegar and sugar or honey. Stir to combine, then return the ribs to the cooker. Season with salt. Close the lid and bring up to high pressure. Cook for 30 minutes for tender ribs that will still hold up to grilling, or 45 minutes for meat that will fall off the bone. Allow to drop pressure naturally.

Remove the ribs from the pressure cooker. Reduce the cooking liquor down until it is syrupy. Either serve the ribs as they are, with the reduced sauce poured over, garnished with sesame, spring onions (scallions) and coriander (cilantro), if using, or fry or grill them, basting them in the sauce, until blackened.

CLASSIC GLAZED HAM

2KG (4LB 8OZ) WILL SERVE AROUND 8 WITH LEFTOVERS

1 ham or gammon joint

1 onion, studded with 4 cloves

1 tsp allspice berries

1 tsp black peppercorns

2 blades of mace

4 bay leaves

1 sprig of thyme

FOR THE GLAZE

2 tbsp honey or syrup from a jar of stem ginger

1 tbsp Dijon mustard

Zest and juice of ½ orange

Cloves (optional)

VARIATIONS

I love using other kinds of liquid when boiling a ham and have used everything from cola, ginger beer, pineapple juice and cider to fizzy pineapple and grapefruit drink. Cooking in a liquid with a higher sugar content gives a denser, firmer meat, which is especially good sliced in sandwiches. You can use the liquid of your choice or dilute it with water – it will still give a strong, interesting flavoured stock.

I am giving you two options for cooking the ham – choose the method that suits you best. Method 1 involves steaming the ham on a trivet. This takes less time to come up to pressure as you use less liquid and results in a denser ham, excellent for slicing and a concentrated stock. Pressure cook for 11 minutes per 500g (1lb 2oz). Method 2 involves poaching the ham as you completely or partially (depending on size of the ham), immerse the ham in liquid. This gives you an excellent stock, useful for all sorts of things (especially soups, pulses and pastas) and a slightly softer finish. Pressure cook for 10 minutes per 500g (1lb 2oz).

To cook ham hocks or knuckles on the bone, use the second method and cook for a blanket 30 minutes.

Make sure when buying a ham that it will fit in your pressure cooker with at least a quarter clear for the steam.

Check whether your ham has been soaked or not. If not, leave to soak in cold water overnight, or put in your pressure cooker and cover with cold water. Close the lid and bring up to high pressure. Immediately remove from the heat and leave to drop pressure naturally. Drain, discarding the water, then rinse out the pressure cooker and give the ham a rinse too. Weigh the ham so you can work out the cooking times.

Return the ham to the pressure cooker and add the onion and aromatics. At this point you can either put around 2cm (¾in) water into the base of your pressure cooker and place the ham on a trivet to steam, or you can completely or partially cover with water again, then close the lid and bring up to pressure. Cook at high pressure for 10–11 minutes per 500g (1lb 2oz), then allow to drop pressure naturally.

Preheat your oven to 200°C (400°F/Gas 6). Mix the honey, mustard and orange zest and juice together. Remove the ham skin and trim the fat. Score with a diamond pattern and push cloves into the corners of the diamonds if you like. Brush with the glaze and oven cook for 20 minutes.

PORK-STUFFED CABBAGE ROLLS

SERVES 4-6

16 Savoy cabbage leaves

FOR THE STUFFING

250g (9oz) minced (ground) pork or sausagemeat

1 tbsp tomato purée

1 onion, finely chopped

3 garlic cloves, finely chopped

1 small carrot, grated

50g (1¾oz) mushrooms, finely chopped

50g (1¾oz) fresh breadcrumbs

25g (1oz) Parmesan cheese, grated (optional)

Zest of 1 lemon

½ tsp dried sage, crumbled

½ tsp dried oregano, crumbled

Sea salt and freshly ground black pepper

OPTIONAL SAUCE

Tomato sauce (see page 332 or 333)

OPTIONAL TOPPING

25g (1oz) fresh breadcrumbs

25g (1oz) cheese, such as Cheddar, grated

2 tbsp finely chopped parsley or dill

Savoy cabbage works best for this recipe as it is the easiest cabbage to pry whole leaves from. If you want to use a tightly furled green or white cabbage (make sure it is round), and are finding it difficult, there is actually a pressure cooker solution – core the cabbage, then steam the whole thing at high pressure for 2 minutes. The leaves will then come away cleanly. It is still, however, a faff, so stick with an easier cabbage if you can.

I suggest making this with one of the tomato sauces on page 332 or 333, but I like it just with sour cream with some caramelized onions (see page 331) stirred through. It is possible to cook cabbage parcels in the sauce, but the texture is, I think, better if they are steamed. A happy medium is to combine after cooking – see below for details.

Put 2cm (¾in) water in your pressure cooker and balance the cabbage leaves on a trivet or steamer basket. Bring up to high pressure and release pressure immediately. The leaves should now be pliable enough to use without the stems breaking when you roll them. Trim the thickest part of the stem away.

Make the stuffing by mixing all the ingredients together and seasoning with salt and pepper. Divide into 16 and shape into logs. Place each log at the base of a cabbage leaf, fold in the sides and roll. Arrange in your steamer basket.

Put around 2cm (¾in) water in the base of your cooker. Insert the trivet and balance the steamer basket on top. Close the lid and bring up to high pressure. Cook for 12 minutes, then allow to drop pressure naturally.

Arrange the cabbage rolls on a serving dish and spoon over the heated sauce. Alternatively, layer with the sauce, sprinkle with the breadcrumbs, cheese and herbs, and put under a hot grill for 5 minutes.

CHORIZO WITH POTATOES AND VEGETABLES

SERVES 4

1 tbsp olive oil

100g (3½oz) cooking chorizo, sliced

2 tbsp sofrito (see page 330) or 1 small onion, finely chopped

750g (1lb 10oz) any potatoes, unpeeled and cut into 3cm (1¼in) chunks

150g (5½oz) frozen broad (fava) beans

200g (7oz) canned chopped tomatoes

200g (7oz) kale, roughly torn

1 small bunch of flat-leaf parsley

Squeeze of lemon juice (optional)

Sea salt and freshly ground black pepper

This is a useful dish to have when you want to make something substantial in one pot in a hurry. It takes so little time I can make it first thing in the morning for the lunch Thermoses. Part of the reason for this is that using the chorizo means you are putting flavour into the dish in a really easy but effective way and don't need to add garlic etc. It works with other types of meat, including leftovers, and any vegetables that won't go mushy in the time. Frozen beans, peas, sweetcorn, spinach are ideal.

Heat the olive oil in your pressure cooker. Add the chorizo and sofrito or onion and cook for 2–3 minutes until the chorizo has given out lots of its oil. Stir in the potatoes and cook for a minute or two, stirring until they are well-coated with the oil.

Add the broad (fava) beans (you don't have to defrost them first), then the canned tomatoes. Add just a splash of water, then season with salt and pepper. Put the kale on top. Close the lid and bring up to high pressure. Cook for 5 minutes, then allow to drop pressure naturally.

Stir in the parsley, and serve as is or with a squeeze of lemon juice.

SAUSAGES WITH SAUERKRAUT

SERVES 4

1 tbsp olive oil

8 sausages of your choice

1 large onion, thickly sliced

½ tsp juniper berries, lightly crushed

½ tsp caraway seeds

3 garlic cloves, finely chopped

½ green cabbage, shredded

1 large jar of sauerkraut, rinsed if you want to reduce the sourness (650g/1lb 7oz drained weight)

1 tbsp wholegrain mustard

1 eating apple, peeled, cored and sliced

100ml (3½fl oz) cider

100ml (3½fl oz) double (heavy) or sour cream (optional)

Sea salt and freshly ground black pepper

Even though I have used pressure cookers for years, I am still amazed at how quickly some things cook. Here is one such example – 2 minutes high pressure seems incredible, but it really does work in that time. I do sometimes use my own sauerkraut for this, but the large jars I can get in the Polish supermarkets near me are excellent. Some will have all kinds of things added to them, but I prefer to buy those that are just cabbage and salt and add in my own flavours.

If you want to add potatoes to this, instead of cooking them separately, you can increase the cooking time without any harm coming to the rest of the ingredients, but it is also worth decanting this to a casserole to keep warm and making mashed potatoes to serve with it.

Heat the oil in your pressure cooker and add the sausages. Cook on a high heat, turning regularly, until browned – around 4–5 minutes. Remove from the cooker and set aside.

Add the onion, juniper berries, caraway seeds and garlic and sauté for a minute or two, just to start them off, then add the cabbage and sauerkraut. Stir in the mustard and apple, then pour over the cider. Make sure you deglaze the base of the cooker well at this point, then season with salt and pepper. Return the sausages to the cooker.

Bring up to high pressure and cook for 2 minutes only. Release pressure naturally, then if using, stir in the cream and simmer for an additional couple of minutes.

VARIATION

Bigos
Take 500g (1lb 2oz) pork ribs or belly pork and fry in 1 tablespoon of olive oil until well browned. Add 100ml (3½fl oz) cider and cook at high pressure for 30 minutes. Fast release. Remove the meat and cooking liquor from the pressure cooker and set aside. Follow the main recipe, replacing the sausages with a Polish-style smoked sausage, thickly sliced. Stir in an optional 1 teaspoon each of sweet and hot paprika after you have sautéed the onions, then add the pork cooking liquor and 100g (3½oz) canned tomatoes along with the cider. Return the pork to the pressure cooker with the sausages. Serve with the sour cream on the side.

QUICK SAUSAGE CASSEROLE

SERVES 4

1 tbsp olive oil

8 sausages

1 large onion, cut into slim wedges

2 large carrots, cut into chunks

200g (7oz) waxy or floury potatoes, thickly sliced

3 garlic cloves, finely chopped

1 tbsp wholegrain mustard

½ tsp dried sage, crumbled

150ml (5fl oz) cider or white wine

½ green pointed cabbage or similar, thickly sliced

2 leeks, cut into thick rounds

Sea salt and freshly ground black pepper

A simple, homely one-pot, saving on fuel and washing up as the greens are cooked in the same cooker. This means the pressure cooking is done in two stages to make sure the leeks and greens won't overcook – the only thing you need to look out for is that if you use floury potatoes, they will leach starch into the gravy, so you must make sure the base of the cooker has nothing sticking to it before you do the second cook.

Heat the oil in your pressure cooker and add the sausages. Brown on all sides, then remove from the cooker.

Add the onion, carrots, potatoes and garlic. Sauté for a couple of minutes, then stir in the mustard. Add the sage, season with salt and pepper, then pour in the cider or white wine.

Close the lid and bring up to pressure, then cook at high pressure for 4 minutes. Release pressure, then give a quick stir to make sure nothing is sticking to the base of the cooker, then add the cabbage and leeks. Close the lid again, bring up to pressure, then immediately remove from the heat. Allow to drop pressure naturally.

PORK AND DILL MEATBALLS WITH BRAISED BUCKWHEAT AND BEETROOT

SERVES 4

FOR THE MEATBALLS

500g (1lb 2oz) minced (ground) pork (or chicken or turkey will also work well)

50g (1¾oz) breadcrumbs (optional)

1 small egg (optional)

1 large garlic clove, grated

1 small bunch of dill, finely chopped

½ tsp hot smoked paprika

Zest of ½ lemon

Sea salt and freshly ground black pepper

FOR THE BRAISE

2 tbsp olive oil

1 onion, finely chopped

150g (5½oz) beetroot, peeled and very finely diced

2 large garlic cloves, grated or crushed

1 tsp sweet smoked paprika

50g (1¼oz) toasted buckwheat

200g (7oz) canned chopped tomatoes

150g (5½oz) any type of kale or chard, shredded

TO SERVE

A few dill fronds

Sour cream

For this recipe, I'm giving you a choice regarding the meatballs. Just using pork will make them quite firm, which is great in the context of this dish; breadcrumbs and egg will make them much softer.

The texture of the beetroot in this dish is deliberately al dente. If you prefer it softer, you can add an extra minute of cooking at high pressure. The buckwheat will be softer, but will be none the worse for it.

First make the meatballs. Mix everything together and season with plenty of salt and pepper. Divide into 16 balls. Heat 1 tablespoon of the olive oil in your pressure cooker – or in a separate pan – and lightly fry the meatballs for a couple of minutes on the top and bottom (don't worry about the sides). If frying in the pressure cooker, remove.

Add the remaining olive oil to the pressure cooker. Add the onion and beetroot. Sauté on a high heat until the onion has turned translucent, then stir in the garlic, paprika and buckwheat. Cook for another couple of minutes. Stir in the tomatoes and kale, and season with salt and pepper. Pour in 150ml (5fl oz) water, then stir again.

Add the meatballs to the pressure cooker, arranging them on top of the vegetables and buckwheat. Bring up to high pressure and cook for 3 minutes, then allow to drop pressure naturally. The beetroot will still have some bite and the buckwheat will have swelled and softened.

Serve with a scattering of dill and spoonfuls of sour cream.

POULTRY

Chicken remains one of our most popular things to eat, which is why there are a fair few recipes here and in other chapters; the focus, however, is primarily on cooking a whole bird or chicken pieces, rather than breast fillets. The reasons for this are various – firstly, there is much more value in buying a whole bird or on-the-bone or intact thighs or drumsticks, not just in terms of money spent, but in terms of flavour. Meat cooked on the bone will always taste better, and the pressure cooker makes short work of tenderizing it. Cooking a whole bird – either by poaching or pot-roasting – is really economical in terms of how much fuel it takes compared to roasting in an oven, making it even better value for money. Finally, if you have a whole bird, you have a carcass for stock (see page 325) and chicken for leftovers, probably enough for several meals.

If you do want to use chicken breasts in any of the recipes in this chapter, you will need to reduce the cooking time substantially, as they will only take a couple of minutes at high pressure with natural release. And if you want to convert any of your conventional recipes, just bear in mind that you should reduce the amount of liquid by at least a third.

What kind of chicken? If you are wanting to use the whole bird and go on to make stock, there is no doubt that you will get better value out of a properly reared, free-to-roam chicken – the bones will be stronger from use, they will not be top heavy (all breast) and they will give out much more collagen into the stock and cooking liquor. This is better for the texture of your finished dish, better in terms of flavour, and better in terms of your health. It is better in terms of sustainability too. Much of this comes down to what chickens and other poultry are fed. Intensively reared chickens are frequently fed a diet that includes a lot of soya, most of which is imported and grown on cleared land, primarily in the Amazon. There is a lack of labelling on this, but organic chickens are safe and any decent butcher or producer should be able to answer your questions on this front. And so too should your supermarket. Such chickens are more expensive to buy but no more expensive than primarily buying plastic wrapped chicken breast fillets, so it is well worth making the switch to a greener chicken that is better for you and will provide you with more meals via leftovers and stock.

This chapter does focus mainly on chicken and duck, but wherever relevant I do mention where you can substitute them for game birds or rabbit – quite a lot of the recipes will adapt very well to them. Look to the variations for guidance on this.

HOW TO POACH CHICKEN (AND OTHER BIRDS)

There is more than one way of doing this, but in recent years I have come round to the 'Zero Minute' method developed by Amy and Jacky of the excellent pressurecookrecipes.com. It is very simple – cover the chicken with liquid, bring up to high pressure, then – the recipe is written for electric pressure cookers – set to 0 minutes pressure, 20 minutes natural release.

This also works well with stovetop pressure cookers, but without the necessity to time for 20 minutes – opening it when it has naturally dropped pressure will give you a perfectly cooked chicken. It is, however, important to make sure your chicken is completely covered in cold liquid, at the outset.

You can use this method to poach whole chickens, pieces of chicken or even filleted chicken breasts or thighs and as long as the chicken is covered with liquid, it will work every time. If you want to make absolutely sure your chicken is cooked through (and this is advisable, especially if you are using a free-range chicken, which will often stay a little pink around the bone), use a probe thermometer. It should read at least 72°C (162°F) wherever you position it in the chicken.

Is it worth doing? I have compared the timings and it takes a similar time to making the pot-roast chicken on page 102. The chicken cooks beautifully – the flesh will be very tender and the skin should be parchment-thin – no flabbiness. You also end up with a pot full of a very light chicken stock that is great to use for any dish to which you are going to add aromatics. It can also be used as a first-stage stock – if you aren't serving the poached chicken whole, you can strip off all the chicken from the carcass for easier storage, add the bones back into the broth along with aromatics and vegetables and make a richer chicken stock – see page 325 for instructions on what to add.

1 chicken, untrussed

A mixture of aromatics, such as garlic, herbs (thyme, rosemary, tarragon, oregano, coriander/cilantro), ginger

Sea salt

TO POACH A WHOLE CHICKEN

First rub the surface of the chicken with plenty of salt and add one third of any aromatics to the cavity. Make sure it is untrussed – you don't want the legs fastened tight against the body as this will result in uneven cooking. Place in the pressure cooker with any remaining aromatics, then cover with cold water. Make sure that the chicken is at least 90% covered if using an electric pressure cooker, completely covered if using a stovetop. Add 2 teaspoons of salt.

Close the lid and bring up to high pressure. As soon as it has come up to high pressure, remove from the heat. If using an electric pressure cooker, time 20 minutes natural release. If using a stovetop, just let it drop pressure naturally. Check the thickest, densest part of the chicken – it should read at least 72°C (162°F) on a probe thermometer.

WHAT TO DO WITH A POACHED CHICKEN?

Well, use it in the three best receptacles for leftovers, the three S's – soups, salads and sandwiches. Add to pasta and rice dishes – there are plenty of recipes dotted around this book that will adapt to cooked chicken. Use the poaching liquid to make a cream-enriched velouté and make a chicken pie. Layer it up with potatoes or other vegetables for a gratin or crumble. So many possibilities.

Overleaf are a couple of ideas for a complete meal using poached chicken.

POACHED CHICKEN SALAD

SERVES 4

FOR THE CHICKEN (AND LEFTOVER BROTH)

2 chicken breasts

25g (1oz) piece ginger, thinly sliced

3 garlic cloves, thinly sliced

1 lemongrass stem, bruised with the back of a knife

4 makrut lime leaves

Light chicken stock or water, to cover the breasts

Sea salt

FOR THE SALAD

100g (3½oz) baby corn

100g (3½oz) Tenderstem broccoli

100g (3½oz) green beans

½ Chinese (napa) cabbage or a cos (romaine) lettuce, shredded

1 large carrot, julienned

1 large bunch of coriander (cilantro), roughly chopped

A few mint leaves

6 radishes, sliced

4 spring onions (scallions), shredded

FOR THE DRESSING

2 tbsp fish sauce

2 tbsp lime juice

½ tsp palm sugar or light soft brown sugar (to taste)

1 garlic clove, finely chopped or grated

5g (⅛oz) piece ginger, grated

2 red chillies, finely chopped (deseeded if you like)

Using chicken pieces instead of a whole chicken when poaching is quicker and it will often result in a stronger flavoured liquor because the ratio of chicken to water is higher. Use the cooking liquor as a base for a Thai curry or broth, or to make the chicken noodle soup on page 178.
This recipe has the added benefit that the vegetables steam in the same pot while the chicken is poaching.

First poach the chicken and steam the vegetables for the salad. Put the chicken breasts in your pressure cooker with the aromatics and cover with water or light chicken stock. Season with plenty of salt. Put the trivet in the pressure cooker and balance the steamer basket on top. Put the baby corn, broccoli and green beans on the steamer basket – in that order so the baby corn is on the bottom. Close the lid, bring up to high pressure, then immediately remove from the heat. Leave to drop pressure naturally. You will find that the greens are just al dente and the chicken will be cooked through.

While the chicken is cooking, make the salad dressing by whisking all the ingredients together.

Take the chicken breasts and shred them with 2 forks. Arrange the Chinese (napa) cabbage or lettuce over a large platter, then top with the cooked vegetables and the carrot, herbs, radishes, spring onions (scallions) and chicken. Very lightly turn over with your hands or salad tongs, then drizzle over the dressing. Serve immediately.

LEFTOVER ZERO-MINUTE CHICKEN GUMBO

SERVES 4–6

FOR THE CHICKEN AND SEASONING

Around 250g (9oz) leftover chicken, with some skin, off the bone as you like

2 tbsp Cajun seasoning

OR

2 tsp garlic powder

2 tsp sweet smoked paprika

1 tsp onion powder

1 tsp ground pepper

1 tsp dried oregano

1 tsp dried thyme

1 tsp cayenne pepper

½ tsp allspice

FOR THE ROUX

75g (2½oz) oil, butter or dripping (any fat skimmed from making stock is good), plus extra for frying

75g (2½oz) plain (all-purpose) flour

FOR THE GUMBO

200g (7oz) smoked sausage, sliced into rounds, or ham from a small hock, pulled into chunks (optional)

½ portion of the green pepper sofrito (see page 330)

4 garlic cloves, chopped

750ml (26fl oz) chicken stock

3 bay leaves

250g (9oz) okra, trimmed, or any robust green

A few dashes of Tabasco sauce

This transforms gumbo from a labour-intensive, special-occasion dish into something that can be achieved much more quickly thanks to the pressure cooker and a few building blocks – leftover chicken and stock, the 'holy trinity' sofrito found on page 330 and a large batch of spice mix that can also be substituted with a good Cajun seasoning. There is still the matter of making the roux, but that can also be made in advance if you prefer.

Duck, ham hock, plain sausage with lots of greens, or seafood also all work very well here. Use this recipe as your guide and your experiments or conversions from conventional recipes won't go wrong.

First fry the sausage (if using) and chicken. Heat a little fat or oil in a frying pan (skillet) and fry the sausage until seared on both sides, then remove. If using the spices, mix together and toss the chicken in half the spices or the Cajun seasoning. Add the chicken and fry until lightly coloured and crisp round the edges. Set aside.

Next, make the roux. Melt the fat or oil in your pressure cooker and add the flour. Cook, stirring pretty much constantly, until the roux is a rich, chestnut brown – do not stint on this, as the roux will provide a wonderfully nutty flavour to the finished dish, but be very careful – if you take it too far it may burn and everything will taste bitter.

Stir in the sofrito, another teaspoon of the seasoning and the garlic. You will find that the roux immediately thickens as if you were making a béchamel. Stir to combine, then add all the stock and stir to completely deglaze the bottom of the cooker. Continue to stir until you are sure the sauce around the vegetables is smooth enough. Add the bay leaves, then start adding the remaining ingredients – the sausage first, topped by the chicken and finally the okra or any other greens on top.

Close the lid and bring up to high pressure. Cook for 3 minutes, then remove from the heat and allow to drop pressure naturally. Stir and season to taste, adding a little Tabasco sauce to bring all the flavours together. Serve over rice with hot sauce on the side.

POACHED CHICKEN WITH SUMMER VEGETABLES AND NEW POTATOES

SERVES 4–6

1 small chicken

3cm (1¼in) piece of cinnamon bark

1 large sprig of tarragon

1 piece of pared lime zest

600g (1lb 5oz) new or salad potatoes, unpeeled (optional)

25g (1oz) butter

500g (1lb 2oz) vegetables, such as leeks, green beans, asparagus or courgettes (zucchini)

This can be made with chicken breasts or on-the-bone pieces in place of a whole chicken. The difference in cooking time will not affect the potatoes adversely.

Put the chicken, aromatics and potatoes (if using) in your pressure cooker and cover with water. Poach as descibed on page 95. Remove from the pressure cooker. Strain and reserve the liquid.

Melt the butter in the pressure cooker and add the vegetables. Ladle over a little of the poaching liquor. Bring up to high pressure and immediately fast release for al dente vegetables or leave for increments of 30 seconds for softer (see page 248 for more details on this).

Divide the chicken and vegetables between 4–6 shallow bowls. Serve with the salsa verde or tarragon cream sauce.

SERVE WITH

Salsa Verde

Blitz 1 bunch of parsley with 2 garlic cloves, 2 tablespoons of capers, zest of 1 lime, 1 tablespoon of red wine vinegar and 4 tablespoons of olive oil.

OR

Tarragon Cream Sauce

Put 100ml (3½fl oz) of the poaching liquor in a small saucepan with 1 large sprig of tarragon, 1 sliced garlic clove and 1 piece of lime zest. Reduce by half, then add 150ml (5fl oz) single (light) cream. Simmer gently until starting to thicken, then strain and beat in an egg yolk. Stir in 1 tablespoon of finely chopped tarragon and a squeeze of lime juice.

GREEN CHILLI CHICKEN

SERVES 4-6

FOR THE SALSA

Zest and juice of 2 limes

1 large bunch of coriander (cilantro), roughly chopped

At least 2 green chillies (preferably jalapeño)

1 Scotch bonnet or habanero, preferably green or yellow

2 garlic cloves

Sea salt and freshly ground black pepper

FOR THE CHICKEN

1 tbsp olive or coconut oil

1 large onion, sliced

4 garlic cloves, chopped

1 tsp cumin seeds

½ tsp dried oregano

½ tsp ground cinnamon

½ tsp ground allspice

6 chicken thigh fillets, roughly sliced

2 chicken breasts, thickly sliced

100ml (3½fl oz) well-flavoured chicken stock

100g (3½oz) tomatillos or green tomatoes (optional)

TO GARNISH

A few sprigs of coriander (cilantro)

A few green chillies, sliced

This is one that doesn't have a massive amount of sauce, but if you happen to have tomatillos, you can add some to bulk it up.

A little tip – if you make double the amount of the salsa and add 1 teaspoon of salt to the half you are not using in this recipe, it will store in the fridge indefinitely as it will very slowly ferment in the way of the Japanese yuzu kosho. It is then a great addition to poached chicken or fish, or stirred through any grain.

This recipe will work well with tacos, but I really like it with quinoa flavoured with coconut (see page 201 for how to cook quinoa) with perhaps some roast squash or pumpkin on the side (see page 264).

First make the salsa. Put all the ingredients in a food processor with 1 teaspoon of salt and plenty of black pepper. Blitz until you have a green purée – you don't need to break it down completely, just make sure everything is very evenly and finely chopped. You will probably have to push down the sides a few times.

Heat the oil in your pressure cooker. Add the onion and sauté until starting to soften, then add the garlic, cumin seeds, oregano and ground spices. Stir for a minute or two, then add the chicken. Stir until completely coated with the spices, then pour in half of the salsa and chicken stock. If you have tomatillos or tomatoes, stir in. Season with salt and pepper.

Close the lid and bring up to high pressure. Cook for 2 minutes, then leave to drop pressure naturally. Stir in the remaining salsa to brighten up the rather murky looking sauce. Serve with a few sprigs of coriander (cilantro) and sliced green chillies.

POT-ROAST CHICKEN WITH FREEKEH

SERVES 4–6

FOR THE CHICKEN

15g (½oz) butter

1 tbsp Baharat spice

1 tsp finely grated lemon zest

1 chicken, trussed

1 sprig of mint, plus extra to garnish

2 garlic cloves, bruised

Sea salt

FOR THE POT

1 tbsp olive oil

1 onion, finely chopped

4 garlic cloves, grated or finely chopped

100g (3½oz) cracked freekeh, soaked for 5 minutes

100g (3½oz) frozen broad (fava) beans, defrosted (optional)

200ml (7fl oz) chicken stock or water

Juice of 1 lemon

150g (5½oz) greens

There are a few variations of this here because I wanted to show just how versatile a pot roast can be. You can make it in a very simple form – a quick browned chicken, a few aromatics and minimal liquid, then 15 minutes high pressure – but it also lends itself very well to being a complete one-pot meal. Grains work particularly well but even potatoes will sit comfortably around the chicken, even with the longer cooking time.

You can also reverse sear a pot-roast chicken if you prefer. This means cooking the chicken without the initial searing and browning at the end for a crisper skin. You can put it under the grill, use a blowtorch or carefully fry in a pan or use an air-fryer lid.

Mix the butter, spice mix and lemon zest together with ½ teaspoon of salt and rub over the chicken. Put the mint and garlic inside the chicken cavity. Heat the olive oil in your pressure cooker or in a separate pan and brown the chicken all over. Remove the chicken from the pressure cooker and add the onion and garlic. Sauté for a minute or two, then add the freekeh, broad (fava) beans, if using, and stock or water. Return the chicken to the pressure cooker and squeeze over the lemon juice. Bring up to high pressure and cook for 15 minutes, then allow to drop pressure naturally. Remove the chicken from the pressure cooker and cover loosely with foil to rest. Add the greens to the cooker and return to high pressure. Fast release. Spoon the freekeh and greens around the chicken and serve garnished with a little more mint.

SPICED POT-ROAST CHICKEN WITH WILD RICE AND A QUICK CORIANDER CHUTNEY

This is a lovely way to eat chicken and rice together. The amount of liquid usually needed to cook the rice has been increased a little, which helps it cook in the time, and it gives a beautifully creamy finish – as if you'd made a brown or wild rice risotto.

Pot-Roast Chicken *continued*

Put a few fresh curry leaves (optional), a few coriander (cilantro) stems and 2 bruised garlic cloves into the chicken cavity. Mix 15g (½oz) butter with the zest of 1 lime and 2 teaspoons of your favourite curry powder and rub over the chicken. Sear as on page 102. Remove and add 1 finely chopped onion, 2 tablespoons of coriander stems and 4 finely chopped garlic cloves to the pressure cooker. Sauté for 2 minutes, then add another 2 teaspoons of curry powder, 150g (5½oz) wild or brown rice and 250ml (9fl oz) chicken stock or water. Dot with butter. Return the chicken to the pressure cooker and cook as on page 102. Serve with a quick coriander chutney – blitz 1 large bunch of coriander with the zest and juice of 1 lime, 1 teaspoon of honey, a pinch of ground turmeric and 2–3 green chillies. Temper this with yogurt, if you like.

POT-ROAST CHICKEN WITH 40 GARLIC CLOVES

I don't always add this many garlic cloves (it's around 3–4 bulbs), it will work with less; I do find the more garlic I use, the creamier the gravy and the less temptation to add crème fraîche at the end. Brown the chicken as above. Put herbs in the cavity and in the base of the pressure cooker; tarragon works beautifully, so does thyme or bay, or even all three. Add the garlic cloves, unpeeled, 100ml (3½fl oz) vermouth or white wine and 100ml (3½fl oz) chicken stock. Cook as on page 102. Remove the chicken and garlic from the pot. Squeeze out all the garlic cloves and return to the cooker, then mix with the cooking liquor. Add crème fraîche and more chopped herbs if you like or for a counterpoint to the creamy savouriness, a squeeze of lemon or lime juice.

POT-ROAST CHICKEN WITH A FAVOURITE STUFFING

If you want to add any kind of stuffing to the chicken, you should increase the high pressure cooking time to 20 minutes to ensure the centre is completely cooked. An alternative for sausage-meat-based stuffings is to shape into balls, brown and cook alongside the chicken.

TIMINGS FOR POT-ROASTING OTHER BIRDS

Poussin and quail need less time to cook, game birds slightly longer as they need to tenderize. Here are quick ideas for all:

POUSSIN WITH CELERIAC AND LENTILS

You can halve the quantities to serve 2 if your pressure cooker won't hold 2 poussin, but it should, just. Heat 1 tablespoon of olive oil in your pressure cooker and brown the birds. Remove and quickly sauté a finely chopped onion. Add a few unpeeled garlic cloves, 1 sprig of thyme, around 150g (5½oz) each diced celeriac (celery root) and carrot and 50g (1¾oz) brown lentils. Pour over 150ml (5fl oz) vermouth, white wine or stock. Season well. Return the birds to the cooker and bring up to high pressure. Cook for 10 minutes, slow release.

QUAILS IN BAY-SCENTED VINEGAR

I avoided quails for years because it is so hard to ethically source them, but this has at last started to change. They need very little cooking at all, just 2–3 minutes after you have seared them. This is based on a Spanish-style adobo and has a very herbal, Mediterranean vibe to it.

Make an optional marinade with 1 dried, crumbled bay leaf, 1 teaspoon of dried oregano, 2 sliced garlic cloves, 2 tablespoons of olive oil, 2 tablespoons of red wine or sherry vinegar and a few pieces of lemon or orange zest. Add 1 teaspoon of salt and lots of black pepper. You can add chilli or pepper flakes for heat or smokiness if you like. Pour over 4–6 quails, then leave to marinate for at least 1 hour. Pat dry, then heat 2 tablespoons of olive oil in your pressure cooker and sear the quails, then pour over the marinade along with 3 bay leaves. Cook at high pressure for 3 minutes and natural release. Remove the quails from the pressure cooker and put under a hot grill if you like. Add an optional 100ml (3½fl oz) orange juice to the liquid left in the pressure cooker and reduce by half before serving with the quail. You can cook vegetables alongside if you like – either give them a quick sauté after the quails have been seared and leave in the pressure cooker or wrap greens in foil and place on top.

PHEASANT WITH BACON, CHESTNUTS AND CABBAGE

You are likely to just get 1 pheasant in the cooker so this is probably best for 2 people. If you want to serve 4, joint pheasants into breast and leg portions. Heat 1 tablespoon of olive oil in the pressure cooker and sear a seasoned pheasant well. Remove. Cut 1 eating apple into wedges and sear on the cut sides. Remove. Add 1 finely chopped onion with 100g (3½oz) bacon lardons. Add 150g (5½oz) whole chestnut mushrooms and 3 chopped garlic cloves, 2 bay leaves and 1 sprig of thyme. Pour over 75ml (2½fl oz) cider and 50ml (1¾fl oz) chicken stock or water. Bring up to high pressure and cook for 15 minutes (pheasant will be cooked through in 10 minutes, but needs longer to tenderize). Leave to drop pressure naturally and remove the pheasant from the cooker. Cover the pheasant in foil and leave to rest. Roughly chop 1 green or Savoy cabbage and add to the pot, along with 75g (2½oz) crumbled chestnuts and the seared apple pieces. Season with salt and pepper. Bring back up to high pressure, remove from the heat and leave to stand for 2 minutes before fast releasing the remaining pressure. Stir in 50ml (1¾fl oz) double (heavy) cream and serve with the pheasant.

A QUICK GAMEY RAGÙ

You can turn any meat from a pot-roast into a quick ragù. They will always benefit from being cooked with some fat, so bacon or similar is always a good idea. And always cook for a little longer so the meat is falling off the bone. Follow the recipe above, but omit the apple, chestnuts and cabbage and replace the cider with Marsala. Add 15g (½oz) dried porcini mushrooms to the pressure cooker along with the bacon lardons. Halve the mushrooms instead of leaving them whole. Increase the cooking time of the pheasant to 20 minutes (you want it falling off the bone). After cooking, strip the meat from the pheasant and roughly chop it. Return to the pot and add 50–75ml (1¾–2½fl oz) double (heavy) cream. Taste for seasoning and add a squeeze of lemon juice if necessary.

GLAZED CHICKEN WINGS

SERVES 4

12 chicken wings or drumsticks

FOR THE MARINADE

Zest and juice of 2 limes

4 garlic cloves, roughly chopped

2 spring onions (scallions), (greens included), roughly chopped

1 chilli pepper (Scotch bonnet is good), roughly chopped

1 tbsp rum

2 tsp curry powder (West Indian is good)

½ tsp dried thyme

Sea salt and freshly ground black pepper

FOR THE GLAZE

50g (1¾oz) butter

1 tbsp rum

2 tbsp tomato ketchup

1 tsp hot sauce

This is a really useful thing to do when you want to cook or tenderize chicken that is to be finished off in another way – for example, barbecued. Use cheap cuts – wings or drumsticks – marinate, steam, then smother in sauce and grill or barbecue. The advantages are in the texture – firm, dry skin and beautifully tender meat.

See the body of the recipe below – with favourite Caribbean-style flavours – for more details, but the basic method is to put well-seasoned, on-the-bone chicken in the steamer basket and cook for 4 minutes, then natural release.

Put the marinade ingredients in a food processor with plenty of salt and pepper. Blitz until fairly smooth. Put the chicken in a bowl and cover with the marinade. Leave for at least 1 hour – you can cover and leave overnight in the fridge if you like.

When you are ready to steam the chicken, scrape off most of the marinade and put it in the base of your pressure cooker. Cover with 2cm (¾in) water. Add the trivet and steamer basket and pile in the chicken pieces. Bring up to high pressure and cook for 4 minutes, then allow to drop pressure naturally. Don't discard the liquid – it can be strained and used as a light chicken stock or as the base for soup.

Mix together the glaze ingredients and brush over the chicken pieces. Barbecue over direct heat, turning and basting regularly as you go, or put under a hot grill for a few minutes on each side until the chicken looks sticky and lightly charred in places. Alternatively, use the air fryer function if you have one on your electric multi-cooker.

CHICKEN STEW AND DUMPLINGS

SERVES 4

1 tbsp olive oil

4 chicken thigh fillets, skin on, cut into large pieces, or around 300g (10½oz) cooked chicken, pulled into large pieces

1 onion, thickly sliced

3 celery sticks, thickly sliced

600g (1lb 5oz) root vegetables (any combination of carrot, parsnip, turnip, celeriac/celery root, potato, Jerusalem artichoke, swede/rutabaga – NOT sweet potato or squash, they will disintegrate in the time)

A bouquet garni of 2 bay leaves, 1 large sprig of thyme, 2 sprigs of flat-leaf parsley, 1 sprig of tarragon

1 litre (35fl oz) well-flavoured chicken stock

150g (5½oz) kale or chard, roughly torn or chopped

2 leeks, cut into chunks

Sea salt and freshly ground black pepper

FOR THE DUMPLINGS

150g (5½oz) self-raising (self-rising) flour

1 tsp baking powder

1 tsp dried herbes de Provence

1 small bunch of flat-leaf parsley, finely chopped (optional)

50g (1¾oz) suet or butter

The general rule about cooking suet dumplings in the pressure cooker has always been – don't. However, I was sure it could be done, and it really can – this method results in lovely soft, pillowy dumplings that steam in the same time it takes the stew to cook underneath. They can then be dropped into the liquid at the end to take on some of the flavour of the broth.

This stew is a great receptacle for any root vegetables and leftovers – I have added roast potatoes, stuffing, and sausagemeat before. If you want to make it completely about leftovers, use cooked chicken and stock from your roast chicken carcass. If you want less robust greens (green beans, shredded cabbage, broccoli/sprouting broccoli), add these with the leeks.

First make the dumplings. Put all the ingredients into a bowl and add just enough water to bind them into a fairly dry, slightly sticky dough. Divide into 8 balls and set aside.

Heat the olive oil in the pressure cooker and sear the chicken fillets, skin-side down, until crisp and well browned. Remove from the cooker and roughly cut up.

Add the onion, celery and root vegetables to the pressure cooker. Stir just to help deglaze the base of the cooker, then add the bouquet garni and season with salt and pepper. Pour over the chicken stock, add the kale or chard and return the chicken to the cooker, skin-side up, pushing it just under the liquid.

Put the trivet on top of the stew, then the steamer basket on top of that. Put the dumplings in the steamer basket.

Close the lid and bring up to high pressure. Cook for 5 minutes, then allow to drop pressure naturally. Remove the dumplings, steamer basket and trivet. If using cooked chicken, add to the pressure cooker now, along with the leeks, making sure you push them well into the broth, then remove the dumplings from the steamer basket and rest them on top of the leeks. Bring up to high pressure once more and, as soon as pressure is reached, fast release. Serve immediately while piping hot.

COQ AU VIN

SERVES 4–6

1 tbsp olive oil

100g (3½oz) bacon lardons

200g (7oz) button mushrooms

1 tbsp plain (all-purpose) flour

1 chicken, jointed, or the equivalent in pieces

50ml (1¾fl oz) brandy or cognac (optional)

1 onion, finely chopped

1 carrot, cut into wedges

4 garlic cloves, finely chopped

1 bay leaf

1 large sprig of thyme

300ml (10½fl oz) red wine

150ml (5fl oz) chicken stock

1 portion of roast shallots (see page 264)

Sea salt and freshly ground black pepper

TO SERVE

Parsley, finely chopped

This is traditionally a labour-intensive and expensive meal to make, primarily because of the amount of wine used. Pressure cooking obviates the need for quite so much wine as the liquid doesn't evaporate, and the alcohol cooks off without the need for the long reduction first; this also means saving time at multiple stages.

You can use a whole chicken for this, jointed into 8–10 pieces – there is always someone who wants breast, after all – but keep everything on the bone. Alternatively, use a mixture of thighs and drumsticks.

Heat the olive oil in your pressure cooker and add the bacon lardons. Fry until crisp, then remove with a slotted spoon and add the mushrooms. Sauté until browned all over, and remove. Season the flour with salt and pepper and use to dust the chicken. Fry the chicken, skin-side down, until well browned. If using, warm the brandy or cognac through on a ladle or small saucepan, then set alight and pour over the chicken.

Remove the chicken from the pressure cooker, add the onion and carrot and sauté until soft. Add the garlic, bay leaf and thyme and pour in the red wine. Allow to bubble and reduce by half, stirring at the same time to deglaze the base of the cooker. Add the chicken stock, then return the chicken and mushrooms to the pressure cooker, making sure the chicken is skin-side up. Bring up to high pressure and cook for 10 minutes, then allow to drop pressure naturally.

Return the bacon to the cooker along with the roast shallots, and leave to heat through for a few minutes. Serve the chicken with the vegetables and bacon lardons, with the red wine sauce poured over, garnished with a little chopped parsley.

VARIATION

Coq au Riesling
Cook in exactly the same way, substituting red wine for white and adding tarragon to the herbs – 1 large sprig with the thyme, then more chopped as a garnish. Finish off with up to 50ml (1¾fl oz) cream if you like.

BRAISED CHICKEN THIGHS WITH FENNEL AND NEW POTATOES

SERVES 4

2 tbsp olive oil

1 fennel bulb, cut into wedges

1–2 chicken thighs per person, skin on

1 onion, thickly sliced

3 garlic cloves, finely chopped

A large pinch of saffron, ground with a pinch of sea salt (optional)

1 sprig of oregano

1 piece of pared lemon zest

100ml (3½fl oz) white wine

200g (7oz) salad or waxy potatoes, thickly sliced or halved if small

Sea salt and freshly ground black pepper

TO SERVE

Fresh oregano, finely chopped

Lemon wedges

This takes some time to brown the chicken well and to get some caramelization on the fennel, but then the cooking time is minimal. If you want to save even more time, skin the chicken thighs, which obviates the need for browning them.

Heat 1 tablespoon of the olive oil in the base of your pressure cooker. Add the fennel, cut-side down, and cook on a high heat until well browned. Remove from the cooker, then add the remaining olive oil and the chicken thighs, skin-side down. Cook for several minutes until the chicken skin is well browned and some of the fat has rendered out, then remove. Don't worry about browning the flesh side.

Remove from the cooker and add the onion. Sauté just enough to deglaze the pan, then add the garlic, saffron (if using), oregano and lemon zest. Pour in the white wine, then add the potatoes. Arrange the fennel and chicken on top.

Season with salt and pepper, then close the lid and bring up to high pressure. Lower the heat until it is the right temperature to maintain pressure, and cook at high pressure for 3 minutes. Leave to drop pressure naturally. Serve with finely chopped fresh oregano and lemon wedges for squeezing at the table.

VARIATION

Pheasant
Use pheasant breasts or legs for this. Keep the cooking times the same for breasts, but increase to 10 minutes for the legs – they will cook in less time, but they need a bit longer to be perfectly tender.

CHICKEN WITH LETTUCE, LEEKS AND PEAS

SERVES 4

1 tbsp olive oil

100g (3½oz) bacon lardons

2 little gem lettuces, halved

6–8 chicken thighs, skin on

3 garlic cloves, finely chopped or grated

75ml (2½fl oz) white wine

2 sprigs of tarragon

100ml (3½fl oz) chicken stock

15g (½oz) butter

200g (7oz) petit pois

2 leeks, cut into rounds

50ml (1¾fl oz) single (light) cream

Sea salt and freshly ground black pepper

TO SERVE

Leaves from 1 sprig of tarragon, finely chopped

A few years ago I wrote a book devoted to chicken and a version of this was one of the most popular recipes in it. The cooking time, conventionally, is upwards of around 1 hour, this reduces it down to around 20 minutes, all in, even less if you use filleted thighs.

Any leftovers are good roughly chopped and cooked with rice or pasta. Or layered with sliced potatoes to make a gratin.

Heat the olive oil in your pressure cooker. When it is hot, add the bacon lardons and the little gems, cut-side down. When the bacon has browned and the underside of the lettuces have taken on some colour, remove from the pressure cooker.

Season the chicken thighs on both sides, then fry, skin-side down, until well browned and becoming crisp. Remove from the cooker and add the garlic. Sauté for a minute, then add the white wine. Allow to bubble up and stir to deglaze the cooker, then return the chicken to the cooker, making sure you leave it skin-side up. Tuck in the sprigs of tarragon. Pour over the chicken stock. Close the lid and cook for 6 minutes at high pressure, then fast release.

Add the butter to the pan and pour in the peas. Place the leeks on top, followed by the little gem lettuces. Bring up to high pressure again, then immediately remove from the heat and leave to stand for 2–3 minutes before releasing any remaining pressure. Stir in the cream and leave to simmer for a further 2–3 minutes. Serve garnished with a sprinkling of finely chopped tarragon.

VARIATIONS

Using thigh fillets (preferably with the skin on), reduce the first cooking time to 2 minutes.

This is really good with grilled artichoke hearts in place of the lettuce. Add at the same time as the leeks.

When in season, add asparagus or use it to replace the little gems. Lay on top of the leeks.

Turn into a one pot: Add 400g (14oz) new or salad potatoes to the cooker before the first HP cook.

CHICKEN OR RABBIT WITH VINEGAR AND MUSTARD

SERVES 4

1 tbsp olive oil

8 chicken pieces (on the bone but skinned) or 1 rabbit, jointed

25g (1oz) butter

1 onion, finely chopped

3 garlic cloves, finely chopped

25ml (1fl oz) sherry or cider vinegar

100ml (3½fl oz) chicken stock

2 sprigs of tarragon

1 tbsp Dijon or tarragon mustard

Leaves from a few sprigs of tarragon, finely chopped

75ml (2½fl oz) double (heavy) cream (optional)

Sea salt and freshly ground black pepper

My default approach when wanting a bit of acidic bite is to reach for the citrus fruits but very occasionally only the astringency of vinegar will do. I love the uncompromising combination of vinegar and mustard; if you want a mellower finish, add the cream.

Heat the olive oil in your pressure cooker. Season the chicken or rabbit with salt and pepper and fry until lightly browned on all sides. Remove from the cooker.

Add the butter to the cooker. When it has melted and foamed, add the onion and garlic and cook briefly for a couple of minutes. Pour in the vinegar and stock and season again. Add the tarragon and return the meat to the cooker. Bring up to high pressure and cook for 8 minutes. Leave to drop pressure naturally.

Remove the meat from the cooker again and stir in the mustard and tarragon leaves. Taste and decide whether you want to mellow the sauce with cream or not. If so, stir it in and return the chicken or rabbit to the pot. Allow to sit for a couple of minutes before serving.

PULLED CHICKEN FOR TACOS

SERVES 4

1 tbsp olive or vegetable oil

1 onion, chopped

1 red pepper, thinly sliced

1 tsp chipotle paste (or similar)

1 tsp garlic powder

1 tsp ground cumin

½ tsp ground cinnamon

½ tsp allspice

1 tsp dried oregano

200g (7oz) canned chopped or fresh tomatoes

2 chicken breasts, skinned

2 chicken thigh fillets, skinned

Sea salt and freshly ground black pepper

TO SERVE (OPTIONAL)

Taco shells or warm corn tortillas

Coriander (cilantro) or pickled jalepeños

Salsa or guacamole

Sour cream

Grated cheese

Refried beans

Serve this with all your favourite additions – guacamole, sour cream, grated cheese, coriander (cilantro) and perhaps some refried beans. If you don't have the individual spices, you can use a taco seasoning instead.

Heat the oil in your pressure cooker and add the onion and red pepper. Sauté on a high heat for 2–3 minutes, just to coat with the oil and start to brown, then stir in the chipotle paste, spices and oregano. Add the tomatoes with 100ml (3½fl oz) water and season with salt and pepper. Place the chicken on top.

Close the lid and bring up to high pressure. Cook for 3 minutes, then natural release. Remove the chicken from the cooker and shred with a couple of forks. While you are doing this, leave the cooker on a low heat, uncovered, so the sauce can reduce down. Add the chicken back to the cooker. Stir so it becomes coated in the reduced sauce and simmer for another couple of minutes so it is piping hot. Serve with any or all of the serving suggestions.

VARIATIONS

Use leftover chicken
You can just make the sauce (cook for 2 minutes at high pressure) and add any cooked or poached chicken (see page 95) instead – simply shred and warm through in the sauce.

Turn into a quick rice dish
Add 100g (3½oz) well-rinsed basmati rice and 150ml (5fl oz) water to the pressure cooker – the rice cooks in the same time as the sauce and chicken. This is a favourite 'cheat' filling for burritos in my household.

To cook using frozen chicken
The chicken doesn't take too much longer to cook from frozen – add an extra 2 minutes at high pressure.

CHICKEN WITH OLIVES AND PRESERVED LEMON

SERVES 4

2 tbsp olive oil

1 chicken, jointed, or 8 chicken pieces, bone in

1 large onion, finely sliced

3 garlic cloves, finely chopped

A large pinch of saffron, ground with ½ tsp sea salt

1 tsp ground ginger

½ tsp ground cinnamon

½ tsp ground turmeric

½ tsp ground cardamom

150ml (5fl oz) chicken stock

Juice of ½ lemon

1 tbsp preserved lemon, finely chopped (see the quick preserved lemons on page 336)

20 large green olives, preferably unpitted and cracked

Sea salt and freshly ground black pepper

TO SERVE

Small bunches of coriander (cilantro), flat-leaf parsley or mint, finely chopped

Using on-the-bone pieces of chicken – including on-the-bone breast – works very well in the pressure cooker when you aren't adding other vegetables that will become too soft during the longer cooking time. The cooking time here also ensures that the skin will become parchment-thin – no flabbiness.

The sharpness of this dish works very well with the bulgar wheat pilaf on page 203, otherwise serve with couscous.

Heat the olive oil in your pressure cooker. Season the chicken with salt and pepper, then add to the cooker and brown on all sides. Remove from the cooker and add the onion, stirring until the base of the cooker is clean. Add the garlic and spices and cook for a further minute. Pour in the chicken stock and lemon juice, then stir in half the preserved lemon. Return the chicken to the cooker and add the olives.

Bring up to high pressure and cook for 10 minutes. Remove from the heat and leave to drop pressure naturally. Taste and stir in more of the preserved lemon if you think it needs it.

Serve sprinkled with the herbs.

CHICKEN WITH MUSTARD AND GRAPES

SERVES 4

1 tbsp olive oil

1–2 chicken thighs per person, skin on, filleted if you like

200ml (7fl oz) red wine

1 tbsp Dijon mustard

A few sprigs of tarragon, left whole, a few leaves reserved for garnish

20 seedless black or red grapes

Sea salt and freshly ground black pepper

This is so good. Grapes keep their integrity very well in the pressure cooker, they just plump up very pleasingly. Use a fragrant, sweet variety if you can. The ingredients are pared right down in this one, I don't feel it needs onion or garlic. A good substitution for chicken is pheasant, using the breasts or legs, increasing the cooking time to 10 minutes if using the legs.

Heat the olive oil in your pressure cooker. Add the chicken thighs, skin-side down, and fry until a rich, crisp brown. Fry for a couple of minutes on the reverse side, then remove and strain off most of the fat that will have rendered out of the skin.

Add the red wine and bring to the boil, then whisk in the mustard. Season with salt and pepper and add the tarragon. Return the chicken to the cooker and dot around the grapes. Bring up to high pressure. Cook for 3 minutes if using filleted thighs, 5 minutes if bone-in. Allow to drop pressure naturally.

VARIATIONS

Also excellent with a jointed rabbit, guinea fowl or whole quail.

Pasta
This makes an excellent pasta dish and is in fact my favourite way to eat it. Before returning the chicken to the pan, sprinkle 250g (9oz) small pasta (I like really tiny pasta shells) and top with water or stock until the pasta is just covered. Add the chicken and grapes. Bring up to high pressure, cook for 4 minutes, then slowly release the pressure over a couple of minutes.

HUNTER'S CHICKEN

SERVES 4

1 tbsp olive oil

1–2 filleted chicken thighs per person

1 red onion, cut into wedges

3 garlic cloves, finely chopped

1 large sprig of thyme

Leaves from 1 sprig of rosemary, finely chopped

100ml (3½fl oz) red wine

1 x 400g (14oz) can chopped tomatoes

50g (1¾oz) pitted black olives

25g (1oz) capers

Sea salt and freshly ground black pepper

TO SERVE

A few rosemary leaves, very finely chopped

This has shades of a cacciatore about it – it's a very robust and savoury dish that is great with a creamy potato or celeriac (celery root) gratin. And the leftovers work particularly well added to pasta – see page 122 for how to make one-pot pasta with leftovers.

Heat the olive oil in your pressure cooker and add the thighs, skin-side down. Brown well, then remove. Add the onion and sauté for a couple of minutes, then add the garlic, thyme and rosemary. Pour over the wine and leave to bubble for a minute or two, then stir, pushing around the bushy sprig of thyme as this really helps to deglaze the pan.

Pour in the tomatoes, olives and capers, and stir. Season with a little salt (the olives and capers add plenty) and lots of black pepper. Place the chicken on top, bring up to high pressure and cook for 3 minutes. Allow to drop pressure naturally. Sprinkle with the rosemary before serving.

VARIATIONS

Mellow this out considerably by replacing the thyme and rosemary with tarragon, the red wine with white and the canned tomatoes with fresh. Omit the olives and capers and garnish with more fresh tarragon.

Add red or green peppers. Cut into strips and add at the same time as the onions.

Also good using rabbit, guinea fowl or poussin.

WEST-INDIAN-STYLE CHICKEN CURRY

SERVES 4

FOR THE CHICKEN

6 skinless, chicken thigh fillets, cut into large pieces

4 garlic cloves, finely chopped

10g (¼oz) piece ginger, finely chopped

1–2 Scotch bonnet chillies, finely chopped

Zest and juice of 1 lime

Sea salt

FOR THE CURRY

1 tbsp olive oil

15g (½oz) butter

1 tsp light soft brown sugar

1 onion, sliced

1–2 tbsp West Indian curry powder

2 carrots, cut into chunks

1 large potato, cut into chunks

2 bay leaves

1 large sprig of thyme

200ml (7fl oz) coconut milk

1 tbsp tamarind paste or 1 tsp concentrate

1 tbsp sherry or golden rum

TO SERVE

4 spring onions (scallions), finely sliced (including the greens)

Lime wedges

My favourite comfort-food curry. The thing to look out for here is that Scotch bonnets vary enormously in terms of heat. If you are worried about your curry being too hot, make sure you deseed and devein the pepper (wearing gloves if you want to take extra care). You can always add hot sauce later to compensate if it turns out to be too mild.

This is excellent with the rice and peas on page 212.

Season the chicken pieces with salt, then put in a bowl. Add the garlic cloves, ginger, Scotch bonnet(s), lime zest and juice. Leave to marinate for at least 1 hour.

Heat the oil and butter in your pressure cooker. When the butter starts to foam, stir in the sugar until it dissolves and starts to caramelize. Add the onion and curry powder, followed by the chicken and its marinade. Stir until everything is well combined and coated with the caramelly butter. Add the carrots, potato and herbs, then pour over the coconut milk. Stir in the tamarind paste.

Bring up to high pressure, and cook for 4 minutes. Leave to drop pressure naturally and stir in the sherry or rum. Garnish with the spring onions (scallions) and serve with the lime wedges.

VARIATION

Chicken on the bone
To use chicken thighs on the bone (preferably skinned) or drumsticks, or even a whole chicken in pieces, you will need to cook this for longer. Do not include the potatoes and carrots in the first cook. Bring up to high pressure and cook for 5 minutes, then fast release. Add the potatoes and carrots and cook for a further 3 minutes at high pressure, then natural release.

CHICKEN LEGS WITH MARSALA

SERVES 4

1 tbsp olive oil

4 chicken legs

1 onion, finely sliced

10g (¼oz) dried mushrooms, soaked in warm water (optional)

250g (9oz) mixture of fresh mushrooms (chestnut, wild, field), sliced

1 garlic clove, finely chopped

1 sprig of thyme

1 sprig of tarragon

75ml (2½fl oz) dry sherry or Marsala

100ml (3½fl oz) double (heavy) cream or crème fraîche

TO SERVE

A few sprigs of finely chopped tarragon, flat-leaf parsley or chervil

When you pressure cook meat with alcohol you don't need as much as you do when cooking conventionally – the natural release method and the fact that pressure cookers are sealed vessels means that all the flavour compounds remain in the cooker and will concentrate. This recipe is a good example of this as a classic Chicken with Marsala will usually use three times the amount of alcohol.

A chicken leg will cook through in just a few minutes, but needs longer to tenderize; if your chicken legs look as though they came from particularly muscular chickens, use the longer cooking time.

Heat the olive oil in your pressure cooker. Brown the chicken legs on both sides until a golden crust has developed. Remove from the pressure cooker. Add the onion and stir to deglaze the cooker. Strain the dried mushrooms, if using, reserving the soaking liquor, then finely chop. Stir into the onion along with the fresh mushrooms and cook until the mushrooms have collapsed down a little. Stir in the garlic and add the herbs.

Pour in the sherry or Marsala and add 50ml (1¾fl oz) of the mushroom soaking liquor. Put the chicken on top. Close the lid and bring up to high pressure. Cook for 8–10 minutes, then allow to drop pressure naturally.

Remove the chicken from the cooker again and stir in the cream or crème fraîche. Allow to simmer for a couple of minutes, then serve the chicken with the sauce, garnished with some finely chopped herbs.

LEFTOVERS

If you have any of the sauce or chicken left, this makes a good base for an all-in-one pasta dish for 1–2 people. Start with a little oil and fry some bacon lardons. Add the reserved sauce and any chicken if you have it, then stir in a portion or two of dried pasta. Add enough water to just cover and a couple of cubes of frozen spinach if you like. Bring up to high pressure, cook for 4-5 minutes, then normal release. Stir the spinach through if using.

VARIATIONS

This is another one that will work really well with pheasant or partridge. Keep the high pressure cooking time the same.

QUICK CHICKEN CURRY

SERVES 4

1 tbsp olive oil

1 large onion, finely sliced

1 tsp cumin seeds

4 garlic cloves, crushed
or grated

15g (½oz) piece ginger, grated

1 tbsp medium curry powder or
spice mix (see below)

6 chicken thigh fillets, skinned
and diced

200g (7oz) canned chopped
tomatoes

Sea salt and freshly ground
black pepper

**FOR THE SPICE MIX
(OPTIONAL)**

1 tsp ground turmeric

1 tsp ground coriander

½ tsp ground cinnamon

½ tsp ground cardamom

½ tsp ground fenugreek

A pinch of ground cloves

TO SERVE

Rice or chapatis

A few green chillies, finely sliced

A few sprigs of coriander
(cilantro)

Lime wedges

**This is an everyday curry that can be made faster if
you make batches of the onion, garlic and ginger on
page 329.**

Heat the olive oil in your pressure cooker. Add the onion
and fry on a high heat for a few minutes until starting
to brown. Add the cumin seeds, garlic, ginger and curry
powder or spice mix and sauté for another 2 minutes,
stirring constantly.

Add the chicken and stir to coat in the spices. Add
the tomatoes with 100ml (3½fl oz) water and season
with salt and pepper. Close the lid and bring up to high
pressure. Lower the heat to maintain pressure and cook
for 3 minutes, then leave to drop pressure naturally.

Turn the chicken over in the cooking juices a couple
of times, reducing down a little if necessary. Serve
with rice or chapatis, garnished with green chillies and
coriander (cilantro), alongside wedges of lime to squeeze
at the table.

SPICED CHICKEN LIVERS

SERVES 4

1 tbsp olive oil

400g (14oz) chicken livers

1 large red onion, sliced into thin wedges

400g (14oz) Tenderstem broccoli

Sea salt and freshly ground black pepper

FOR THE SAUCE

4 garlic cloves, crushed or grated

25g (1oz) piece ginger, grated

1 tbsp chilli sauce (I use sriracha or a Scotch-bonnet-based one; use whatever you like)

2 tbsp light soy sauce

Zest and juice of ½ orange

½ tsp ground turmeric

A pinch of ground cinnamon

OPTIONAL EXTRA

150g (5½oz) cooked Puy lentils or similar

TO SERVE

1 small bunch of coriander/ cilantro (optional)

Chicken livers are quick to cook anyway, but pressure cooking them makes them incredibly tender and gives the sauce a chance to develop its flavour. This dish is real pick-me-up food – one of the first things we turn to in our household when fatigued or suffering from a cold.

Quick braises like this work particularly well in sauté-pan-sized pressure cookers, but can be cooked in any size. Just make sure if you are using a particularly deep pot that you give the livers plenty of space to sear – do this in two batches if necessary.

First make the sauce by whisking together all the ingredients and adding 50ml (1¾fl oz) water.

Heat the olive oil in your pressure cooker. Add the chicken livers and very briefly sear on all sides. Remove from the cooker and add the onion. Stir to deglaze the pan, then pour in the sauce.

Return the livers to the pressure cooker and turn over in the sauce once or twice. If using the lentils, add to the cooker at this point and add an extra 50ml (1¾fl oz) water. Season with salt and pepper, then lay the broccoli on top of the livers. Close the lid and bring up to high pressure. Immediately remove from the heat and leave to drop pressure naturally.

Great on their own, with perhaps some bread for mopping up the pan juices, or serve over rice or noodles, garnished with plenty of coriander (cilantro), if you like.

CHICKEN OR TURKEY MEATBALLS WITH GIANT COUSCOUS

SERVES 4

2 tbsp olive oil

1 red onion, sliced into wedges

1 large bunch of chard, stems and leaves separated and sliced

3 garlic cloves, finely chopped

75g (2½oz) giant couscous

2 tsp spice mix (see below) or ras el hanout

2 large pieces of pared lemon zest

500ml (17fl oz) chicken stock

Juice of 1 lemon

FOR THE MEATBALLS

400g (14oz) minced (ground) chicken or turkey

40g (1½oz) fresh or dried breadcrumbs

1 small onion, finely chopped

Zest of 1 lime

½ tsp allspice

A large pinch of ground cinnamon

A large pinch of hot chilli powder or flakes

1 tsp dried mint

Sea salt and freshly ground black pepper

FOR THE SPICE MIX (OPTIONAL)

2 tsp ground turmeric

1 tsp ground cinnamon

1 tsp ground cumin

1 tsp ground coriander

1 tsp ground ginger

½ tsp allspice

½ tsp ground cardamom

½ tsp black peppercorns

¼ tsp ground cloves

TO SERVE

2 tbsp preserved lemon (see page 336)

Small bunches of mint and coriander (cilantro), finely chopped

There are a lot of ingredients in this recipe, but for all that, it is fairly quick to put together. And the flavours here will also work well with diced chicken – perhaps just do a quick marinade with the same aromatic ingredients listed under the meatballs, then fry the chicken at the beginning of the cooking process with the onion.

First make the chicken balls – mix all the ingredients together with plenty of seasoning. Form into fairly small balls – around 35g (1¼oz) each. If you want to brown them before cooking (by no means essential), heat a little olive oil in a pan and fry them briefly on two sides. Set aside.

If making the spice mix, stir all the spices together and put in an airtight jar – you won't need all of the mix for this recipe.

Next, heat the olive oil in your pressure cooker. Add the onion and chard stems and cook on a high heat until starting to take on a little colour around the edges. Add the garlic and giant couscous and stir until coated in the olive oil. Stir in the spices and lemon zest.

Add the stock and dot around the chicken balls. Pile the chard leaves on top, then bring up to high pressure. Cook for 3 minutes at high pressure, then leave for 5 minutes off the heat before releasing the rest of the pressure.

Add the lemon juice and serve with some preserved lemon and plenty of herbs.

DUCK LEG CURRY

SERVES 4

FOR THE PASTE

2 shallots

5g (⅛oz) piece ginger, peeled

5g (⅛oz) piece galangal, peeled (optional)

6 garlic cloves, peeled

2 lemongrass stems, roughly chopped

2–3 red bird's eye chillies, roughly chopped

½ tsp ground cardamom

½ tsp ground turmeric

½ tsp ground cumin

½ tsp ground coriander

1 tsp shrimp paste

FOR THE CURRY

1 tsp olive or coconut oil

2 large duck legs, skinned or unskinned (see introduction)

1 onion, thickly sliced

1 large carrot, sliced

A handful of fresh curry leaves

400ml (14fl oz) coconut milk

1–2 tbsp fish sauce

400g (14oz) potatoes (any sort), cut into chunks

200g (7oz) fresh pineapple, cut into chunks

Juice of ½ lime

TO SERVE

Fresh coriander (cilantro)

Jasmine rice

As duck legs contain much, much more fat than chicken, they do need a bit of extra care and attention. This is partly because the pressure cooker is just so efficient at rendering fat – most of it will end up on top of your sauce. Your options are: skin the duck legs and render the fat separately; reduce the amount of fat by partially skinning; or fry until most of the fat is rendered out. Or accept that you will need to skim – strain the liquid, then wait for the fat to collect on top and set. Store the fat in the fridge and use for frying, sautéing and roasting.

This is quite a rich curry so I find 2 duck legs ample for 4 people. You can increase the amount if you like.

Roughly chop all the paste ingredients and put in a small food processor. Season with salt and pepper and blitz until well broken down, adding a little water if necessary.

Heat the oil in your pressure cooker. Add the duck legs, skin-side down if unskinned, and fry for several minutes until a rich brown. Turn over and fry for a few more minutes. Remove from the pressure cooker and remove all but 1 tablespoon of the rendered fat.

Add the onion and carrot and sauté for a few minutes until starting to soften, then stir in the curry leaves. When they have crackled, add the curry paste and stir until the aroma intensifies. Pour in the coconut milk and add 1 tablespoon of the fish sauce. Return the duck to the pressure cooker and add the potatoes and pineapple. Close the lid and bring up to high pressure. Cook for 10 minutes, then allow to release pressure naturally.

If you have opted to leave the skin on you will need to skim the liquid. Remove the duck and the vegetables from the pressure cooker, pour off the remaining liquid into a container and leave it to settle until the fat collects on top for easy removal. If the duck is skinless, you don't need to skim. Pull the duck meat into large chunks. Reassemble the curry with the meat, vegetables and liquid and heat through. Add the lime juice and adjust for seasoning, including an extra dash or two of fish sauce if you think it needs it.

CRISPY AROMATIC DUCK

SERVES 4–6

4 duck breasts, legs or a combination

1 tsp Chinese 5 spice

2 tsp groundnut oil

Sea salt

TO SERVE

Chinese pancakes

½ cucumber, shredded lengthways

1 bunch of spring onions (scallions), shredded lengthways

Hoisin sauce

I get a lot of messages asking me whether it is possible to cook (or part cook) certain dishes in a pressure cooker and this was one of them. Thanks Lou, you made me think this one through and it really works!

It still takes a bit of time, this. In part because of the overnight salting, which isn't essential but the results will be better for it. You can use breast or legs, or a combination. I tend to buy a duck, use the breasts to make a half portion of this and the legs for confit (see page 130), but any combination works.

Prick the skin of the duck all over with a fork, a skewer or the point of a knife. Mix the 5 spice with 1 teaspoon of salt and rub all over the skin and flesh of the duck. Put in the fridge, preferably overnight.

Remove the duck pieces from the fridge and pat dry with kitchen towel. Heat 1 teaspoon of the oil in your pressure cooker and swirl to coat the base, then add the duck pieces, skin-side down. Leave to fry for around 5 minutes until they have started to brown and the fat is rendering out. Sear briefly on the flesh side, then leave flesh-side down – the fat will render through the flesh as it cooks, helping with both flavour and texture.

Close the lid and cook at high pressure for 30 minutes, then allow to drop pressure naturally. You should find that most of the fat has rendered out into the pressure cooker.

Remove the pieces from the pressure cooker. If you want to crisp up the skin, heat the remaining oil in a frying pan (skillet) and sear, skin-side down, for a couple of minutes. Remove to a board and shred with a couple of forks.

Serve with warm Chinese pancakes and accoutrements.

DUCK CONFIT

SERVES 4

4 duck legs

4 bay leaves

1 tsp dried thyme

1 tsp juniper berries, crushed

1 tsp black peppercorns, crushed

1 tsp fennel seeds, lightly crushed

3 tbsp sea salt

2 tbsp duck fat

4 garlic cloves, thinly sliced

I've tried a few versions of this, including using a jar of duck fat in the pressure cooker to see what would happen (not advisable), but this is what works best. This method also works well with other meats, including chicken, pork and rabbit. It produces a very soft, tender meat, which is particularly good for rillettes or potted meat.

If you want to store the duck for any length of time (ie, longer than a week), when it has finished cooking, push into a sterilized jar and pour over warmed duck fat. When the fat has set again, you can keep it chilled indefinitely.

Put the duck legs in a non-reactive dish. Mix the aromatics with the salt, then rub this all over the duck legs. Cover and leave in the fridge overnight.

Brush off the duck legs and pat dry with kitchen towel (they should look moist as the salt will have drawn some liquid out of them).

Heat the duck fat in your pressure cooker. Add the legs, skin-side down, sprinkle with the sliced garlic and start the frying process. As soon as you start to see some fat rendering out of the legs and some steam appear, close the lid on your pressure cooker and bring up to high pressure. If you are nervous about not adding liquid, add 75ml (2½fl oz) water, but it honestly isn't really necessary. Cook at high pressure for 20 minutes, then fast release. Turn the legs over and close the lid again and cook for another 20 minutes. This time allow to drop pressure naturally.

Remove the legs from the pressure cooker. Pour off the remaining contents into a pot or jar. The fat and liquid will separate, giving you a deep brown jelly stock below and white spoonable fat above.

The duck can now be used in other recipes or stored in duck fat until needed.

DUCK BRAISED WITH RED CABBAGE AND POTATOES

SERVES 4

2 tbsp olive oil

1 quince or firm eating apple, peeled and cut into wedges

A pinch of ground ginger

1 tsp honey

½ red cabbage, cut into slim wedges

200g (7oz) duck meat, finely diced

1 tsp Chinese 5 spice

1 garlic clove, finely chopped

50ml (1¾fl oz) Shaoxing rice wine

50ml (1¾fl oz) light soy sauce

1 tbsp ketjap manis (optional)

500g (1lb 2oz) waxy or salad potatoes, such as Charlotte or Pink Fir, sliced

TO SERVE

3 spring onions (scallions), shredded

This is remarkably fast, after some initial prep. The duck is there for flavour and can be successfully replaced with diced pork, any leftover cooked meat or even mushrooms.

Heat 1 tablespoon of the olive oil in your pressure cooker. Toss the quince or apple in the ginger and drizzle over the honey. Fry for a couple of minutes on each side until lightly browned, then remove.

Add the red cabbage to the pressure cooker and fry on both sides for 2 minutes until it is starting to brown. Remove.

Toss the duck in the Chinese 5 spice. Add the remaining oil to the pressure cooker and fry the duck briefly for a couple of minutes, then add the garlic. Pour in the rice wine, soy sauce and the ketjap manis, if using.

Return the red cabbage to the cooker along with the potatoes and toss gently to coat. Place the quince or apple on top. Bring up to high pressure and cook for 3 minutes, then allow to drop pressure naturally.

Serve with a garnish of spring onions.

FISH AND
SEAFOOD

If speed is your only consideration, there is very little need for a pressure cooker when cooking most fish and seafood. Not only that, many types of fish need careful handling – overcooking can lead to disintegration on one hand, rubbery texture on the other. So most recipes in this chapter are the result of much thought and experimentation – and have proven to me that the pressure cooker can be indispensable. Here are the main ways in which I use it:

Stocks, broths and soups – It will create the most wonderful stocks (see page 326), broths and sauces, for use in a myriad of soups, casseroles and braises, using mainly waste material.

Tenderizing – It will make short work of all the types of seafood that usually need slow, low cooking to tenderize – think squid and cuttlefish, octopus and molluscs such as conch and whelk.

Pressure steaming – It will pressure steam large crustaceans, such as lobster and crab, in a fraction of the time it normally takes you to bring a large vat of water to the boil – you will save time, money and water, and will create an intensely flavoured stock at the same time.

Softening bones – The pressure cooker was initially created to soften fish – you can cook oily fish, such as sardines, pilchards and mackerel, to the point that the bones are soft and edible; the same texture you find in tins. This is great if you prefer using fresh fish but want soft bones or if you are feeding small children.

Preparing salt-preserved fish – The pressure cooker makes short work of soaking anything salted. For example, saltfish can take up to 3 days of soaking in regularly refreshed water to hydrate and bring the salinity down to an acceptable level for eating. You can achieve this in a pressure cooker in roughly 30 minutes.

Cooking en papillote – Fish cooks very well in parcels that are normally baked in the oven or steamed. Doing this saves time and seals in flavour, and you can also cook other food alongside.

One-pot cooking – Finally, pressure cooking makes any kind of one-pot fish cooking easy as you can use it to create the sauce or cook the vegetables before adding the fish. You can then either cook the fish under low or high pressure or leave it to simmer conventionally.

HOW TO COOK SHELLFISH

Cover the base of your pressure cooker with 1–2cm (½–¾in) water or stock and maybe a splash of wine or vermouth. Add any aromatics you like – pared lemon or lime zest, garlic, pepper, bay leaves – then add the shellfish. Bring up to low pressure and cook for 2 minutes. Remove from the heat and leave to stand for a minute. Release the remaining pressure and remove from the cooker. This will work for all kinds of large seafood that have similar thickness of shells and flesh.

It is really as simple as that. Shave off a minute for large shrimp or langoustine; add a minute if you are cooking particularly large or thick crab or lobster. The cooking liquor will have taken on some of the flavour and aroma of the shellfish in that short time and can be used as a light stock. And of course, once you have used the shellfish meat, you can use all the debris to make a stock – see page 326.

PRAWNS AND FETA IN TOMATO SAUCE

SERVES 4

2 tbsp olive oil

1 red onion, very finely chopped

2 garlic cloves, finely chopped

1 tsp fennel seeds

1 tsp dried oregano

100ml (3½fl oz) white wine

1 x 400g (14oz) can chopped tomatoes

A pinch of ground cinnamon

1 tbsp ouzo or similar (optional)

1 block of feta (around 200g/7oz)

200g (7oz) peeled prawns (shrimp)

Sea salt and freshly ground black pepper

TO SERVE

Green salad

Bread

The Greek classic, saganaki, which is yet another way with tomato sauce. It is the tomato sauce that takes up most of the time here. The prawns (shrimp) and cheese cook pretty much instantly.

Heat the olive oil in your pressure cooker. Add the onion and sauté for a few minutes until starting to look transparent, then add the garlic, fennel seeds and oregano. Season with salt and pepper.

Pour in the white wine and allow to bubble up until almost completely evaporated. Stir in the tomatoes and cinnamon. Rinse out the can with 75ml (2½fl oz) water and add this to the cooker. Close the lid and bring up to pressure. Cook for 5 minutes and fast release.

Stir in the ouzo, if using. Add the feta – you can leave in a single block or you can dice. Push the prawns (shrimp) into the sauce. Bring up to high pressure again and release pressure immediately.

Serve with a green salad and bread.

SEAFOOD BOIL

SERVES 4

500g (1lb 2oz) waxy potatoes, preferably red, halved if large

4 corn on the cob, cut in half

500g (1lb 2oz) kielbasa or similar smoked sausage, cut into chunks

1 large onion, cut into wedges

4 bay leaves

1.5kg (3lb 5oz) crustaceans, such as langoustine, large prawns (shrimp), lobsters or lobster tails, crab claws

FOR THE SPICE MIX

2 tbsp Old Bay Seasoning

OR

1 tsp mustard powder

1 tsp paprika

1 tsp garlic powder

1 tsp dried thyme

1 tsp cayenne pepper

1 tsp ground black or white pepper

1 tsp celery or onion salt

½ tsp allspice

¼ tsp ground cinnamon

FOR THE SAUCE

75g (2½oz) butter

3 large garlic cloves, grated or crushed

Hot sauce, to taste (optional)

Lemon juice, to taste (optional)

TO SERVE

Lemon wedges

This is great fun. And – stay with me here, don't laugh – it is one of the best reasons I can think of for taking your pressure cooker on holiday to the coast with you. The freshest seafood and al fresco dining without having to wait half the day for a large vat of water to come up to the boil.

This serves 4 hungry people reasonably well, and will just fit into a 4.5-litre (156-fl oz) pressure cooker. You can increase or reduce the quantities of anything as you please, it is the timings that are important.

A smoked sausage is ideal for this recipe, but don't feel limited by this – I once made it with fresh garlicky sausages, and just browned them first.

First make the spice mix if that's what you are using. Mix everything together. Put the potatoes in the base of your pressure cooker and put the corn on the cob and sausage on top, followed by the onion. Tuck in the bay leaves. Pour in 150ml (5fl oz) water, and sprinkle over half of the spice mix.

Close the lid and bring up to high pressure. Cook for 3 minutes and fast release. Arrange all the shellfish on top and sprinkle over the rest of the spice mix. Bring up to low pressure this time. Cook for 1 minute for prawns (shrimp) or langoustines and 2 minutes for lobster tails or crab, then remove from the heat. Leave to stand for 1 minute, then release pressure.

Melt the butter and garlic together in a separate pan. Ladle all the seafood, sausages and vegetables over a large platter with lemon wedges. Whisk around 100ml (3½fl oz) of the cooking liquor left in the pressure cooker into the butter and taste – adjust the flavour with a little more hot sauce if you like, and/or a squeeze of lemon juice.

And with the debris, try making a broth or go all out and make the bisque overleaf.

Seafood is very expensive and is definitely a treat in our house, so it is really worth trying to get as much out of it as possible. Making a stock is one way, but it also occurred to me that these particular leftovers would make an excellent spicy bisque.

FOR A SPICY BISQUE

Take any shells and heads left over from the boil. Put 1 tablespoon of olive oil in your pressure cooker and add 1 roughly chopped onion, fennel if you have it, and carrot (or simply use around 3–4 tablespoons of any of the sofritos on page 330). Cook on a high heat without stirring until lightly charred/browned on the bottom, then stir and add the seafood debris. Sauté for another minute or two, then pour in a scant 25ml (1fl oz) brandy or rum. Leave it to reduce, then stir in 2 tablespoons of tomato purée. Stir again until the purée looks as though it is separating. Pour in 100ml (3½fl oz) white wine and add 1.2 litres (40fl oz) of fish stock or water. Season with salt and pepper, tuck in any herbs you like and perhaps a piece of pared lemon or orange zest.

Bring up to high pressure and cook for 5 minutes. You can strain to use as a broth (excellent in a seafood ramen, see page 175), or you can remove the zest and herbs and blitz in a blender until smooth. Push through a sieve, then a sieve lined with muslin (cheesecloth) or kitchen towel to remove any grittiness.

Reheat and adjust the seasoning as you like. This will make a fairly thin bisque. For a thicker one, blitz in some cooked rice or anything else you like to thicken it. It is rich as is, but you could also add cream.

Use the bisque to add richness to seafood or fish stock when making pasta or rice dishes as well as soups. It will make an intense risotto, especially with a lot of lemon and crab meat stirred in at the end.

FISH WITH BRAISED CABBAGE AND BACON

SERVES 4

1 tbsp olive oil

150g (5½oz) bacon lardons

1 onion, cut into thin wedges

50ml (1¾fl oz) white wine, cider or vermouth

50ml (1¾fl oz) water or fish or vegetable stock

1 cabbage (a small Savoy or a pointed green or hispi cabbage are ideal), shredded

4 thick, skinless cod fillets

50g (1¾oz) Cheddar cheese, grated (optional)

Sea salt and freshly ground black pepper

TO SERVE

50ml (1¾fl oz) double (heavy) cream

1 small bunch of flat-leaf parsley, finely chopped

This is such a comforting one-pot dish and I still can't quite believe how fast it is. If you have the sauté pressure cooker, do it in this as it is a great stovetop-to-table dish. Fish should really be cooked at low pressure, but 1 minute at high and a gentle comedown does not do it any harm.

Heat the olive oil in your pressure cooker. Add the bacon lardons and onion, and sauté on a medium–high heat until the bacon has crisped up and the onion has started to brown. Turn up the heat and add the wine, cider or vermouth and allow it to boil off. Turn down the heat, add the water or stock, then arrange the shredded cabbage on top.

Season the cabbage and give it a quick stir. Season the cod with salt and pepper, then divide the cheese between the fillets, if using. Arrange over the cabbage, then bring up to high pressure. Cook for 1 minute only, then remove from the heat and leave to stand for 2 minutes. Release the remaining pressure gently.

Carefully remove the fish from the pressure cooker and keep warm. Stir in the cream and stir on a low heat for a minute or two, then return the fish to the cooker and put under a hot grill for a minute or two if you like, or simply just plate up. Serve garnished with parsley.

VARIATIONS

To add carbs for a one-pot meal: To add beans, take 250g (9oz) cooked white beans, stir into the cabbage before cooking and proceed as above. To add potatoes, take 200g (7oz) floury potatoes, peel and slice or dice. Sauté the bacon and onion as above, then add the potatoes and 100ml (3½fl oz) water and cook at high pressure for 2 minutes. Fast release. Stir in the cabbage and proceed as above.

Add bivalves: A handful of clams, mussels or cockles added to this works really well. Make sure they are well cleaned and tightly closed before you cook them, then add to the pressure cooker at the same time as the fish. Make sure there is enough room in the pressure cooker for them to open!

FISH WITH PAPRIKA POTATOES

SERVES 4

2 tbsp olive oil

2 red onions, sliced into wedges

500g (1lb 2oz) new or salad potatoes, diced

1 large garlic clove, grated or crushed

½–1 tsp hot paprika

½ tsp fennel seeds

1 sprig of rosemary (optional)

100ml (3½fl oz) red wine

200g (7oz) canned chopped tomatoes

50g (1¾oz) pitted black olives

600g (1lb 5oz) skinless fish fillets (see intro)

Zest of 1 lemon, very finely planed (optional)

Sea salt and freshly ground black pepper

TO SERVE

Flat-leaf parsley leaves, chopped

I use a robust cod loin or hake for this dish, or anything thick and meaty that can be cut into 4 thick fillets.

Heat the olive oil in your pressure cooker. Add the red onions and potatoes. Sauté on a high heat until both are taking on some colour. Add the garlic, paprika, fennel seeds and rosemary, if using, and stir for a couple more minutes. Season with plenty of salt and pepper.

Pour in the red wine and let it bubble for a minute or two, then add the tomatoes and 100ml (3½fl oz) water. Stir, then close the lid and bring up to high pressure. Cook for 2 minutes, then release pressure quickly. Make sure the potatoes are almost knife tender (their cooking can be inhibited by tomatoes). Stir in the black olives.

Season the cod and rub with the lemon zest if using. Arrange on top of the potatoes. Bring up to low pressure and cook for 2 minutes, then allow to drop pressure naturally. Garnish with a little parsley.

VARIATION

This is a good one to add a fennel bulb to. Cut a fennel bulb into wedges and brown on the cut sides. Remove from the cooker, then arrange around the fish before cooking.

FISH SOUP

SERVES 4-6

FOR THE BROTH

500g (1lb 2oz) large prawns (shrimp)

1 tbsp olive oil

1 tbsp tomato purée

2 large tomatoes, puréed or finely chopped

3 tbsp onion or fennel sofrito (only if you have it, page 330)

100ml (3½fl oz) white wine

1 piece pared orange zest

A pinch of saffron

1 bay leaf

1.2 litres (40 fl oz) fish stock (see page 326 or use shop-bought)

Sea salt and freshly ground black pepper

FOR THE SOUP

2 tbsp olive oil

1 fennel bulb, cut into slim wedges

2 leeks, white parts only, thinly sliced

500g (1lb 2oz) mixture of filleted fish, cut into large chunks

24 mussels, clams or cockles, cleaned (optional)

1–2 tsp pastis or ouzo

Leaves from 2 sprigs of parsley, chervil or tarragon, finely chopped

FOR THE ROUILLE

50g (1¾oz) white breadcrumbs

1 large garlic clove, crushed or grated

½ roasted red pepper (see page 268)

½ tsp hot chilli powder

1 egg yolk

This is based on the classic bouillabaisse, complete with rouille. Like many of the fish and seafood recipes in this book, the value of the pressure cooking isn't in the last stage, which is when the fish or seafood is cooked, but in the time you save making the stock and then the broth. Use this method to make your favourite fish soups, stews and casseroles and you won't go far wrong.

First make the broth. Peel and devein the prawns (shrimp). Heat the olive oil in your pressure cooker and add the prawns. Sear quickly on both sides, then remove from the pressure cooker and set aside. Add the heads and shells to the pressure cooker. Fry on a high heat until they have turned pink, then stir in the tomato purée. Continue to cook, stirring, until the tomato sauce starts to separate from the oil and the aromas start smelling rich. Stir in the tomatoes and sofrito, if using.

Pour in the white wine and allow it to bubble up, then add the orange zest, saffron and bay leaf. Pour in the stock. Season with salt and pepper, then bring up to high pressure and cook for 5 minutes. Allow to drop pressure naturally. Strain through a sieve, pushing through any pulp from the tomatoes and sofrito.

Reserve 50ml (1¾fl oz) of the broth, scooping up some of the red droplets of oil as you do so. Before you make the soup, make the rouille. Soak the bread in the reserved broth until it is completely absorbed, then squeeze it out. Put the breadcrumbs, garlic, red pepper, chilli powder and egg yolk into a food processor and blitz until smooth and well combined. Start dripping in the oil while the motor is still running – when it has emulsified properly, pour in a steady stream until you have used it all up and have a creamy orange mayonnaise. Set aside.

Next, prepare the croutons ready for the grill. Rub the slices of baguette with the garlic and arrange over a baking tray. Sprinkle with the cheese. Preheat your grill to high.

Fish Soup *continued*

200ml (7fl oz) neutral-tasting oil
(I prefer groundnut)

50ml (1¾fl oz) light-flavoured
olive oil

FOR THE CROUTONS

12 slices of baguette, cut on the
diagonal

2 garlic cloves, cut in half

100g (3½oz) Gruyère or similar,
grated

Finally, make the soup. Put the olive oil in your pressure cooker. Add the fennel wedges and sauté until nicely browned on the cut sides. Add a ladleful of the broth, bring up to high pressure and cook for 1 minute. Release pressure quickly. Add all the remaining broth to the pressure cooker followed by the leeks, then the pieces of fish and any molluscs, if using. Close the lid again, bring up to high pressure and immediately remove from the heat. Allow to drop pressure naturally and discard any molluscs that haven't opened. Stir in the ouzo or pastis, if using, then add the seared prawns and allow them to heat through in the broth.

Garnish with a few parsley, chervil or tarragon leaves. Put the croutons under the grill for 2–3 minutes. Serve the soup with the croutons and rouille.

STEAMED WHOLE FISH WITH GINGER AND GARLIC

SERVES 4

100g (3½oz) mangetout (snow peas), green beans or asparagus

1 courgette (zucchini), cut into rounds

100g (3½oz) baby corn, halved lengthways

4 spring onions (scallions), sliced at an angle

15g (½oz) piece ginger, cut into slim batons

2 garlic cloves, sliced

2 smallish fish – sea bream or bass are ideal, cleaned and gutted, heads removed if you like

2 tbsp dark soy sauce

2 tbsp mirin

1 tsp sesame oil

Sea salt and freshly ground black pepper

Whole fish will steam really well in the pressure cooker. You can do this using the trivet and steamer basket, layering up the vegetables before placing the fish on top, but it is easier to just put them in the base of the pressure cooker and as you are cooking at low pressure rather than high, they won't overcook in the time.

Put a very thin layer of water on the base of the pressure cooker and then add the vegetables. Sprinkle over half the ginger and garlic.

Cut diagonally into the fish – 3 slashes on each side – and season with salt and pepper. Place on top of the vegetables and sprinkle over the remaining ginger and garlic.

Mix the soy sauce, mirin and sesame oil together and drizzle half of it over the fish.

Close the lid, bring up to low pressure and cook for 2 minutes. Leave to drop pressure naturally. Carefully remove from the pressure cooker. Flip the fish over and place on a platter. Drizzle over the remaining sauce. Serve with the vegetables and perhaps some noodles or steamed rice.

HOT AND SOUR FISH

SERVES 4

FOR THE FISH

Zest and juice of 1 lime

1 tsp Kashmiri chilli powder

1 tsp ground turmeric

1 garlic clove, crushed

600g (1lb 5oz) firm white fish fillets, skinned and cut into large chunks

Sea salt and freshly ground black pepper

FOR THE SAUCE

1 tbsp coconut oil

1 onion, finely sliced

1 tsp mustard seeds

3 garlic cloves, crushed or grated

15g (½oz) piece ginger, grated

1 tsp ground turmeric

1 tsp Kashmiri chilli powder

¼ tsp ground cinnamon

150g (5½oz) fresh tomatoes, puréed or finely chopped

400ml (14fl oz) coconut milk

1 tsp concentrated tamarind paste

TO GARNISH

1 tsp coconut oil

12 fresh curry leaves

A few sprigs of coriander (cilantro)

This is based very loosely on a Goan fish curry – it is very simplified but I don't think the flavour suffers in any way – the marinade and the pressure cooking of the sauce ensures this.

Firstly, put the lime zest and juice, chilli powder and turmeric in a bowl with 1 teaspoon of salt and plenty of ground black pepper. Add the fish and turn over gently until completely covered, then add the garlic and just enough water to cover. Leave to marinate while you prepare the sauce.

Heat the coconut oil in your pressure cooker. Add the onion and cook on a medium heat until starting to change colour. Add the mustard seeds and keep cooking until they pop. Add the garlic, ginger and spices and stir for a further minute. Add the tomatoes, coconut milk and tamarind paste. Season with salt.

Close the lid and bring to high pressure. Adjust the heat until it is just high enough to maintain pressure, then cook for 3 minutes. Allow to drop pressure naturally.

Drain the fish, then add this to the sauce. Either close the lid and bring up to low pressure, then immediately remove from the heat to drop pressure naturally, or leave to simmer in the sauce, uncovered, for 4–5 minutes until the fish is just cooked through.

Heat the coconut oil in a separate pan and add the curry leaves. Fry until they are crackling and turning brown. Serve the curry garnished with the curry leaves and coriander (cilantro).

FISH EN PAPILLOTE

SERVES 4

400g (14oz) new or salad
potatoes, thickly sliced

A few sprigs of mint

2 tbsp olive oil

2 small courgettes (zucchini),
thinly sliced on the diagonal

200g (7oz) green beans or
asparagus, trimmed

4 wild salmon steaks or fillets

A few sprigs of basil, mint or dill

2 garlic cloves, finely sliced

2 tbsp capers

8 slices of lemon

Generous knob of butter

Sea salt and freshly ground
black pepper

Cooking fish in parcels is usually done in the oven and often requires par-cooking vegetables first so they steam in the same time as the fish. This simplifies things a bit, not least because you can cook potatoes at the same time underneath.

Most green vegetables will cook well in these parcels, you could also add julienned pepper or carrot or whole cherry tomatoes. You can also use any fairly thick fillets of fish. Make sure, however, that you use baking paper not foil – foil-wrapped parcels will take much longer and you will end up overcooking the potatoes.

Put the potatoes and mint sprigs in the base of your pressure cooker and season with salt. Add enough water to generously cover. Add a trivet and steamer basket.

Cut 4 pieces of baking paper. Brush the centre of each one with olive oil, then arrange the vegetables over the top. Season the salmon with salt and pepper and place on top of the vegetables. Sprinkle with the herbs, garlic and capers, then top with the lemon slices.

Fold each piece of parchment into a parcel around the salmon and vegetables. Place in the steamer basket.

Close the lid and bring up to high pressure. Cook for 3 minutes, then remove from the heat and fast release the pressure. Remove the fish parcels from the pressure cooker and transfer to 4 plates. Drain the potatoes and transfer to a serving bowl with the butter.

Open the parcels at the table.

SMOKED MACKEREL AND ROOT VEGETABLE GRATIN

SERVES 4

15g (½oz) butter, plus extra for greasing

1 large parsnip, peeled and thinly sliced

150g (5½oz) waxy potatoes, such as Charlotte, thinly sliced

1 leek, very finely sliced

3 smoked mackerel fillets, skinned and broken up into small pieces

2 tbsp horseradish cream

½ tsp plain (all-purpose) flour

150ml (5fl oz) double (heavy) cream

Sea salt and freshly ground black pepper

The flavours in this dish are based on a Diana Henry recipe – I thought it was very clever putting smoked mackerel fillets in a gratin like this. You could use cold-smoked trout instead if you prefer. If you aren't keen on parsnip, you can replace it with half a small celeriac (celery root) instead. This recipe is crazy-fast when you consider how long it would take in an oven, even after par-boiling the vegetables.

Melt the butter in the base of your pressure cooker. Remove from the heat and then layer the root vegetables, leek and smoked mackerel together. Start with a layer of root vegetables – arrange a third of them on the base of the pan, then add half the mackerel and leeks. Dot with half the horseradish, then season with salt and pepper. Repeat, then finish with the remaining root vegetables.

Put the flour in a bowl and whisk in a little of the cream until it is lump-free. Gradually mix in the rest of the cream (do not whisk at this stage, you don't want it to thicken), then add 25ml (1fl oz) water. Pour this over the contents of the pressure cooker.

Cut a round of baking paper to fit inside the pressure cooker and butter one side of it. Place this, butter-side down, on top of the contents of the pressure cooker.

Close the lid and bring up to high pressure. Cook for 3 minutes at high pressure then remove from the heat. You can fast release if you like – it will be cooked – but I leave it for a few minutes to help it settle.

Serve straight from the pan. It is very good with the red cabbage on page 260, which you could cook first, transfer to a saucepan or serving dish and warm through just before serving.

SQUID WITH WHITE BEANS AND 'NDUJA

SERVES 4

1 tbsp olive oil

1 large onion, finely sliced

500g (1lb 2oz) squid or cuttlefish, cleaned and sliced

3 garlic cloves, finely chopped

1 tsp dried oregano

50g (1¾oz) 'nduja (or harissa)

100ml (3½fl oz) red wine

200g (7oz) canned chopped tomatoes

500g (1lb 2oz) cooked cannellini beans (see page 210)

200g (7oz) cavolo nero, torn (optional)

Sea salt and freshly ground black pepper

FOR THE PANGRATTATO (OPTIONAL)

1 tbsp olive oil

25g (1oz) breadcrumbs

2 garlic cloves, finely chopped

Leaves from 1 small bunch of flat-leaf parsley or coriander (cilantro), finely chopped

This is a rich and fiery way to eat squid. 'Nduja, the spicy Calabrian soft salami, can now be bought in jars that keep indefinitely in the fridge. If you want a non-meat version, you could use a harissa paste instead.

A pangrattato is a good way of getting a bit of crunch into a dish such as this, without having to put it under the grill.

Heat the olive oil in your pressure cooker. Add the onion and fry on a high heat until starting to brown. Add the squid or cuttlefish and continue to cook on a high heat until it has turned opaque.

Add the garlic and oregano, then stir in the 'nduja or harissa. Stir so it coats the onion and squid, then pour in the red wine. Bring up to the boil, and stir to make sure the bottom of the cooker is completely deglazed. Add the tomatoes and beans. Add 100ml (3½fl oz) water and season with salt and pepper. Add the cavolo nero, if using, and close the lid. Bring up to high pressure and cook for 5 minutes, then remove from the heat and allow to drop pressure naturally.

If you want to serve it with the pangrattato, make this separately in a frying pan (skillet). Fry the breadcrumbs in the olive oil until crisp and brown, then stir in the garlic. Cook for a further minute, just to mellow the garlic a bit, then remove from the heat and stir in the herbs. Alternatively, serve with a sprinkling of chopped herbs.

VARIATIONS

To turn into a one-pot pasta dish (with or without the beans) Cook as above. Add 200g (7oz) uncooked pasta with the beans and stir to combine, then add enough water to just cover. Bring up to high pressure and cook for 5 minutes. Fast release. Add any other fish or seafood (or seafood mix) and leave to sit on top for a minute or two until just cooked, then stir through.

This can be cooked with dried beans too – the squid doesn't suffer from very lengthy cooking. Quick soak 150g (5½oz) cannellini beans, then proceed as above, adding 300ml (10½fl oz) water or stock instead of 100ml (3½fl oz) water and cooking for 15 minutes instead of 5.

FISH FILLETS WITH SAFFRON, LEEKS, RAISINS AND PINE NUTS

SERVES 4

4 fish fillets, skinned if possible

½ tsp ground cardamom

Zest of 1 lime

1 tbsp olive oil

15g (½oz) butter

4 leeks, finely sliced

A large pinch of saffron, soaked in a little warm water

50ml (1¾fl oz) vermouth or dry sherry

30g (1oz) raisins

25g (1oz) pine nuts

Sea salt

TO SERVE

A few sprigs of mint, flat-leaf parsley or chervil

This is a very fragrant, mellow dish that I make with skinned fillets of fish or goujons – you can use white or oily fish here; sea bass will work but so will mackerel. If you prefer to use fish with the skin on, I would recommend crisping it up with a blowtorch if you have one – putting it under the grill will overcook the fish.

This is particularly good with the freekeh, lentil and broad bean pilaf on page 204, but if you serve them together, you might want to omit the fried onions.

Pat the fish fillets dry with kitchen towel. Mix the cardamom and lime zest with ½ teaspoon of salt and sprinkle over the fillets. Set aside for a few minutes.

Heat the olive oil and butter in your pressure cooker. Add the leeks with a pinch of salt and sauté, turning regularly, until glossy with butter. Add the saffron, including the soaking water, followed by the vermouth, raisins and pine nuts. Bring to the boil, then lay the fish fillets on top.

Close the lid and bring up to low pressure. Cook for 1 minute, then remove from the heat. Leave to stand for 1 minute, then release the remaining pressure. Garnish with a few sprigs of mint, parsley or chervil.

PRESSURE-COOKING SALTFISH

The main advantage to preparing saltfish in the pressure cooker will become obvious to you when you read the method – in a few minutes you will have saltfish ready to use, as opposed to days of soaking and regularly changing the water. It is not the only advantage, however. From the second boil onwards, you can add aromatics, which will start getting right to the heart of the fish, and so add depth and flavour to your finished dishes; in other words, the pressure cooker is adept at pushing salt out while pushing flavour in.

There is a huge variation in the type of saltfish that can be bought, from large thick white fillets, often cod, to much smaller pieces that have been salted on the bone. The flavour tends to be better on the bone and is what I will usually use if I am making anything heavily spiced; fillets that will flake into large pieces are better for brandade.

The method is simple. Rinse the saltfish well. It is likely to have a thick crust of salt on it, much of which might just break off.

Put the saltfish in your pressure cooker, cover with water, bring up to high pressure, remove from the heat and allow to drop pressure naturally.

Strain the fish and return it to the pressure cooker, this time breaking it up a bit. This is important if your saltfish is particularly thick as it will give you more even results.

Cover with water again, along with any aromatics you like – I usually add a couple of bay leaves, a few black peppercorns and a few allspice berries, perhaps a slice of Scotch bonnet.

Strain again and taste – it should still be slightly salty, but not unpleasantly so. If you are using very thick pieces of fish, you might want to repeat the process one more time, but it isn't usually necessary – any tiny bit of excess salt still lingering will just help season any dish you use the fish in.

Flake the fish or pull into chunks, removing any skin and bones as you go.

Your saltfish is now ready to use. Try it in Caribbean favourites such as saltfish and ackee, or in crisp, chewy little fritters, or lightly braised in place of any of the fish fillets in the previous recipes in this chapter (especially page 140) or try one of the recipes on the following pages.

BRANDADE – SALTFISH AND POTATO DIP

SERVES 4

250g (9oz) saltfish (unprepared weight)

2 bay leaves

A few allspice berries

1 blade of mace

1 piece of pared lemon zest

2 garlic cloves, thinly sliced

100ml (3½fl oz) whole milk

125g (4½oz) small floury potatoes, left whole

1 garlic clove, grated or crushed

2 tbsp parsley, finely chopped

50ml (1¾fl oz) olive oil

50ml (1¾fl oz) single (light) cream

This is a classic way to use saltfish. It is a useful thing to make when you have some mashed potato to use up as the quantities are not set in stone – some brandades are made without any potato at all.

Prepare the salt fish as described on page 154. Flake the fish and put in your pressure cooker with the aromatics and milk. Bring up to high pressure and cook for 2 minutes, then allow to drop pressure naturally. The milk will look slightly curdled, but that doesn't matter in this instance. Strain, discarding the bay leaf, allspice, mace and lemon zest.

Put the potatoes in the steamer basket and place over 2cm (¾in) water. Bring up to high pressure and cook according to size – see how to bake potatoes on page 270. Remove from the pressure cooker. As soon as they are cool enough to handle, peel and discard the skin. Mash, preferably by pushing through a ricer.

Put the strained fish, garlic and parsley in your stand mixer or food processor and beat, drizzling in the olive oil and then the cream. Finally, add the mashed potato, keeping the mixing to an absolute minimum to prevent it going gluey.

Pile into a serving bowl and serve with crackers or crudités.

SALTFISH WITH CHICKPEAS AND CHILLI

SERVES 4

FOR THE SALTFISH PREPARATION

250g (9oz) saltfish (unprepared weight)

1 tsp allspice berries

2 bay leaves

Juice of 1 lime

Freshly ground black pepper

FOR THE DISH

2 tbsp olive oil

1 onion, diced

1 red or green pepper, diced

1 Scotch bonnet, finely chopped

2 garlic cloves, finely chopped

1 sprig of thyme

100g (3½oz) canned or fresh tomatoes, puréed

500g (1lb 2oz) cooked chickpeas (see page 210)

1 tsp sherry vinegar

TO SERVE

Flat-leaf parsley or coriander (cilantro), finely chopped

Lime wedges

This is loosely based on a Caribbean favourite of mine – adding coconut milk (see Variations) turns it into a wetter dish, similar to a rundown.

First prepare the saltfish as described in the method on page 154, adding the allspice berries and bay leaves to the second 'soak'. Strain the saltfish and toss in the lime juice. Season with a little pepper.

Wash out your pressure cooker and add the olive oil. Add the onion, red or green pepper and Scotch bonnet and cook gently for a few minutes, until the onion is starting to look translucent. Add the garlic, thyme, tomatoes, chickpeas and sherry vinegar. Stir in the saltfish and close the lid. Bring up to high pressure and cook for 2 minutes, then allow to drop pressure naturally.

Sprinkle with herbs and serve with lime wedges. Good with fried flatbreads or toast.

VARIATIONS

Replace the chickpeas (garbanzo beans) with ackee. Cook the saltfish as above without the chickpeas, then gently stir in the ackee and simmer for a couple of minutes – this is a great breakfast dish.

Turn into a stew
Add 200ml (7fl oz) coconut milk and other vegetables – squash or pumpkin, peppers and aubergines (eggplants) make good additions.

CARBS

When I wrote my first book on pressure cooking, it was pressure cooking pasta and risotto that proved most controversial. There are still people who are very resistant to the idea of pressure-cooker risotto, despite many excellent Italian cooks swearing by the method; all I can say about this is please try it once, you may well be converted. As for pasta, in recent years the traditional method of cooking pasta in large quantities of water has been challenged by those who prefer the absorption method. Pressure-cooked pasta uses this method, it's just faster.

The advantages of cooking pasta by absorption are – primarily, you will be conserving water as there is no need to bring a large pot of water to the boil. Secondly, you will be saving fuel by using just one ring on your hob as these pastas are generally one-pot dishes. Thirdly, there is a saving of time too – it can take forever for a large pot of water to come up to the boil, even if you've used freshly boiled water. When you start using a pressure cooker, you will find that frequently the whole meal is cooked in the time it would normally take for you to get the pasta on to cook.

There are limitations to this way of cooking. You must be careful about the type of pasta you choose, focusing on types that will cook evenly. This means that you have to be able to arrange the pasta in even layers in your pressure cooker. Short-form pastas work best as they cover the base of the cooker. Long forms – the exception being those formed into 'nests' – are tricky because most need breaking to fit and it is impossible to get them to fit in a way that will use up the surface area of the cooker efficiently. This means it is necessary to add more liquid than usual and you will end up with a wetter sauce. The same issues apply to noodles, which is why I only recommend cooking noodles in the pressure cooker in soups where plenty of liquid is expected, not for drier dishes.

The absorption method is the most common method I use for rice and other grains. I have found that I am much more likely to eat certain grains (wild rice, quinoa, barley) now I can cook them so quickly; it has especially meant that I am eating many more wholegrains, particularly in salads. Being able to cook them so quickly is also really helpful when I am time-pressed – it means that I often manage a rice (or pasta) dish first thing in the mornings for the school Thermoses. It makes risotto achievable on an evening when I can't start making dinner until late.

This chapter contains the recipes that need the most precision in terms of both quantities and timings. If you stick to these, you will hopefully find the recipes very flexible. The key to adaptation is working out how much time ingredients need to pressure cook; for example, if making a chicken pilau with diced, off-the-bone chicken, you can cook it with the rice as they take the same length of time to cook. If cooking a lamb biryani, however, you would need to cook the lamb first to tenderize, before adding the rice. Working these things out becomes second nature very quickly as you use your pressure cooker.

HOW TO PRESSURE COOK PASTA

If you want to cook pasta on its own, the method is simple.

Heat 1 tablespoon of olive oil in your pressure cooker. Add the pasta, paying special attention to getting it into an even layer and filling any gaps. Season with salt and just cover with water or stock, adding a couple of ladlefuls more if you want to incorporate any cooking liquid into the sauce later. Add another tablespoon of oil – this will help reduce foam and make it easier for you to open your pressure cooker post-cooking.

Bring up to high pressure, cook for 4 minutes and remove from the heat. Leave for 30 seconds or so, just so the starch has a chance to settle down, then fast release. Do not let it sit without opening the lid as this will result in overcooked pasta. It should be just al dente. Strain off any liquid and reserve for making a sauce.

This works well if you are going to add any pre-cooked or raw sauces (eg, stirring in pesto or chopped fresh tomatoes), but at this point you can also wilt in greens such as spinach or grated courgette (zucchini), or make any traditional sauces where cooking liquid is usually added. For example, make *cacio e pepe*, stirring in plenty of black pepper and Pecorino, with enough cooking water to coat the pasta.

ALL-IN-ONE PASTAS WITH SAUCE

These are very simple to make and you can adapt any of the pasta recipes in this book – they should give you a good idea about what will work and what won't. There are also a lot of dishes in this book that I have highlighted as working well as pasta sauce bases. However, there are a few things to bear in mind and watch out for:

Tomatoes – The mainstay of many pasta sauces, they are often flagged as being difficult because they can trigger a burn alarm in electric pressure cookers or scorch in a regular pressure cooker before it has reached high pressure. If you make sure the base of the cooker is deglazed and enough water is stirred in, or in the case of electric pressure cookers, use the ceramic liner as opposed to the stainless-steel pot, you should be OK, but if you find this does happen, you can put the tomatoes/tomato sauce on top instead, without stirring, until the cooking is completed. Other starchy sauces can also be tricky in this regard, such as leftover beans or lentil ragùs. Again, make sure they are well stirred in with the pasta and water, or put on top, not left to sit on the base of the cooker.

Adding vegetables – Greens in particular will become very soft and mushy when cooked by this method; kales and chard being the obvious exception. If you want to incorporate greens into your sauce, cook them first, separately (see page 248 for a full explanation), then remove from the cooker and proceed with the rest of your recipe, stirring the greens through to heat after you have released pressure. If there is room, you can also wrap them in foil and place on top to steam while the pasta cooks. Alternatively, if you like very soft courgettes (zucchini), beans etc, you can add them at the beginning. Just avoid overcooking vegetables such as broccoli and cauliflower as they will disintegrate.

Liquid levels – Always make sure the pasta is just covered – and no more – with water or stock. Very occasionally, you might find that the pasta has not absorbed all of the liquid, leaving your sauce a little thin. This can happen for a variety of reasons, mainly because slightly too much liquid has been added or because vegetables have given out too much water. One thing to counter this is to throw in a handful of unrinsed split red lentils to the cooker at the same time as the pasta – they will disintegrate and help thicken the sauce. The other option is to simply put the lid back on and leave to stand for a few minutes – the sauce should thicken naturally in this time.

Pasta bakes – Cooking the pasta and sauce together in the pressure cooker speeds up the first part of the process and you can still transfer to an ovenproof dish and put in the oven if you like. However, in order to avoid turning on the oven, consider the alternatives. Firstly, if using a sauté-pan pressure cooker, you can cover the handles with a triple layer of foil and safely put under the grill for a few minutes (or use an air-fryer attachment if you have one). Secondly, replace browning with a sprinkling of something like a pangrattato (fried breadcrumbs with aromatics) instead. Thirdly, consider whether you want a brown, crisp finish – sometimes just putting cheese on top of pasta and replacing the lid to let it melt in the ambient heat is a really comforting thing to do.

WINTER MINESTRONE

SERVES 4

2 tbsp olive oil

2 small red onions, cut into wedges

1 large carrot, cut on the diagonal

2 celery sticks, thickly sliced

100g (3½oz) smoked or unsmoked bacon, diced (optional)

3 garlic cloves, finely chopped

½ butternut squash or similar, peeled and diced

100g (3½oz) short pasta

250g (9oz) cooked beans, such as cannellini, butter (lima) beans or borlotti

100ml (3½fl oz) red wine

750ml (26fl oz) smoked ham, chicken or mushroom stock (see page 324)

A Parmesan rind (optional)

A bouquet garni of thyme, flat-leaf parsley and rosemary sprigs

2 tomatoes, finely diced

1 large bunch of cavolo nero, kale or chard, roughly chopped

Sea salt and freshly ground black pepper

TO SERVE

Parmesan, grated

Finely chopped flat-leaf parsley

This is a good pasta dish to get started with. The amount of pasta is small, obviously, but it makes its presence felt as the starch it releases during the pressure-cooking time will help thicken the broth.

I don't give variations for this one as it is by its nature a receptacle for whatever you have to put in it, but stick to fairly robust vegetables if you can. You can also pare it right down, especially if you have any building block recipes such as sofrito (see page 330) in the fridge or freezer. A little fried garlic and bacon, if using, some cooked beans, pasta and greens makes a really good soupy meal without any wine, herbs or other vegetables.

Heat the olive oil in your pressure cooker. Add the onion wedges, carrot, celery and bacon, if using. Fry on a high heat until the bacon is crisp and the vegetables are browning around the edges. Add the garlic and squash. Stir for a minute or two.

Stir in the pasta and beans, then pour over the red wine. Bring to the boil and simmer for a couple of minutes, then add the stock, Parmesan rind, if using, the bouquet garni and the tomatoes. Season with salt and pepper.

Close the lid and bring up to high pressure. Cook for 4 minutes, then remove from the heat. Fast release the pressure. Push the greens into the liquid, then close the lid again. Bring up to pressure, then immediately remove from the heat and fast release. Remove the lid, stir the greens through the soup, then leave to stand for a few minutes.

Remove the bouquet garni and the Parmesan rind. Serve with grated Parmesan and plenty of parsley.

PASTA WITH TOMATO SAUCE

SERVES 4

1 tbsp olive oil

1 onion, finely chopped

3 garlic cloves, finely chopped

1 tsp dried oregano

A pinch of ground cinnamon

25g (1oz) split red lentils (optional)

300g (10½oz) short pasta

1 x 400g (14oz) can chopped tomatoes

1 sprig of basil

Sea salt and freshly ground black pepper

There are other recipes for tomato sauce in this book (see pages 332 and 333), which of course can be used with pasta in place of this one, following the guidance on page 160. This is what I consider to be the absolute basic recipe for use when I'm in a hurry and don't have any tomato sauce made up.

Heat the olive oil in your pressure cooker and add the onion. Sauté until the onion is starting to soften, then add the garlic, oregano and cinnamon. Season with salt and pepper and stir for a minute or two. Stir in the lentils, if using, followed by the pasta. Add just enough water to cover the pasta, then pour the tomatoes on top. Add the basil. Close the lid and bring up to high pressure. Cook for 5 minutes, then leave to stand for up to a minute and manually release the pressure slowly. Remove the basil and stir through the tomatoes.

VARIATION

Meatballs with Tomato Pasta
This is the best sauce to go with classic meatballs. If you want to make the meatballs from scratch, sauté 1 finely chopped onion in 1 tablespoon of olive oil until soft and add 2 finely chopped garlic cloves. Put 400g (14oz) minced (ground) beef in a bowl and add 35g (1¼oz) fresh breadcrumbs, 1 egg, plenty of seasoning, 1 teaspoon of dried oregano and the onion and garlic. Mix thoroughly. Form into around 16 balls. You can either fry them lightly first in olive oil before dropping them on top of the pasta, or simply add uncooked. A little finely chopped bacon is also good fried with the onion.

QUICK AND EASY PASTA SAUCES

PASTA WITH BACON, CHILLI AND GREENS

Heat 1 tablespoon of olive oil in your pressure cooker. Sauté 1 onion or 2 tablespoons of sofrito (page 330) with 100g (3½oz) bacon lardons, 2 chopped garlic cloves, ½ teaspoon of dried herbs and ½ teaspoon of chilli flakes. Pour in 50ml (1¾fl oz) white wine and allow to boil off, then add a handful of split red lentils and 250g (9oz) short pasta. Add enough water or stock to cover and put 100g (3½oz) kale on top. Bring up to high pressure, cook for 5 minutes, then remove from the heat. Leave for 30 seconds, then slowly release the pressure. If you want to use tender greens, such as sprouting broccoli or cime di rapa, cook these first according to the instructions on page 248, then remove from the cooker, cook the pasta and stir through before serving.

PASTA WITH FETA AND CHERRY TOMATOES

While I was writing, a version of this dish, originally created by Finnish blogger Jenni Häyrinen, was absolutely everywhere on social media. Feta cooks beautifully in the pressure cooker, to a soft creaminess.

Heat 1 tablespoon of olive oil in your pressure cooker. Add 250g (9oz) short pasta and 1 teaspoon of dried oregano and stir quickly, then cover with cold water or stock. Season, then top with a 250g (9oz) feta block, 250g (9oz) cherry tomatoes and ½ head of garlic. Drizzle over another 1 tablespoon of oil. Cook as above. Remove the garlic and squeeze the flesh from the skins. Add back to the pressure cooker with a few basil leaves. Stir to combine. Serve with extra cheese if you like and plenty of pepper.

PASTA WITH COURGETTES, ROCKET AND LEMON

You have two options with the courgettes (zucchini) here. If they are very small and firm, they will do well cooked with the pasta without disintegrating or leaching out too much liquid. If they are large, or you would just prefer more of an al dente finish, cook them first according to the instructions on page 248, then add back in at the end. Other greens that work well in this dish, cooked either way include runner (string) or other flat beans or skinned broad (fava) beans.

Heat 1 tablespoon of olive oil and 15g (½oz) butter in your pressure cooker. Add 2 finely sliced leeks, 2 sliced courgettes (zucchini) and 3 finely chopped garlic cloves, and sauté for a couple of minutes until glossy, then stir in 250g (9oz) pasta and the zest of 1 lemon. Pour in enough water to cover the pasta and season with salt and pepper. Cook and release as described opposite, then wilt in 75g (2½oz) roughly chopped rocket (arugula). Add the juice of ½ lemon, 75g (2½oz) grated Parmesan or similar and a few basil leaves. Stir and taste, adding more lemon juice if necessary. Alternatively, cook the courgettes separately, see page 248, and stir in with the rocket.

STORECUPBOARD TUNA PASTA

Heat 1 tablespoon of olive oil and add 1 finely chopped onion. Sauté until starting to take on colour, then add 3 finely chopped garlic cloves or 1 teaspoon of garlic powder, along with a large can of tuna, drained, 2 tablespoons of sliced black or green olives, 2 tablespoons of capers, the zest of 1 lemon and ½ teaspoon each of chilli flakes and dried herbs (I like rosemary). Add 250g (9oz) short pasta and add either 3 tablespoons of tomato purée or 200g (7oz) tomatoes. Pour in enough water to cover and cook as above. Serve with basil; cheese strictly optional.

CREAMY SAUSAGE PASTA

A quick and comforting dish that works well with other types of minced (ground) meat. Heat 1 teaspoon of olive oil in your pressure cooker and add roughly 200g (7oz) sausagemeat or sausages with their casings removed. Break up, then add 1 finely chopped onion and sauté until the sausage is well browned. Add 2 chopped garlic cloves and ½ teaspoon of dried sage, then stir in an optional 1 tablespoon of tomato purée and 25g (1oz) split red lentils, followed by 100g (3½oz) roughly chopped greens. Pour in 100ml (3½fl oz) white wine and bring to the boil, then stir in 250g (9oz) pasta and enough water or stock to cover. Cook as before. Stir in 100g (3½oz) cream cheese or crème fraîche. Leave to stand for a few minutes (this will help the sauce thicken). Serve with plenty of cheese. There are numerous variations – try adding 100g (3½oz) peeled and diced squash along with the greens, vary the sausage you use (chorizo is good but use half the quantity), turn into a hearty red wine and tomato sauce by replacing the white wine with red, adding 200g (7oz) tomatoes to the pasta and omitting all or half the cream cheese.

PASTA WITH CHICKPEAS

Cook 200g (7oz) chickpeas (garbanzo beans) as on page 210, adding a few garlic cloves, sprigs of rosemary, 1 roughly chopped carrot and onion after the soak or quick soak and using vegetable or chicken stock in place of water if possible. Drain, reserving the cooking liquid. Blitz 150g (5½oz) of the cooked chickpeas in half the cooking liquid until roughly puréed.

Heat 3 tablespoons of olive oil in your pressure cooker. Sauté 100g (3½oz) finely diced pancetta (optional, this is also very good vegan) and 4 chopped garlic cloves, then stir in 3 chopped tomatoes. Add the whole chickpeas and 250g (9oz) pasta – traditionally a flat one, but anything goes. Season and add enough of the chickpea water and any additional stock to generously cover – you want this quite soupy. Tuck in more rosemary. Cook at high pressure for 4 minutes, then normal release. Stir in the puréed chickpeas along with some very finely chopped rosemary and leave to stand for a few minutes before serving.

QUICK ALL-IN-ONE BOLOGNESE

SERVES 4

1 tbsp olive oil

300g (10½oz) minced (ground) beef

1 large onion, finely chopped

10g (¼oz) dried mushrooms, crumbled

3 garlic cloves, finely chopped, or 1 tsp garlic powder

½ tsp dried oregano

1 sprig of thyme or ½ tsp dried thyme

A large pinch of sugar

2 tbsp tomato purée

100ml (3½fl oz) red wine

25g (1oz) split red lentils

250g (9oz) spaghetti or linguine, broken in half

200g (7oz) canned chopped tomatoes

Sea salt and freshly ground black pepper

TO SERVE

Parmesan, grated

I offer this recipe with a caveat. I thought it important to include because spaghetti Bolognese is a very popular recipe, especially with children, and the internet is awash with one-pot pressure-cooker versions of it. However, there is no getting away from the fact that if you use a long pasta it will not be the same as if you had cooked the pasta and sauce separately. You will have to accept two things. First, the pasta has to be broken in half to fit into your cooker and will therefore be shorter than you are used to. Secondly, because the pasta has to be completely immersed in liquid to cook evenly and there isn't an even way of arranging the pasta, you do end up with much more sauce than you would normally expect. Adding the lentils does help with this as it means the sauce won't be watery. If you are happy with this, then embrace it, rename it 'spaghetti casserole' or similar and use the same process for any other sauce that takes your fancy. Alternatively, use nests of long pasta or stick with short forms.

Heat the olive oil in your pressure cooker. Add the beef and onion. Sauté until the beef is cooked – you will find it will give out a lot of liquid, you want it to look quite dry before you start adding the remaining ingredients. Crumble in the mushrooms and stir in the garlic or garlic powder and herbs. Stir for a couple of minutes, then stir in the sugar and tomato purée. Pour in the wine and deglaze the base of the cooker, thoroughly.

Sprinkle in the red lentils, then arrange the spaghetti over the top in a spiral, then add just enough water to cover. Season with salt and pepper, then pour over the tomatoes. Bring up to high pressure and cook for 4 minutes and leave to drop pressure naturally for 5 minutes. Release any remaining pressure.

Stir the contents of the pot so all the pasta is coated with the sauce. Leave to sit for a few minutes. Serve with plenty of Parmesan.

MAC 'N' CHEESE

SERVES 4–6

1 tbsp olive oil

15g (½oz) butter

150g (5½oz) smoked or unsmoked bacon, diced

1 bunch of spring onions (scallions), greens and whites separated, finely chopped

500g (1lb 2oz) elbow macaroni

1 large tomato, finely chopped or puréed

1 tsp hot sauce (or to taste) or 1 Scotch bonnet, finely chopped

1 large sprig of thyme

750ml (26fl oz) water or stock

350ml (12fl oz) whole or evaporated milk

200g (7oz) hard cheese, such as Cheddar or Gruyère, grated

75g (2½oz) mozzarella or other stretchy cheese, such as Gouda or Ogleshield

Sea salt

It has taken many, many attempts to get this recipe just right. The main version here has flavours I associate with the Caribbean macaroni pie. You can use this recipe as an alternative to any béchamel-based version – see below for other variations. A note on the cheese – you don't have to add mozzarella or Ogleshield but it will give a degree of stringiness to the dish that kids will love.

Heat the olive oil and butter in your pressure cooker and add the bacon. Fry until crisp, then add the whites of the spring onions (scallions). Stir to coat, then stir in the macaroni, tomato, hot sauce and thyme sprig. Season with salt and pour over the water or stock. Close the lid, bring up to high pressure and cook for 5 minutes.

Manually slow release the pressure (being careful because the macaroni contains starch, see page 160). Pour in the milk or evaporated milk, then stir in all the cheese and the spring onion greens. Remove the thyme.

Stir on a low heat to separate the clumps of macaroni and until the cheese has melted and coats the macaroni with a thick sauce. Serve immediately.

VARIATIONS

Traditional
For a more traditional mac 'n' cheese, replace the spring onions (scallions) with 1 small finely chopped onion. Omit the tomato, hot sauce and thyme. Whisk 1 tablespoon of Dijon mustard into the milk before adding to the macaroni.

Baked
Transfer to an ovenproof dish and sprinkle with an extra 50g (1¾oz) mixture of hard and stretchy cheese or a mixture of 25g (1oz) cheese and 25g (1oz) fresh breadcrumbs. Put under a hot grill for 5 minutes or in an oven preheated to 200°C (400°F/Gas 6) for 30 minutes.

Greens
Include a few cubes of frozen spinach or fresh greens, such as chard or kale, to the macaroni and stir this through with the milk and cheese at the end. Or, wilt in fresh spinach or rocket (arugula) and stir through.

Seafood
Add prawns (shrimp – preferably North Atlantic), crab or lobster. If you have the shells, fry these in the oil first, deglaze the pan with some of the stock, and strain. Discard the shells and add the liquor back into your stock, topping up to the full amount if necessary. Add the seafood after you have melted in the cheese.

RETRO TUNA CASSEROLE

SERVES 4-6

1 tbsp olive oil

15g (½oz) butter

1 onion, finely chopped

100g (3½oz) mushrooms, finely chopped or puréed

1 large garlic clove, grated or crushed

1 tsp garlic powder

1 tsp plain (all-purpose) flour

1 x 160g (5¾oz) can tuna

250g (9oz) short pasta

150g (5½oz) frozen sweetcorn or peas (optional)

300ml (10½fl oz) whole milk

100g (3½oz) cheese, grated (Cheddar is good)

Sea salt and freshly ground black pepper

This dish – a family favourite – reminds me of student days as it was the one thing almost everyone knew how to make – but usually by using condensed soup as the sauce. I can't bring myself to do that in this recipe but I'm hoping you won't miss it.

Heat the olive oil and butter in your pressure cooker. Add the onion and mushrooms and sauté until the mushrooms have given out liquid and are looking dry. Stir in the garlic, garlic powder and flour and stir for a minute or two, then add the tuna and pasta.

Add just enough water to cover the pasta and season with salt and pepper. Stir to thoroughly deglaze the bottom of the pan. Sprinkle the sweetcorn or peas over the top, if using.

Close the lid and bring up to high pressure. Cook for 5 minutes, then remove from the heat and leave the cooker to calm down for up to a minute, then steadily but quickly release the rest of the pressure. Put back on a low heat and stir in the milk – you should see the sauce around the pasta immediately thicken.

Sprinkle with cheese and replace the lid, allowing the cheese to melt over the pasta, or transfer to an ovenproof dish or cover the handles of your pressure cooker, sprinkle with cheese and put under the grill until the cheese has melted and started to brown.

GREEK CHICKEN AND PASTA

SERVES 4-6

1 tbsp olive oil

3 chicken thigh fillets, skin on

1 fennel bulb, trimmed and cut into wedges

1 onion, finely chopped

2 garlic cloves, finely chopped

Zest and juice of 1 lemon

1 sprig of tarragon

½ tsp dried oregano

¼ tsp ground cinnamon or allspice (optional)

100ml (3½fl oz) white wine (optional)

300g (10½oz) kritharaki, manestra or orzo

Stock or water to cover the pasta (around 400ml/14fl oz)

Sea salt and freshly ground black pepper

TO SERVE

1 small bunch of flat-leaf parsley, finely chopped

Smoked chilli flakes

The best pasta to use for this dish is kritharaki, which is pretty much identical to manestra or orzo, so use any of those interchangeably. You could also use other kinds of short pasta, but you will need more liquid – just make sure you use enough to cover.

I have used chicken thighs with the skin still attached because that does give the best flavour, but you can use diced thighs if you prefer. This will save time as you will not need to brown them in the same way and you can just add them to the pressure cooker along with the onions.

Heat the olive oil in your pressure cooker. Add the chicken thighs, skin-side down, and fry until they are a deep golden brown and nicely crisp. Remove. Add the fennel wedges and fry on each side until lightly caramelized. Remove. Add the onion and garlic and sauté for a couple of minutes, then stir in the lemon zest, tarragon, oregano and cinnamon or allspice, if using. Deglaze with the white wine, making sure you scrape up any brown residue stuck to the base of your cooker.

Pour in the pasta and just enough stock or water to completely cover it. Season generously with salt and pepper. Return the chicken thighs to the pressure cooker, skin-side up, and arrange the fennel wedges around them. Season again, then pour over the lemon juice.

Bring up to high pressure and cook for 5 minutes. Remove from the heat and leave to stand for a couple of minutes, then release any remaining pressure. Remove the chicken and roughly slice, discarding the bones and any very flabby pieces of skin, then stir through the pasta along with the parsley. Serve with chilli flakes, if you like.

STUFFED PASTA SHELLS

SERVES 2 AS A MAIN, 4 AS A STARTER

18-20 large pasta shells
(conchiglioni)

1 tbsp olive oil

1 portion of tomato sauce (see
page 332)

2 blocks of mozzarella or similar
stretchy, melting cheese

FOR THE STUFFING

250g (9oz) frozen spinach blocks

150g (5½oz) ricotta

2 garlic cloves, grated or finely
chopped

Zest of 1 lemon

A few grates of nutmeg

Sea salt and freshly ground
black pepper

Having tomato sauce ready to go is a boon for busy people, but the beauty of pressure cooking is that even if you don't, it is short work making a batch for this recipe. You can make it even speedier by just following the tomato sauce recipe up to the point when you cook under pressure, then proceed as below.

Portion wise, this recipe is slightly limited in quantity because the shells need to be arranged in a single layer. I would say it will feed 2 generously, 3 very well and for 4 people it's a full meal if supplemented with something else, or a generous starter.

I use my sauté-pan pressure-cooker for this dish as it is a good oven-to-table size.

First defrost the spinach. Once drained and squeezed of liquid, it should give you around 75-85g (2½–3oz). Finely chop, then put in a bowl with the remaining stuffing ingredients plus plenty of seasoning. Use to stuff the shells, making sure each shell is full – the shells will expand as they cook.

Drizzle the olive oil over the base of your pressure cooker, followed by the tomato sauce. Arrange the stuffed shells over the sauce, then pour water around them (trying to avoid pouring it over them), making sure it comes all the way up the sides. Close the lid and bring up to high pressure. Cook for 5 minutes, then allow to drop pressure naturally for 2 minutes before releasing the rest of the pressure.

Tear over the cheese to cover the top and leave on a low heat for a short while until the cheese has melted. Alternatively, cover the handles of your pressure cooker with foil and put under a hot grill for a few minutes.

NOODLES

After experimenting a lot with cooking noodles, I have come to the conclusion that they work very well cooked in the pressure cooker in soups, but not for all-in-one drier dishes. The reason for this is that noodles, like long forms of pasta, don't cook evenly unless completely submerged in liquid. As it takes more liquid to completely submerge the noodles than they need to absorb to be perfectly al dente, you will always end up with either overcooked, overplump noodles or too much liquid. I have tried cooking with small amounts of liquid that the noodles can collapse down into, but the results have been too inconsistent. Having said that, noodles do cook well in soups, and more importantly, the pressure cooker is perfect for making the accompanying broths.

A good broth is the result of a decent, homemade stock (see page 324), which is infused with various aromatics to get the depth of flavours you want. What I have discovered when making broth-based soups is that a pressure cooker injects that flavour very quickly and easily into the broth, giving excellent results regardless of whether you use your own homemade stock or a bought equivalent. A homemade stock made with lots of collagen-rich bones and offcuts will still give you the best results texturally, but flavourwise, a bought one will work. The exception is with bought vegetable stocks – these tend to be a bit too dominantly herbal, especially for the following soups and I would be more inclined to use an instant dashi, miso or 'umami' base instead.

For any soup of this type, follow the same method – add whole or lightly crushed aromatics to the stock, bring up to pressure, cook at high pressure for 1 minute, then remove from the heat and leave to drop pressure naturally. In the time it takes for the pressure to drop and the liquid to cool, the stock will take on the flavour of the aromatics – strain just before you need to use it. This makes it ideal for preparing ahead.

You can then cook the main components of the dish in the pressure cooker. Most noodles (except vermicelli) will cook in the time it takes for the pressure cooker to come up to pressure, which is useful as it is also the amount of time most greens and finely sliced meat or vegetables will take to cook too. If you want more control, you can cook according to the packet instructions instead.

These recipes may have long lists of ingredients but they are all incredibly quick – there is no sautéing and very little preparation – in fact, most of the prep is in the garnishes. This means that a traditionally quite laborious soup can suddenly become quite achievable on an evening when you are time-pressed.

RAMEN

SERVES 4

FOR THE BROTH

1 portion of ramen stock (see page 328) or 1.5 litres (52fl oz) chicken stock

2 pieces of konbu (each the size of a bacon rasher)

25g (1oz) dried shiitake (optional)

25g (1oz) piece ginger (optional)

4 garlic cloves, left whole, squashed (optional)

FOR THE SEASONING (TARE)

2 tbsp dark soy sauce

1 tbsp mirin

2 tsp soft light brown sugar

FOR THE SOUP

1 tbsp neutral-tasting oil, such as groundnut, grapeseed or sunflower

4–8 slices of char siu or chasu (see page 79), or 2 cooked chicken breasts (see page 94), sliced

4 blocks of noodles

1 head of Chinese (napa) cabbage or equivalent in pak choi (bok choy), sprouting broccoli, Brussels sprout tops, trimmed and cut into wedges

TO SERVE (OPTIONAL)

Spring onions (scallions), roughly cut

A handful of beansprouts

4–8 tamago eggs (according to appetite, see page 38)

Sesame or chilli oil

More tare seasoning or equivalent

This is a composite recipe that relies on a number of building block recipes to assemble – but you can take shortcuts with any of those steps, so it can be as complicated or as simple as you like. I like the deeply savoury seasoning of tare with all the ramens I make – at its simplest, it is a combination of soy sauce, mirin and sugar that are simmered together until syrupy. You can also add other intensely savoury ingredients such as bacon, dried shrimp or anchovies.

You can cook the noodles in the broth as described below, but if you are using long noodles, fresh noodles or simply prefer to cook separately, you can do so.

Put the stock and konbu in your pressure cooker and add the dried shiitake, ginger and garlic if using. Close the lid on your pressure cooker, bring up to high pressure and cook for 5 minutes. Allow to drop pressure naturally.

Strain the stock. Return it to the pressure cooker. Make the seasoning by heating the soy, mirin and sugar together until the sugar has dissolved. Add 1 tablespoon of this to the broth and taste – keep adding a little more until it is seasoned to your liking.

Heat the oil in a pan and add the slices of char siu or chasu. Fry until slightly browned around the edges, then add to the pressure cooker. Push in the blocks of noodles and put the greens on top.

Bring up to high pressure and immediately remove from the heat and fast release. Divide the greens, meat and noodles between 4 deep bowls and pour over the broth. Garnish with any or all of the remaining ingredients.

SIMPLE BEEF PHO

SERVES 4

FOR THE BROTH

1 litre (35fl oz) beef stock

4 garlic cloves, thinly sliced

25g (1oz) piece ginger, thinly sliced

1 small piece of cinnamon stick (around 4cm/1½in), broken up

3 star anise

2 cloves

A few black peppercorns, crushed

1 tbsp dark soy sauce

1 tbsp fish sauce

1 tsp palm sugar or light soft brown sugar

FOR THE PHO

1 bunch of spring onions (scallions), sliced, white and green parts separated

1 carrot, cut into batons

200g (7oz) egg noodles

200g (7oz) Chinese greens

Sea salt (optional)

TO SERVE

200g (7oz) sirloin steak, preferably frozen

1 small bunch of coriander (cilantro) and/or mint

Lime wedges

Soy sauce

Chilli or sesame oil

Make this with the homemade stock on page 324 or a shop-bought equivalent.

First make the broth. Put the stock and all the aromatics, sauces and sugar into your pressure cooker. Bring up to high pressure, cook for 1 minute, then turn off the heat and leave it to drop pressure naturally. Leave sealed until you have prepped everything else, including the beef – this should be sliced as thinly as possible and is much easier to do if it is at least semi-frozen.

Strain the broth and discard all the aromatics. Transfer back to your pressure cooker and taste for seasoning – add salt and a little more soy sauce if necessary. Add the spring onion (scallion) whites and carrots to the broth, then push in the noodles. Top with the Chinese greens.

Return to high pressure and immediately remove from the heat and fast release. Divide the sliced beef between 4 bowls. Top with the greens, followed by the noodles, then cover with broth. Serve with the spring onion greens, coriander (cilantro) and/or mint and lime wedges. You can also put soy sauce and chilli or sesame oil on the table for drizzling.

QUICK AND EASY NOODLE SOUPS

QUICK CHICKEN NOODLE SOUP

Make exactly as on page 176 but use a chicken stock base. Add 2 chicken breasts to the cooker with the stock when you add the aromatics for infusing. They will poach perfectly in the same timings. Remove from the stock, then slice or shred.

QUICK DUCK NOODLE SOUP

Use a chicken or duck base. Shred 1 portion of Crispy Aromatic Duck (see page 128) or finely slice a couple of duck breasts and cook with the noodles and greens.

MUSHROOM AND SEAWEED NOODLE SOUP

Make as the broth on page 176, replacing the beef stock with vegetable or dashi stock (page 329) and adding 15g (½oz) dried sliced shiitake or wild mushrooms and 1 tablespoon of dried dulse seaweed. Strain, but add the shiitake back to the broth. Add a variety of vegetables (halved baby corn, mangetout/snow peas, asparagus as well as greens) and some sliced fresh mushrooms. Bring up to high pressure and fast release. Garnish with a little more ground dulse. Also good with udon noodles (cooked separately).

SEAFOOD LAKSA

Use a fish stock as a base but reduce to 600ml (21fl oz). Instead of the aromatics listed on page 176, fry heads and shells from 500g (1lb 2oz) raw or cooked prawns (shrimp), or crab or lobster shells in 1 teaspoon of coconut oil before adding the stock and proceeding as above. Strain and reserve. Heat 1 tablespoon of coconut oil and add 3 tablespoons of laksa paste (you can take a shortcut by using a bought one, or a red curry paste or use the rendang-style paste on page 61). Fry the paste with 1 teaspoon of shrimp paste, if you have it, until aromatic, then pour in the stock along with 400ml (14fl oz) coconut milk, 2 teaspoons of palm sugar and 2–3 tablespoons of fish sauce. Add flat rice noodles, raw prawns, raw mussels or other molluscs and any greens you like, bring up to high pressure and fast release. Add any already cooked seafood at this point and allow to warm through. Serve with lime wedges and handfuls of laksa leaves (rau ram). For a very rich broth, stir in a couple of tablespoons of brown crab meat before serving.

OX CHEEK AND PEPPER NOODLE SOUP

Roughly chop 200g (7oz) ox cheek and sear in 1 tablespoon of oil in the pressure cooker. Remove the meat. Cut 1 onion in half and brown the cut sides. Stir in 1 tablespoon of tomato purée, then add the aromatics, including 1 tablespoon of lightly crushed peppercorns, and the stock. Return the meat to the cooker. Cook for 45 minutes at high pressure and drop pressure naturally. Remove the meat and pull apart. Strain the broth and proceed as on page 176, adding the meat back into the cooker with the noodles.

DUMPLINGS

You can steam all kinds of dumplings – bought or homemade – in the pressure cooker and it will be much quicker than steaming them conventionally. To do this, lightly oil your steamer basket and add the dumplings, well spaced out, then steam over water.

For cooked dumplings, bring up to high pressure and immediately remove from the heat and leave to drop pressure naturally. For frozen cooked dumplings, cook for 1 minute at high pressure and also leave to drop pressure naturally. For uncooked dumplings, they will need 3 minutes at high pressure, natural release.

You can also steam bao buns and other types of dim sum this way – the filled spherical bao buns will take 3 minutes at high pressure, natural release, while the folded will take 5 minutes at low pressure, natural release. If you make your own bao buns, there are plenty of recipes in this book that you can use as fillings – for example try shredding the ribs recipe on page 83, or the char siu on page 79.

However, I wanted to know if it was possible to make proper, crisp-bottomed potstickers, which are a family staple – it takes quite a while to cook them conventionally, as they have to be done in batches and we never eat fewer than 20 at a time. The good news is that it is, as long as you invest in some Teflon-coated fabric or Bake-O-Glide. The Teflon-coated fabric is essential here – it isn't just that pressure cookers aren't non-stick, as you can prise the dumplings off without too much difficulty, it's just that in the time they take to cook, they will burn without it.

The timings for these very much depend on the size of pressure cooker you have and the thickness of the wrappers you use. The ideal for this is a 2.5–3-litre (87–105fl oz) pressure cooker, which depending on brand comes as a small saucepan shape or as a sauté pan – see page 6 for details of these. These will come up to pressure very quickly with minimal liquid and so will cook these perfectly after 2 minutes of high pressure. However, a larger pressure cooker – even a regular 4.5-litre (157fl oz) one – will cook these differently. I add the same amount of water, then time from the moment I start cooking for 2½ minutes, regardless of the pressure it is at.

For these timings, please try to get gyoza wrappers that are a little thinner than dumpling wrappers. Alternatively, you will have to add an extra minute on to the timings.

POTSTICKERS

SERVES 4–6

A bag of potsticker or gyoza wrappers

Groundnut oil, for greasing

FOR THE FILLING

200g (7oz) Chinese (napa) cabbage, very finely shredded

3 spring onions (scallions), finely chopped

15g (½oz) piece ginger, grated

3 garlic cloves, grated

200g (7oz) minced (ground) pork

1 tbsp dark soy sauce

1 egg

Sea salt and freshly ground black pepper

FOR THE DIPPING SAUCE

2 tbsp dark soy sauce

1 tbsp rice wine

1 tbsp chilli oil

1 tsp toasted sesame oil

These are a family favourite and luckily both my children enjoy making them. However, they can take ages to cook, especially when doing multiple batches, so I was really happy that I managed to come up with a faster pressure cooker method. Please read the previous page for more detailed instructions on how to cook – I would just stress that you should aim for the gyoza wrappers that are thinner than dumpling rounds.

First make the filling. Mix all the ingredients together thoroughly and season with salt and pepper. You will find it seems very sticky to start with but knead it and it will firm up nicely.

Take a wrapper and put 1 teaspoon of filling in the centre of it. Wet the edges, then bring together into a cresent shape, pleating on one side as you go. Place on a baking tray until you are ready to cook.

To cook, put round of Teflon-coated fabric in the base of your pressure cooker and drizzle with oil. Arrange some of the dumplings over the base, making sure you leave room between them all and then splash with water – no more than 25ml (1fl oz). Close the lid and bring up to high pressure. Cook for 2 minutes, then fast release in a small pressure cooker or from the moment you close the lid, time for 2½ minutes in a larger pressure cooker and fast release. Repeat until you have cooked all your potstickers.

To make the dipping sauce, simply mix all the ingredients together and taste. Adjust the soy and chilli as you like.

VARIATION

You can also use this cooking method with pierogi. Normally I would cook the pierogi first, then fry with butter and onion – this method allows us to do it in one. Sauté 1 finely chopped onion in oil and butter until golden brown, then add your favourite pierogi and turn over a couple of times in the butter. Add 100ml (3½fl oz) water as the dough will be thicker and need to absorb more, then cook for 3 minutes and fast release. Simmer off any liquid and serve with a little more butter, some finely chopped flat-leaf parsley or dill and a grating of nutmeg.

COOKING GRAINS

Cooking grains in the pressure cooker requires a degree of precision. Most of the following recipes use the absorption method – using just the right amount of liquid the grain needs to swell and cook, no more, so no wasted water – which is by far the most efficient, but it does mean attention has to be paid to liquid-to-grain ratios and timings. Don't try to wing it here, at least to start with.

Measuring by ratio is actually very useful, because it gives you the formula for scaling quantities up and down – the cooking time will always be the same – and makes it easy when adapting other recipes. Pressure-cooker recipes will always have less liquid than conventional recipes because there is much less evaporation.

HOW TO COOK LONG-GRAIN RICE

Several of the following recipes are adaptations of this method – once you can cook basmati rice in the pressure cooker, you can cook any type of long-grain rice and know that as long as you follow the same timings and ratios, you can pretty much adapt to any recipe, including pilafs, plovs, biryanis, jollof, you name it.

The basic ratio is 1:1.5 (or 2:3 if you prefer) and this ratio applies to all kinds of long-grain rice, including brown, black, wild, carmargue red. If using white rice, rinse thoroughly. I do this in a bowl rather than keeping the tap running, simply cover the rice in water, swirl round to release starch and pour off, repeating until the water remains clear. Then place in the pressure cooker with the right amount of liquid (you can use water, stock, coconut milk, just make sure it's cold), salt and any aromatics you like and bring up to high pressure. Cook basmati rice for 2–3 minutes, depending on your pressure cooker, other types of long-grain rice for 3–4 minutes, and any wild or wholegrain rices for 18–20 minutes, then remove from the heat and allow to drop pressure naturally. Remove the lid, cover with a tea towel and place the lid back on loosely, and leave to steam off the heat until very dry and fluffy.

You can also cook wild and wholegrain rice quicker in more water. Cover generously with water, add salt and close the lid. Bring up to high pressure and cook for 8 minutes. Allow to drop pressure naturally, then drain.

ADAPTING THIS METHOD

When deciding how to cook an all-in-one rice dish, you need to work out how long the other ingredients need to cook – specifically, if they should be part-cooked first. So, for example, if cooking chicken off the bone, mince, finely cut meat, there is no need to pressure cook first. If you are using chicken on the bone or tougher cuts of meat on or off the bone, you will need to cook them first before finishing with the rice to make sure they are cooked through and tender. You will also need to make sure the liquid ratios are right, so take into account liquid still in the pressure cooker when measuring the liquid for the rice. See the Fragrant Chicken and Rice (overleaf), which is very adaptable.

You can also use any aromatics you like. Start any rice dish with a sauté of onion or whole spices or whole dried herbs. Flavour with citrus zest or fresh herbs – coriander (cilantro) stems and fresh curry leaves in particular give out wonderful flavours when cooked with rice.

SHORT- AND MEDIUM-GRAIN RICE

The main rule for short-grain rice is that you shouldn't rinse it, as for the most part you want the starch to release into the liquid to create a creamy sauce. For this type of cooking, the grain-to-liquid ratio is 1:2.5, so for every 100g (3½oz) rice, you will need 250ml (9fl oz) liquid.

The main exception to this is sushi, sticky/glutinous rice and other short-grain rices that are often used for stuffing things like vine leaves – think Turkish baldo rice. For these types of rice, you want the end result to be slightly sticky so the rice will clump together, without the starchiness. So rinse thoroughly but gently (better to swirl around in a bowl than roughly handle with a sieve). Then use a 1:1.25/1.5 ratio of grain to liquid, depending on how dry you want the rice. Cook for 6 minutes and allow to release pressure naturally for 5 minutes. It is very important that the rice and water are evenly distributed across the base of the cooker, so make sure you push down any rice from the sides and make sure it is in an even layer.

Treat brown short-grain rice in the same way as white, including the rinsing, and extend the cooking time to 20 minutes.

FRAGRANT CHICKEN AND RICE

SERVES 4

500g (1lb 2oz) diced chicken (preferably a mixture of breast and thighs)

Juice of ½ lemon

3 tbsp yogurt

1 tbsp olive oil

15g (½oz) butter

1 onion, finely chopped

3 garlic cloves, finely chopped

2 bay leaves

50g (1¾oz) golden raisins or chopped dried apricots

300g (10½oz) basmati rice, well rinsed

450ml (16fl oz) chicken or vegetable stock or water

A few drops of orange blossom water (optional)

Sea salt

FOR THE SPICES

2 tsp ground cardamom

2 tsp ground coriander

1 tsp ground cinnamon

1 tsp allspice

½ tsp ground turmeric

½ tsp ground white pepper

A pinch of saffron, ground with a pinch of sea salt

TO SERVE

50g (1¾oz) flaked (slivered) almonds

3 tbsp pomegranate seeds

A few sprigs of herbs, such as mint, parsley, chervil, coriander (cilantro)

This is the recipe to use as a base for any type of pilaf. It uses ground spices instead of whole, as that is more child friendly, and gives an even distribution of gentle flavour and fragrance. You can use whole spices instead but be sparing as pressure cooking will push their flavour into the rice while intensifying it – it is very easy, for example, to use too much cinnamon or clove.

The yogurt marinade is not essential, as the pressure cooker does a very good job of tenderizing the chicken on its own, but it does add an extra dimension, so is worth doing if you have time.

First mix the spices together. Put half of them in a bowl and add another ½ teaspoon of salt. Toss the chicken in the spices, then pour over the lemon juice and yogurt. Mix together so the chicken is completely coated. Cover and leave for at least 1 hour if you have time – it can sit in the fridge overnight if necessary.

Heat the oil and butter together in your pressure cooker until the butter is foaming, then add the onion. Sauté for a minute or two, just so it gets coated with the butter, then add the garlic and the remaining spices. Stir in the chicken, then add the bay leaves and raisins or apricots. Season again with more salt.

Sprinkle in the rice, making sure it is evenly spread, then pour over the stock or water and sprinkle over a few drops of orange blossom water, if using.

Close the lid and bring up to high pressure. Cook for 3 minutes at high pressure, then fast release. Remove the lid, put a tea towel over the cooker and replace the lid. Leave to steam for 5 minutes.

Lightly toast the flaked almonds in a dry frying pan (skillet). Spoon the rice and chicken on to a serving platter or into individual bowls and garnish with the toasted almonds, pomegranate seeds and herbs.

KITCHARI

SERVES 4

1 tbsp coconut oil

1 tsp mustard seeds

1 tsp fennel seeds

1 tsp ground turmeric

1 tsp ground coriander

½ tsp ground cinnamon

1 onion, finely chopped

1 large carrot, coarsely grated

15g (½oz) piece ginger, grated

75g (2½oz) split red lentils, well rinsed

150g (5½oz) basmati rice, well rinsed

Sea salt and freshly ground black pepper

TO SERVE

Green chillies, sliced

Yogurt

A really good vegetarian comfort food dish, this. It is traditionally just lightly spiced lentils and rice, but you can add anything else that pressure cooks in around 3 minutes.

There are lots of ways of eating this. In our house, it is always served quite dry, a bit like a pilaf, but it can also be eaten more like a rice porridge; soupier and with the rice broken down. If you would prefer to do the latter, increase the liquid by 100ml (3½fl oz) and cook for a further minute.

Heat the coconut oil in your pressure cooker. When it has melted, add all the spices, onion, carrot and ginger and stir to combine. Add the lentils and rice, then pour in 400ml (14fl oz) water. Season with salt and pepper. Close the lid and bring up to high pressure. Cook for 3 minutes, then remove from the heat and allow to drop pressure naturally.

Serve with sliced green chillies and a little yogurt.

VARIATIONS

Change the texture
To make it soupier, cook in 600ml (21fl oz) liquid and increase the cooking time by 1 minute.

Vary the vegetables
Replace or add to the carrot with grated or finely chopped squash, pumpkin, sweet potato or parsnip.

CHICKEN CONGEE

SERVES 4

2 chicken drumsticks

100g (3½oz) white rice, well rinsed

10g (¼oz) piece ginger, finely chopped

2 garlic cloves, grated

Sea salt

TO SERVE (OPTIONAL)

4 eggs

A dash of dark soy sauce

A drizzle of chilli oil

One of the cheapest and most nutritious rice dishes you can make. I prefer my congee quite thin – more like a soup than a thick, stand-up-your-spoon-in-it porridge. Texturally, this recipe will give you a result in which the rice is very, very soft, but will not have disintegrated into the liquid; increasing the cooking time by increments of 5 minutes will give you thicker, more broken down results.

Virtually any white rice works in this dish. You can also work in brown or wild rice, see Variation.

Put all the ingredients in your pressure cooker along with 1 litre (35fl oz) of water and 1 teaspoon of salt. Bring up to high pressure and cook for 15 minutes. Allow to drop pressure naturally, then remove the drumsticks from the pot. Discard the skin and bones, and shred the chicken. Return to the cooker.

If you want to add eggs, you can either poach separately, or drop them into the congee to cook for a few minutes. Serve with soy sauce and/or chilli oil, if you like.

VARIATION

To add wild or brown rice to the congee, put 50g (1¾oz) of either in your pressure cooker with all the ingredients apart from the white rice. Cook for 15 minutes, then fast release. Add the white rice and cook for a further 15 minutes, natural release. Proceed as above.

SEAWEED AND MUSHROOM RICE BOWL

SERVES 4

FOR THE RICE

250g (9oz) brown rice

375ml (13fl oz) dashi stock (bought or see page 329)

1 tsp flaked seaweed

10g (¼oz) ginger, grated

½ tsp sea salt

150g (5½oz) chestnut or button mushrooms, left whole or halved

1 tbsp tamari

FOR THE MUSHROOMS (OPTIONAL)

1 tbsp groundnut or other neutral-tasting oil

250g (9oz) shiitake or similar mushrooms, sliced

1 tbsp tamari

A few drops of sesame oil

FOR THE PICKLED VEGETABLES

1 large carrot, julienned

100g (3½oz) radishes, sliced

½ cucumber, cut into half-moons

2 tsp caster (superfine) sugar

1 tsp salt

1 tbsp Japanese rice vinegar

TO SERVE

Sesame seeds

3–4 spring onions (scallions), sliced

This is a type of donburi or rice bowl that can be made with all kinds of toppings. This version has mushrooms steaming over the rice – I have discovered that mushrooms are very adaptable to timings when steamed – they shrink down a little and add mushroom liquor to whatever is cooking below them, but their flavour also intensifies. Because of this you could quite easily make this without the additional sauté of mushrooms and it would be a very satisfying dish.

Put the rice in your pressure cooker along with the stock, seaweed, ginger and salt. Toss the mushrooms in the tamari, then either drop on top of the rice or add the trivet to the pressure cooker and put the mushrooms in the steamer basket. Either way, the mushrooms will steam and intensify in flavour as they cook. Bring up to high pressure and cook for 18 minutes, then allow to release pressure naturally.

Make the pickles by tossing the vegetables in the salt and sugar and placing in a colander to strain. Leave for 30 minutes, then squeeze gently and toss in the vinegar.

If adding the optional mushrooms, heat the oil in a frying pan (skillet) and add the mushrooms. Fry until glossy, then stir in the tamari and drizzle with sesame oil.

To assemble, divide the rice, mushrooms and pickles between 4 bowls and garnish with spring onions (scallions) and sesame seeds.

KEEMA BIRYANI

SERVES 4

1 tbsp coconut oil

1 onion, finely chopped

4 garlic cloves, grated or crushed

25g (1oz) piece ginger, grated

4 tbsp coriander (cilantro) stems, finely chopped

400g (14oz) minced (ground) lamb

1 tbsp mild curry powder

½ tsp ground turmeric

1 tsp nigella seeds

50g (1¾oz) brown lentils

300g (10½oz) peas

100g (3½oz) basmati rice, well rinsed

100g (3½oz) canned chopped tomatoes

FOR THE RAITA

200ml (7fl oz) yogurt

1 tsp dried mint

A handful of coriander (cilantro) leaves, finely chopped

A squeeze of lemon juice

TO SERVE (OPTIONAL)

A few coriander (cilantro) leaves

A few green chillies, finely sliced

A few lemon wedges

Keema peas is a firm favourite in our house, but sometimes I want to make this recipe as it is completely one-pot. If you want to make this without the rice, you can, just omit and reduce the water to 250ml (9fl oz). You can serve with flatbreads, or rice. You can also add the rice later. A very quick meal is to put 100g (3½oz) rice and 150ml (5fl oz) water in your pressure cooker, add a frozen block of keema peas or any other block of minced (ground) meat, lentils, chilli or curry. Bring up to high pressure and cook for 3 minutes as normal, natural release. You will find that the block of frozen keema will be sitting on top of the rice, still in its block but fully defrosted – all you have to do is stir it in.

Heat the coconut oil in your pressure cooker and add the onion, garlic, ginger, coriander (cilantro) and lamb. Stir on a high heat until the meat has lightly browned, then sprinkle in the spices. Stir to combine.

Stir in the lentils, peas and rice, then pour over the tomatoes and 400ml (14fl oz) water. Make sure the rice sits below the water, pressing down with the back of a spoon if necessary. Close the lid and bring up to high pressure. Reduce the heat to maintain high pressure, then cook for 3 minutes. Remove from the heat and allow to drop pressure naturally.

Stir thoroughly to make sure everything is well combined. Mix together all the raita ingredients. Serve garnished with coriander leaves, green chillies and some raita and lemon wedges on the side.

VARIATIONS

A wonderful alternative grain to make this with is bulgar wheat. Change the spicing – use ras el hanout, or baharat or harissa paste (or a simple combination of cinnamon, cardamom and cayenne pepper is good), then replace the rice with the same quantity of bulgar wheat. You might also want to replace the garnish with mint or parsley. Use the ratios and timings on page 201.

A FEW FAST AND ECONOMICAL RICE DISHES

These are the sort of meals that come almost from nowhere – when there's little in the fridge except a few odds and ends and leftovers. They are perfect for school lunch Thermoses as they're so quick to make before school from scratch (I find them less hassle than making a sandwich). They are also the sort of dishes I might have traditionally made with leftover rice – as rice is so quick to make in the pressure cooker it no longer seems like such a time-saver to use leftover rice, so these days I usually make just enough for one meal.

A BASIC FRIED RICE

To which you can add virtually any left-over meat – Chinese ribs, leftover char sui, crispy duck – or vegetables, such as a handful of mushrooms, a single carrot, julienned, ½ pepper, 1 diced courgette (zucchini), a cupful of peas. Or, of course, change the spicing – perhaps stir in some chopped kimchi.

Heat 1 tablespoon of groundnut oil in your pressure cooker. Add 1 sliced onion, 2 finely chopped garlic cloves and 15g (½oz) ginger, cut into matchsticks. Sauté for 3–4 minutes, stir in 200g (7oz) well-rinsed basmati rice and 300g (10½oz) frozen peas and add 300ml (10½fl oz) cold water or stock. Season with salt and pepper and a large pinch of Chinese 5 spice. Bring up to high pressure and cook for 3 minutes. Leave to drop pressure naturally. Push all the rice to one side. Add a little more oil and return to a high heat, then pour in two beaten eggs. Some of the egg will leach into the rice, which is OK, but if the heat is high enough it should be stopped in its tracks. Let the underside cook, then stir or flip and leave to set. Break up and push through the rice. Add a few sliced spring onions (scallions) and plenty of soy sauce, chilli oil or sesame oil.

SESAME CITRUS CHICKEN AND RICE WITH STEAMED CHINESE GREENS

This one uses raw meat and has vegetables steaming above. You can also cook tender vegetables first, then remove and stir through to warm at the end. Try this with cubed aubergine (eggplant) too.

Heat 1 tablespoon of groundnut oil in your pressure cooker and add 3 finely chopped garlic cloves, 15g (½oz) finely chopped ginger and 200g (7oz) diced chicken thighs. Stir on a medium–high heat until the chicken is lightly browned, then pour in 50ml (1¾fl oz) light soy sauce, 1 tablespoon of honey and the zest and juice of 1 lemon or ½ orange. Stir until the chicken is dark brown and glossy. Stir in 200g (7oz) well-rinsed basmati rice along with 300ml (10½fl oz) water or chicken or vegetable stock. Add 3–4 roughly sliced spring onions (scallions). Place in the trivet and add 400g (14oz) Chinese greens on the steamer basket. Cook as in the previous recipe and serve with sesame or chilli oil.

DIRTY RICE

One of the best economical dishes, traditionally made with chicken livers, which I love because a small amount – I will just use 3 or 4 – gives out so much flavour and nutrition and they are so cheap, even if you buy the organic ones. It also makes a good receptacle for leftover cooked meat or any scraps of meat trimmings you can quickly dice. Start with bacon fat, oil or butter in your pressure cooker and add 2–3 tablespoons of the sofrito on page 330 or finely diced onion, green pepper, celery and 2 garlic cloves. Add 3–4 finely diced chicken livers and sauté for a couple of minutes. Stir in some Cajun seasoning if you like (see page 99) or just some cayenne pepper, paprika and dried thyme. Add 300g (10½oz) well-rinsed long-grain rice and 450ml (16 fl oz) water or chicken stock. Cook as per the basic fried rice opposite.

JAMBALAYA

You can develop the idea of dirty rice to make a very fast jambalaya. Use a mixture of diced chicken thighs and smoked garlic sausage (a decent kielbasa in preference over chorizo) in place of the livers and follow the recipe above; after you have sautéed the meats and sofrito and added the same seasonings, stir in 1 tablespoon of tomato purée and 100g (3½oz) chopped tomatoes before adding the rice. If you want to make an occasion of it, after pressure cooking add seafood (large prawns/shrimp, mussels, clams) and place on top of the rice, then leave on a low heat, covered, until the seafood is cooked/heated through. Serve with finely chopped flat-leaf parsley and lemon wedges.

CHILLI CHEESE RICE

This is one I make when I have some leftover black beans, but you can use any cooked beans or lentils (see page 210) or just up the vegetables. Dice 1 red onion, 1 red pepper and 1 courgette (zucchini) and sauté in 2 tablespoons of olive oil. Add garlic, 1 teaspoon of chipotle, the finely chopped stems from 1 bunch of coriander (cilantro) and the zest of 1 lime. Add 150g (5½oz) black beans and 250g (9oz) basmati or long-grain rice with 375ml (13fl oz) stock or water. Cook as per the basic fried rice on page 192, then fluff up and stir through 75g (2½oz) grated Cheddar, 2 chopped tomatoes and the chopped leaves from the bunch of coriander. Leave to stand until the cheese has melted. Serve with lime wedges.

TOMATO AND HOT PEPPER RICE

This is heavily inspired by jollof rice but with a Caribbean twist. Put 1 roasted red pepper, 150g (5½oz) tomatoes and ½–1 Scotch bonnet in a food processor and blitz. Heat 2 tablespoons of olive or coconut oil in your pressure cooker and add 1 diced red onion and red pepper and 3 finely chopped garlic cloves. Sauté for a couple of minutes, then stir in 1 tablespoon of Caribbean curry powder and the pepper/tomato purée. Stir until the mixture looks quite dry, then add 250g (9oz) well-rinsed basmati or long-grain rice and 1 large sprig of thyme. Pour in 375ml (13fl oz) water or stock, bring up to high pressure and cook for 3 minutes. Leave to drop pressure naturally, then leave to stand for 5–10 minutes. Garnish with sliced spring onions (scallions) and lime wedges. Great on its own or with grilled chicken.

RISOTTO

SERVES 4

1 tbsp olive oil

30g (1oz) butter

1 onion, finely chopped

2 garlic cloves, finely chopped

300g (10½oz) risotto rice, such as arborio or carnaroli

100ml (3½fl oz) white wine

750g (1lb 10oz) chicken or vegetable stock

25g (1oz) Parmesan cheese, grated, plus extra to serve

Sea salt and freshly ground black pepper

Here is the basic method for risotto with a few recipe ideas to follow. It is ridiculously easy and has converted no end of people – not only those cooks who found the idea of making risotto daunting, but a few Italian food purists too.

A note on stock – with a fairly plain risotto a decent stock is essential – a bad one has nowhere to hide. Generally speaking, if I had to choose between a stock cube or water, I would probably choose water and pay extra attention to the seasoning. This is particularly important when cooking in a pressure cooker as pressure cooking does intensify flavour and push it into the rice.

You can also use other types of grains to make risotto type dishes. A spelt or farro risotto will take 15 minutes at high pressure and you need a ratio of 1:3 of grain to liquid, a barley risotto will take 18 minutes and will need a ratio of 1:4.5. In both cases I would reduce the amount of grain by a third to 200g (7oz).

Heat the olive oil and half the butter in your pressure cooker. When the butter has melted, add the onion and garlic and stir for a couple of minutes just to get the cooking process started. Add the rice and stir until it is glossy with oil and butter. Pour in the wine and bring to the boil. When it has virtually evaporated, pour in the stock and season with salt, pepper and any aromatics you like. Close the lid and bring up to high pressure. Cook for 5–6 minutes, then manually release the pressure.

Stir in the remaining butter and Parmesan and beat until creamy, then serve with more freshly grated Parmesan.

CITRUS RISOTTO

Follow the recipe opposite exactly, but add lemon or sour orange zest along with the onion and garlic – the best way to use it in this instance is to pare it in strips, then finely shred it. Add a squeeze of juice at the end. A couple of thyme sprigs or bay leaves work well too.

MUSHROOM RISOTTO

There is a certain sniffiness attached to truffle oil, but I honestly think some available today are very good, pack an amazing punch of aroma and flavour and are a more affordable way of getting a touch of luxury into a dish. I can't afford to buy white truffles but I can afford to buy truffle oil and feel no shame in offering it as an addition here.

Soak 15g (½oz) dried porcini mushrooms in warm water. Strain and roughly chop, then add to the pressure cooker along with the onion, 200g (7oz) sliced mushrooms (any, but button, chestnut and cremini are all good), 3 finely chopped garlic cloves, 1 large sprig of thyme and 1 large sprig of tarragon. Use Marsala or vermouth in place of white wine if you like and use chicken or mushroom stock. Finish with a little truffle oil if you like and some more freshly chopped tarragon. You can make this really special occasion stuff if you splash out on some wild mushrooms and sauté them in butter, garlic and tarragon for a garnish.

COURGETTE, LEMON AND CRAB RISOTTO

You can keep this fresh and light-tasting, or turn it into a sumptuous affair by using a rich shellfish stock and/or stirring brown crab meat into the risotto as well as white.

Add 1 finely sliced or grated courgette (zucchini) to the pressure cooker along with the onion, an extra clove of finely chopped garlic and the zest of 1 lemon. Add lemon thyme as well if you have it. Use vegetable, chicken or seafood stock. Stir in 150g (5½oz) white crab meat or 100g (3½oz) small brown shrimp after you have beaten in the butter. Parmesan is strictly optional with this one – I will usually halve the amount or omit it entirely from the risotto, but still grate a little over. Serve with a few torn basil leaves or chervil.

TOMATO RISOTTO

There are so many versions of this, some of which replace the stock with passata. My version has a richness and depth of flavour because of the sun-blushed (semi-dried) tomatoes and sweetness thanks to using very fresh, ripe tomatoes; if I wanted something very rich, I would add tomato purée at the outset, use canned tomatoes, and switch from white wine to red. Regarding the sun-blushed tomatoes – you can also get smoked ones, and adding a few of these along with the non-smoked sort is worth trying at least once – it adds an unexpected dimension to the risotto, which I personally love.

Take 50g (1¾oz) strained sun-blushed tomatoes in oil (if you can substitute some with smoked) and blitz. Use their oil in place of the regular olive oil, then follow the basic risotto recipe, adding an extra clove of finely chopped garlic, either 1 tablespoon fresh oregano or 1 teaspoon of dried, and replacing 100ml (3½fl oz) of stock with 100g (3½oz) fresh puréed tomatoes and adding the sun-blushed tomatoes at the same time. Garnish with a few basil leaves.

SAUSAGE AND RED WINE RISOTTO

Skin 250g (9oz) sausages, then add to the pressure cooker with the onion and garlic and break up as they sauté. Add 1 large sprig of thyme or 1 teaspoon of dried sage along with the rice and use red wine in place of the white. This also works well with other types of meat; try adding chicken livers – use 200g (7oz) roughly chopped, sauté in the oil and butter until just cooked, then remove – they will give flavour to the risotto, then you can stir them back in at the end to warm through. Good with red wine or Marsala.

RISI E BISI

This is perfect storecupboard/freezer comfort food. It is also one of those recipes that many Italians would throw up their hands in horror over, as you should be using the sweetest, freshest, tiniest peas. But I have to be a realist – peas only stay very sweet for a very short window after they have been picked, so buying becomes a very hit-and-miss affair. A fresh green stock as per pages 326–7 is good for this, but really, so is regular vegetable, chicken or smoked ham. And if you're using smoked ham stock, you might want to add a bit of the ham or some bacon too.

Follow the basic risotto recipe but add 900ml (31fl oz) stock instead of 750ml (26fl oz) for a soupier finish and 200g (7oz) fresh or frozen peas. Add any herbs you like – tarragon, basil, chervil, even mint are all good.

To make this gloriously green, you can make a separate pea purée to swirl through at the end. Put 100g (3½oz) peas, 1 chopped garlic clove and 1 sprig of mint in the pressure cooker with 15g (½oz) butter. Season with plenty of salt and pepper. Heat until the butter has melted, then add 50ml (1¾fl oz) stock. Bring up to high pressure and fast release immediately. Remove the sprig of mint, then purée. Add more freshly chopped mint, if you like. Stir through the risotto until it is a uniform green or simply use as a garnish at the table for swirling through.

LEFTOVER CHICKEN RISOTTO

This is an ideal risotto to make when you have roast or pot-roast chicken leftovers and have made a quick chicken stock with the carcass. You can also make it with uncooked chicken – it will cook perfectly with the rice. The squash will be very soft and will break up – that is the point – it will give a wonderful, sweet creaminess to the whole dish.

Follow the method above, adding 200g (7oz) squash or pumpkin and 1 teaspoon of dried sage to the pressure cooker when you add the onion and garlic. Add 200g (7oz) diced cooked chicken along with the stock. Make an optional garnish by frying a few sage leaves in 15g (½oz) butter and pouring over before serving. If using raw chicken, add 300g (10½oz) along with the squash. Don't worry if the squash breaks up when you beat in the butter and Parmesan – it will diffuse its sweetness throughout the whole dish.

RICE WITH SQUID AND CHORIZO

SERVES 4–6

1 tbsp olive oil

100g (3½oz) cooking chorizo, finely chopped

1 onion, finely chopped, or 3 tbsp pepper or fennel sofrito (see page 330)

400g (14oz) cleaned squid, thinly sliced

100g (3½oz) cavolo nero, shredded (optional)

100ml (3½fl oz) white wine

1 tbsp tomato purée

A generous pinch of saffron, soaked in a little warm water

2 sachets squid or cuttlefish ink (optional)

300g (10½oz) white paella rice

750ml (26fl oz) stock or water

Sea salt and freshly ground black pepper

TO SERVE

A few sprigs of finely chopped flat-leaf parsley (optional)

Lemon wedges

This can be a relatively cheap, midweek pleaser; neither squid nor a small amount of chorizo will break the bank. However, you can really elevate it into a dramatic, celebratory dish by using black rice and/or squid ink sachets, see the Variation.

Heat the olive oil in your pressure cooker and add the chorizo. When it has started to crisp up and rendered out plenty of orange-coloured oil, add the onion or sofrito and cook for another minute. Add the squid and stir until it has turned from a transparent silver to a matt white, then stir in the cavolo nero, if using.

Pour in the white wine and allow it to evaporate. Add the tomato purée, saffron and the squid ink sachets, if using. Season with salt and pepper, then pour in the stock. If using the ink, stir until the colour of the liquor darkens to a deep black/brown.

Sprinkle over the rice, then close the lid and bring up to high pressure. Cook for 5 minutes and fast release.

Sprinkle with a little parsley, if you like, and serve with wedges of lemon.

VARIATIONS

Use Italian black rice. Cook for 20 minutes at high pressure – this will not harm the texture of the squid – and allow to drop pressure naturally. You don't need the ink for colour here; the colour of the rice is intense enough, but you can add it for flavour if you like.

You can add all kinds of seafood to this – the best way to do it is to cook as above, then add any ready-cooked seafood you might want to add on top of the rice, then cover but don't close the lid. Leave to steam gently off the heat for a few minutes. If you want to add anything raw, for example mussels, which will add to the general indigo intensity of the dish, leave on a very low heat until they open. Do not attempt to bring back up to pressure as it is likely the rice will catch on the bottom before you manage to do so.

CHICKEN OR RABBIT 'PAELLA' WITH BROAD BEANS AND ARTICHOKES

SERVES 4–6

2 tbsp olive oil

8 chicken or rabbit pieces (breasts, halved, thighs and/or drumsticks)

1 onion, finely chopped, or 4 tbsp green pepper sofrito (see page 330)

3 garlic cloves, finely chopped

100ml (3½fl oz) white wine

2 pieces of pared lemon zest

Leaves from 1 large sprig of rosemary, finely chopped

1 tsp dried oregano

Large pinch of saffron, ground with a little sea salt

1 tsp sweet or hot paprika

750ml (26fl oz) chicken or vegetable stock

2 tomatoes, finely chopped or puréed

300g (10½oz) paella rice

150g (5½oz) broad (fava) beans (frozen is fine)

6 cooked artichoke hearts (the chargrilled ones in oil are best), halved

Sea salt and freshly ground black pepper

TO SERVE

Lemon wedges

Leaves from a bunch of flat-leaf parsley, chopped

This is an on-the-bone version of a paella that needs some cooking of the chicken or rabbit pieces at high pressure before you add the rice. But, it can also be made using diced meat, in which case the extra cooking time is unnecessary, see the Variation for details.

Heat the olive oil in your pressure cooker. Season the chicken or rabbit pieces and add to the pan. Brown on all sides. Remove from the pressure cooker and add the onion or sofrito. Sauté for a few minutes until starting to brown, then add the garlic. Stir for a couple of minutes, then pour in the wine and add the lemon zest, rosemary, oregano, saffron and paprika. Return the chicken or rabbit to the pan and close the lid. Cook for 5 minutes and fast release.

Pour in the stock and stir in the tomatoes. Sprinkle over the rice, trying to make sure it falls around the chicken rather than over it. Add the broad (fava) beans and artichoke hearts. Season with more salt and pepper and bring up to high pressure. Cook for 5 minutes, then remove from the heat. Fast release the pressure, then leave to stand, loosely covered, for a few minutes.

Serve with lemon wedges and plenty of chopped parsley.

VARIATION

If using diced meat, use around 400g (14oz). Cook with the onions, then add the remaining ingredients in the same order as above and cook for just 5 minutes at high pressure in total.

OTHER GRAINS

Like rice, grains are generally best cooked using the absorption method, so again, a degree of precision is necessary with ratios. Too little, and the grain won't be able to absorb as much liquid as it needs to swell and soften, too much, and it may become too soft.

I prefer using an absorption method as the end result is better in terms of both texture and flavour. You use less liquid, and because of this if you are using stock or adding any other aromatics, they will infuse all their flavour into the grain.

GENERAL COOKING INSTRUCTIONS

Rinse. You won't always need to remove starch, but most grains still benefit from washing, and in the case of quinoa it is necessary to remove a bitter outer coating. Drain thoroughly.

Toast. This is optional but it does improve flavour. Heat 1–2 tablespoons of oil in your pressure cooker and sauté until any liquid from washing has steamed off and the grain is giving out a strong nutty aroma. If you want to add any whole or ground spices, now is the time to do so. You can also sauté an onion first if you like.

Add the right amount of liquid (see ratios), using water or stock. Add any other aromatics at this point – fresh or dried herbs, citrus zest, even dried fruit.

Cook for the right length of time for the grain (see timings below). Allow to drop pressure naturally for 5 minutes, then release the remaining pressure. If the grain looks wet, drape over a tea towel

and place the lid back. Leave to stand for a few minutes. DO NOT leave any grains to stand indefinitely and definitely DO NOT leave them with the lid closed. They will continue cooking in the residual heat. Remove from the pressure cooker to cool, spreading out if possible to speed it up.

You can cook some grains at pressure for a shorter period of time by just covering in plenty of water, but really, you are not saving fuel, because the larger volume of water means that your pressure cooker will take longer to come up to pressure and will therefore be on a high heat for longer. This makes sense when you remember that you will normally need minimal heat to maintain high pressure.

There are a couple of grains I don't pressure cook. Firstly, I have tried and tried to make a polenta I am happy with, but have admitted defeat. Secondly, oats. These take longer to cook in the pressure cooker than conventionally. So it is only useful if you are using the keep warm function.

RATIO/TIME

Barley (pearled) – 1:2/18 minutes
Buckwheat groats – 1:1/3 minutes
Bulgar wheat – 1:2/1 minute al dente;
2 minutes softer
Farro – 1:2.5/10 minutes
Freekeh – 1:2/10 minutes
Giant couscous – 1:2.5/1 minute
Millet – 1:3/1 minute
Quinoa – 1:2/1 minute
Spelt – 1:3/12 minutes

BRAISED QUINOA AND BUTTER BEANS

SERVES 4

1 tbsp olive oil

1 onion, cut into wedges

1 green pepper, diced

3 garlic cloves, grated

1 bunch of coriander (cilantro), stems and leaves separated, finely chopped

2 jalapeños or similar, finely chopped

100g (3½oz) quinoa, well rinsed

400g (14oz) cooked butter (lima) beans

100g (3½oz) cherry tomatoes, blitzed to a purée

Sea salt and freshly ground black pepper

TO SERVE

Jalapeños or similar, finely chopped

Sprigs of coriander (cilantro)

Lime wedges

Equally good as a one-pot meal or as a side dish. To keep it vegetarian, try it with the cauliflower florets on page 266. Cook this first, transfer to a serving dish and keep warm and then cook the cauliflower.

This recipe will work with all types of quinoa; I sometimes substitute 25g (1oz) with smoked quinoa that gives an extra dimension to the flavour. If using red or black quinoa, either on their own or as part of a mix, increase the cooking time at high pressure to 2 minutes.

Heat the olive oil in your pressure cooker until hot. Add the onion and green pepper and fry until starting to colour around the edges. Stir in the garlic, coriander (cilantro) stems, jalapeños and quinoa and stir for a couple more minutes.

Add the butter (lima) beans and cherry tomatoes, then add 250ml (9fl oz) water. Season with salt and pepper, then close the lid and bring up to high pressure. Cook for 1 minute only, then leave to drop pressure naturally. Stir through, and serve, garnished with a little more chilli and coriander and with lime wedges on the side.

VARIATIONS

As this has such a short cooking time, you can add most green vegetables without them coming to too much harm. Any type of green bean would work well.

You could turn this into a one-pot chicken dish too. Dice 400g (14oz) chicken thighs, fry with the onion and green pepper and keep the cooking time the same.

BULGAR WHEAT PILAF WITH CARROTS AND DATES

SERVES 4

FOR THE BULGAR WHEAT

1 tbsp olive oil

1 onion, finely chopped

2 large carrots, cut into small wedges

1 garlic clove, crushed

8 dates, sliced

A pinch of allspice

A pinch of ground cinnamon

150g (5½oz) cracked bulgar wheat (coarse)

300ml (10½fl oz) vegetable or chicken stock or water

Sea salt and freshly ground black pepper

TO DRESS (OPTIONAL)

2 tsp preserved lemon or quick preserved lemons (see page 336)

2 tbsp olive oil

Juice of ½ lemon

1 tsp honey

TO FINISH

4 radishes, finely chopped

3 spring onions (scallions), sliced (whites and greens)

A handful of mint and flat-leaf parsley leaves

1 tbsp pumpkin seeds, pistachios or pine nuts

As always when devising recipes for this book, I cooked bulgar wheat plain a few times to get the timings and ratios just right. It made me look at it in a whole new light. When cooked just so, it is nutty, creamy and tender with just a slight bite in the centre – plus as it is so versatile and cooks in such a short period of time, it makes a really useful change from rice.

To cook bulgar wheat plain, heat 1 tablespoon of olive oil in the pressure cooker. Add the bulgar wheat and sauté for a minute or two, then put in double the amount of liquid. Season and bring up to high pressure. Cook for 2 minutes, then remove from the heat and release pressure naturally. This will give a perfect bite for pilafs. If you want a firmer bite, reduce the cooking time to 1 minute.

First, cook the bulgar wheat. Heat the olive oil in your pressure cooker. Add the onion and carrots and sauté on a high heat until the carrots have browned, stirring at intervals. Add the garlic, dates, spices and bulgar wheat and stir for another minute or two. Season with plenty of of salt and pepper.

Pour over the stock or water and close the lid. Bring up to high pressure and cook for 2 minutes. Remove from the heat and allow to drop pressure naturally.

If making the dressing, whisk all the ingredients together and add a little water if necessary. Season with salt and pepper.

Add the radishes and spring onions (scallions) to the pilaf and fluff up. Transfer to a serving dish. Drizzle over some of the dressing and leave the rest on the side. Garnish with the herbs and seeds or nuts.

FREEKEH PILAF WITH LENTILS AND BROAD BEANS

SERVES 4

1 tbsp olive oil

1 large onion, finely chopped

2 garlic cloves

½ tsp ground allspice

¼ tsp ground cinnamon

¼ tsp ground cardamom

100g (3½oz) cracked freekeh, soaked for 5 minutes

100g (3½oz) brown or green lentils, rinsed

250g (9oz) broad (fava) beans (frozen are fine)

25g (1oz) barberries or goji berries (optional)

300ml (10½fl oz) vegetable or chicken stock or water

Sea salt and freshly ground black pepper

TO SERVE

2 tbsp olive oil

1 large onion, sliced

1 small bunch of dill or mint

Seeds from ½ pomegranate (optional)

Freekeh has a very distinctive smokiness that is very appealing with sweeter spices, especially allspice and cinnamon. It is also very filling, so works well in this triumvirate.

Heat the olive oil in your pressure cooker. Add the onion and sauté for a few minutes until it takes on some colour. Add the garlic and spices and stir for another minute.

Drain the freekeh, add to the pressure cooker and sauté for a couple of minutes, then stir in the lentils, broad (fava) beans and barberries or goji berries, if using. Pour in the stock and season with salt and pepper.

Bring up to high pressure and cook for 10 minutes. Remove from the heat and leave to drop pressure naturally.

While the pilaf is cooking, fry the onion for the garnish. Heat the oil in a frying pan (skillet) and add the onion. Fry on a high heat until the onion is crisp and brown. Season with plenty of salt and pepper and drain on kitchen towel.

Stir the dill or mint through the pilaf and garnish with the onion and a few pomegranate seeds, if you like.

GIANT COUSCOUS SALAD

SERVES 4

3 tbsp olive oil

4 spring onions (scallions), thickly sliced

2 medium courgettes (zucchini) or 1 medium aubergine (eggplant), diced

2 garlic cloves, finely chopped

¼ tsp allspice

¼ tsp ground cinnamon

Zest and juice of ½ lemon

100g (3½oz) giant couscous

200g (7oz) salad leaves

200g (7oz) cherry tomatoes

200g (7oz) feta, diced (optional)

50g (1¾oz) pitted olives

Sea salt and freshly ground black pepper

FOR THE DRESSING

½ tsp caraway seeds

Seeds from ½ tsp cardamom pods

¼ tsp ground ginger

1 tsp dried mint

1 small bunch of coriander (cilantro)

1 small bunch of mint

2 green chillies

3 garlic cloves

Zest and juice of 1 lemon

4 tbsp olive oil

TO GARNISH

Any fresh herbs or micro herbs

I really love salads made with cooked ingredients, especially with a grain component, which is another great reason why pressure cookers are for all seasons, not just for hearty winter meals. You can cook the vegetables and couscous together if you like – they will be softer because of the 5 minutes natural release but still perfectly good. I just prefer them slightly more al dente in a salad. If choosing to do this, sauté first, scoop them out, toast the couscous, then place on top so they don't get waterlogged.

Heat 2 tablespoons of the olive oil in your pressure cooker. When it is very hot, add the spring onions (scallions) and courgettes (zucchini) or aubergine (eggplant) and fry very quickly until lightly browned, then add the garlic, spices and lemon zest and juice. Season with salt and pepper and add a scant 50ml (1¾fl oz) water. Close the lid and bring up to high pressure, then release pressure immediately. Remove and leave to cool.

Add the remaining tablespoon of olive oil and the couscous. Stir for a minute or two to toast, then add 250ml (9fl oz) water. Bring up to high pressure, cook for 1 minute, then leave to drop pressure naturally for 5 minutes. Release the remaining pressure, then leave to cool to room temperature.

Make the dressing by toasting the caraway and cardamom seeds and grinding with a pinch of sea salt. Put in a small food processor with the remaining ingredients until you have a green-flecked sauce.

Assemble the salad by arranging the leaves over a platter. Drizzle some of the dressing over the cooked vegetables and couscous and stir briefly, then pile on top of the leaves with the cherry tomatoes, feta, if using, and olives. Drizzle over more of the dressing and garnish with herbs. Serve immediately.

BEANS AND PULSES

My friend Deb brilliantly summed up the main advantage of pressure cookers when it comes to the main ingredients of this chapter: 'I adore pulses, but have no idea whether I want to eat them tomorrow or not.' This is it in a nutshell. There are very few days when some kind of bean or lentil isn't eaten in my household, but I very rarely know in advance what I want to eat when, so the fact that I don't have to soak them overnight is an absolute boon. If you are the type of person who doesn't want to always plan ahead, it will be a boon to you too.

Of course, canned beans can save the day, but there are several disadvantages to canned pulses. Firstly, they never taste as good as those you have cooked yourself, they cost a lot more comparatively speaking (yes, I know there is the cost of cooking them too, but this is cut down dramatically by pressure cooking, see below), and not so good in terms of sustainability – a lined can plus all that water for every 200-250g (7–9oz) beans, as opposed to a small plastic bag (or reusable/paper bag or your own tub if you buy them loose) for 500g (1lb 2oz) will give you 1.2–1.3kg (2lb 11oz–3lb) cooked beans.

Here's an example of the difference in cooking time. For the purposes of this, I am not taking into account the length of time it takes a saucepan of water to come up to the boil, or a pressure cooker to come up to pressure – though you will save time here too as the pressure cooker time is much faster.

To conventionally cook a pot of borlotti beans you need to soak them overnight or do a quick soak, which involves bringing them up to the boil, removing from the heat and leaving to stand for 1 hour. You then have to replace the water, bring back to the boil, fast boil for 10 minutes, then simmer for between 1 hour 15 minutes and 2 hours. You will also need a lot more water – at least twice as much – because so much of it will evaporate during this process and you may well need to top it up.

To pressure cook a pot of borlotti beans, you can still soak them overnight if you like, or quick soak, which involves bringing up to high pressure, cooking for 2 minutes, removing from the heat and leaving to stand for 5 minutes, before releasing the remaining pressure and draining. Then to cook, cover with water again, cook at high pressure for 7–10 minutes, depending on your pressure cooker, then remove from the heat and allow to drop pressure naturally. The beans are still cooking as the cooker drops pressure, but as it is off the heat there is no fuel cost. Alternatively, you can cook from dry and it will take 20–25 minutes at high pressure, plus the time it takes to drop pressure, which again, is off the heat so no fuel costs. And as there is no soaking at all, you are using less water.

To me it's a no-brainer, and I am always shocked whenever I have to recipe-test something conventionally, over how frustratingly long it takes.

I cook a lot of beans in bulk and freeze them in 250g (9oz) portions because then they correspond roughly to the drained weight of a can – useful if following conventional recipes. But the beauty of pressure cooking does mean you don't have to make large quantities at once. In fact, my first proper experience of pressure cooking brought this home to me when my Brazilian sister-in-law cooked black beans from scratch at the end of a busy day house moving. It was second nature to her and made me realize why pressure cookers are so important across South America and the Indian subcontinent where a lot of beans and pulses are eaten. Storing them dry and cooking them as needed – usually after a day at work – is so useful wherever there is limited fridge and freezer space.

HOW TO COOK BEANS

The way I cook beans has changed since I wrote my last pressure-cooker book. For years, I rarely bothered soaking or quick soaking, but after much experimentation I have come to realize that not only does it makes sense from a time and sustainability perspective but also results in a better, more consistent texture. It is especially useful when you are cooking any type of bean that has a tendency to go mushy.

Here is the basic method – this is very useful when you are making soups, stews, chillies, salads and need cooked, intact beans. A 500g (1lb 2oz) bag of beans will normally get you around 1.2–3kg (2lb 9oz–3lb) cooked beans. I portion these up in Tupperware and store in the freezer. If you are going to use them in conventional recipes, it is worth freezing in portions of 230–250g (8¼–9oz) as this is the drained weight of the average can.

Put your beans in your pressure cooker and cover with cold water, making sure you don't fill to beyond the two-thirds mark. Add 1 teaspoon of salt and 1 tablespoon of oil – the oil is important as it helps prevent the released starch in the beans from foaming up and potentially clogging air vents as you fast release some of the pressure.

Bring up to high pressure, then adjust the heat to maintain the pressure and cook for 2 minutes. Remove from the heat and leave to stand for 5 minutes, then release the remaining pressure. Check over the beans.

If there are a few floaters that are still very hard and wrinkly, discard as they will not soften in the same time it takes the rest of the beans to cook. If there are a lot of these, you can separate them from the rest and give them another quick soak to see if that has any effect – if it doesn't, discard them.

Drain the beans and cover with more cold water, again, making sure you don't fill beyond the two-thirds mark. Add 1 teaspoon of salt, 1 tablespoon of vinegar, lime or lemon juice* and 1 tablespoon of oil. Add any aromatics you might want to flavour your beans – herbs or a bouquet garni of whole spices for easy removal are ideal. You can also substitute the water for any kind of stock and/or add coconut milk.

Bring up to high pressure and cook according to which bean you are cooking, see the timings on page 210. Remove from the heat and leave to drop pressure naturally. Be careful here and try to drain them as soon as the pressure has dropped. If you don't, they will continue cooking in the water and you may end up with mushy beans if you leave them for too long. Drain thoroughly. You can now use the beans in any recipe using cooked beans.

A NOTE ON COOKING CHICKPEAS AND MAKING AQUAFABA

Chickpea (garbanzo bean) water – or aquafaba – has become a popular egg-white substitute in recent years, as it can be whipped into meringues, mousses and even mayonnaises. It especially makes superb chocolate mousse. If you want to be able to make this without relying on canned chickpeas, it is important that you don't salt the chickpeas or add oil to the pressure cooker. This is OK if you allow the pressure cooker to drop pressure naturally both when quick soaking and cooking, as it gives any starch time to subside and won't clog up your safety vents. Then strain off the liquid and for best results, bring to the boil, reduce by half, then cool and chill before using in any aquafaba recipes.

* I add just 1 tablespoon here as acidic ingredients do inhibit the ability of beans and pulses to cook, but I have found that adding a very small quantity when cooking does help them keep their integrity (ie, less likely to break down), while still cooking through completely.

BASIC TIMINGS FOR BEANS

These are the basic timings, but please refer to specific recipes for when the beans are cooked with other ingredients – in particular acidic ones, such as smoked meats, tomatoes, citrus and vinegar, as the timings will usually be slightly longer, taking into account the effect of the ingredients and less liquid on the ability of the beans to absorb water.

The numbers below refer to cooking times unsoaked/soaked or quick soaked. The variations take into account the difference in pressure cookers – the higher the PSI, the shorter the cooking time. Newer models of electric pressure cookers should cook beans in the shorter time as will most pressure cookers with a PSI of over 12. However, one tricky issue is that beans and pulses do deteriorate with age and will take longer to cook if they are old. It is virtually impossible to tell how fresh dried beans are and there are times when they simply won't cook properly. This isn't your or the pressure cooker's fault. I find that after doing a long or quick soak, removing any floating, wrinkly beans can help in terms of evenness of cooking. Always go for the shorter time to start with – you can always put it back on afterwards, but you can't do much about overcooked, mushy beans apart from turn them into soups or dips.

Black-eyed peas – 6–9 minutes unsoaked/3–5 minutes soaked

Black beans – 22–25 minutes unsoaked/4–6 minutes soaked

Borlotti beans – 19–22 minutes unsoaked/7–10 minutes soaked

Butter (lima) beans – 12–15 minutes unsoaked/5–7 minutes soaked

Cannellini beans – 25–30 minutes unsoaked/5–8 minutes soaked

Chickpeas (garbanzo beans)/Carlin peas – 28–35 minutes unsoaked/13–20 minutes soaked

Fava (dried broad beans) – 25–30 minutes unsoaked/10 minutes soaked

Flageolet beans – 18–25 minutes unsoaked/6–8 minutes soaked

Whole gungo/Pigeon peas – 25 minutes unsoaked/12–15 minutes soaked

Haricot (navy) beans – 18–25 minutes unsoaked/6–8 minutes soaked

Kidney beans – 25–30 minutes unsoaked/6–8 minutes soaked

Marrowfat peas – 20 minutes unsoaked/6–8 minutes soaked

Pinto beans – 19–22 minutes unsoaked/7–10 minutes soaked

Soybeans – 28–35 minutes unsoaked/20 minutes soaked

A POT OF CANNELLINI BEANS WITH GARLIC AND PARSLEY

MAKES 1.2–1.5KG (2LB 11OZ–3LB 5OZ)

Quick soak 500g (1lb 2oz) cannellini beans as described on page 208. Drain and rinse, then return to the cooker. Add a few unpeeled garlic cloves, a few stems of parsley, 1 tablespoon of red wine vinegar, 2 tablespoons of olive oil and 1 teaspoon of salt. Add enough water so they are well covered (usually around 1.25 litres/44fl oz). Bring up to high pressure and cook for 8 minutes, then allow to drop pressure naturally.

Remove the garlic cloves and the parsley stems. Squish the flesh out of the garlic and return to the pot. Strain the beans, reserving the liquid, which will make a very good stock base for soup.

TO SERVE AS A SIDE DISH

Add lots of finely chopped parsley and dress with a little more olive oil.

These recipes also work with borlotti, pinto and butter (lima) beans:

TO TURN INTO A PURÉE

Take half a portion, drain and add back a ladleful of cooking liquor. Blitz and dress with a little olive oil and a finely chopped spoonful of preserved lemon (see page 336).

TO TURN INTO A SOUP

Sauté 1 finely chopped onion or a couple of leeks in 1 tablespoon of olive oil and 15g (½oz) butter. Add a couple of garlic cloves, then ½ portion of cannellini beans, half of them roughly puréed. Add 850ml (29fl oz) of any stock and cook at high pressure for 1 minute. Allow to drop pressure naturally, then stir in a large handful of finely chopped flat-leaf parsley or chervil. Garnish with a few bacon lardons, ham hock or chorizo and 1 tablespoon of sherry.

A POT OF RED KIDNEY BEANS

MAKES 1.2–1.5KG (2LB 11OZ–3LB 5OZ)

These are so useful for chillies, curries and salads – I use them interchangeably with black beans and pinto beans. Pre-soak 500g (1lb 2oz) red kidney beans as described on page 208. Drain and return to the pressure cooker with 1 large sprig of thyme, 2 bay leaves and 1 teaspoon of allspice berries. Add 2 teaspoons of salt and 1 tablespoon of oil (I usually use coconut) and cover with water again. Bring up to high pressure and cook for 7–9 minutes, depending on your pressure cooker.

TO TURN INTO RED RICE AND PEAS (SERVES 4–6)

Put ½ portion of the cooked kidney beans in the pressure cooker. Add 200g (7oz) well-rinsed basmati rice and 300ml (10½fl oz) coconut milk (or water or stock) and another teaspoon of salt, along with 1 large sprig of thyme and a whole Scotch bonnet, if you like. Bring up to high pressure and cook for 3 minutes. Remove from the heat and leave to drop pressure naturally. Fluff up the rice before serving – it should be tinged pink from the beans – removing the thyme and scotch bonnet first if you have added them.

TO TURN INTO WARM RED KIDNEY BEAN AND BEETROOT SALAD (SERVES 4)

Cook 250g (9oz) red kidney beans as above, adding 300g (10½oz) washed, small-medium beetroot, the stems from 1 small bunch of dill, tied together, and 1 tablespoon of olive oil after the quick soak. Strain, discard the dill stems and rub off the beetroot skins and dice. Toss the beetroot and beans with finely chopped dill and another tablespoon of olive oil.

Add 100g (3½oz) salad leaves, 1 finely sliced red onion, 1 segmented orange, 25g (1oz) walnuts and leaves from 1 small bunch of parsley. Toss in a dressing made from 1 tablespoon of olive oil, 1 teaspoon of wholegrain mustard, 1 teaspoon of red wine or sherry vinegar, the juice from squeezing the discarded orange peel and ½ teaspoon of honey.

A POT OF BLACK BEANS

MAKES 1.2–1.5KG (2LB 11OZ–3LB 5OZ)

This is my base recipe for these beans. Vary the type of chillies, the aromatics, replace the tomato with coconut, but then know you can add what you like to them. Bacon, all kinds of vegetables, you can refry them...I am never without portions of these in my freezer; they are so useful. This method – in part due to the salt in the stock and the acid in the tomatoes – will make sure the beans will not disintegrate but will be very tender inside.

Quick soak 500g (1lb 2oz) black beans as described on page 208. Drain thoroughly. Return the beans to the cooker. Add a bouquet garni of 2 bay leaves, 1 sprig of thyme, 1 teaspoon of lightly crushed allspice berries and a small piece of cinnamon stick. Add 2 tablespoons of tomato purée or purée 200g (7oz) canned chopped tomatoes, plus 2 tablespoons of finely chopped coriander (cilantro) stems if you have them. Just cover with water (around 1.25 litres/44fl oz) and add 1 teaspoon of salt and either 1 tablespoon of coconut oil or 2 tablespoons of olive oil. Bring back up to high pressure and cook for 5 minutes, then allow to drop pressure naturally.

TO TURN INTO A SOUP (SERVES 4)

Heat 1 tablespoon of olive or coconut oil in your pressure cooker. Add 1 diced red onion and 1 diced red pepper. Sauté until starting to soften, then stir in 3 chopped garlic cloves, the zest of 1 lime and 200g (7oz) diced squash or sweet potato. Stir for another minute or two. Take a ½ portion of the cooked black beans and 850ml (29fl oz) of the cooking liquor, and roughly purée half of them to add texture to the soup. Add all the beans to the soup along with 2 teaspoons of hot sauce (chipotle is good) and 1 square of dark chocolate. Stir until the chocolate has melted, close the lid, bring up to high pressure and cook for 1 minute. Leave to drop pressure naturally.

For an optional garnish, finely dice ½ red onion, ½ firm ripe mango, 1 red chilli and mix with the zest and juice of ½ lime and a few sprigs of coriander (cilantro). Or just serve with sour cream.

BLACK BEAN AND BRUSSELS SPROUT TACOS

SERVES 4

½ portion black beans (see page 213)

1 tbsp olive oil

300g (10½oz) Brussels sprouts, trimmed and halved

1 tsp chipotle paste

Sea salt and freshly ground black pepper

TO SERVE (OPTIONAL)

Corn tortillas

Sour cream

Guacamole

Grated hard cheese, such as Cheddar (optional)

Coriander (cilantro) or micro herbs

Pickled jalapeños

Lime wedges

You don't have to use Brussels sprouts in this recipe – any green that will take to this type of roasting will work, as indeed will squash or cauliflower...you get the picture.

Once you have everything assembled, the slowest thing about this dish is heating the tortillas. But you can even do that in the pressure cooker if you don't want to do them individually on the stove. Wrap the tortillas in foil and place on the trivet or steamer basket over water. Bring up to high pressure and immediately fast release. They should be warmed through.

First assemble all the garnishes – apart from heating through the tortillas, this is what will take the most time. Reheat the black beans.

To cook the Brussels sprouts, heat the olive oil in your pressure cooker. Add the sprouts, preferably in a single layer and preferably cut-side down. Fry on a high heat until taking on colour – you want them to look dark brown around the edges. Season with plenty of salt and pepper.

Loosen the chipotle paste with 1 tablespoon of water, then stir into the sprouts. Make sure the heat is turned right up and pour in 75ml (2½fl oz) water. This should create a lot of steam so that if you work very fast at putting on the lid, it should come up pressure pretty much immediately. Cook for 1 minute at high pressure, then fast release. Transfer to a serving bowl with any juices from the cooker.

Serve with as many of the garnishes as you like.

MASALA BEANS

SERVES 4

1 tbsp olive or coconut oil

1 large onion, finely diced

1 large carrot, finely diced

5 garlic cloves, crushed or grated

30g (1oz) piece ginger, grated or finely chopped

2 tbsp finely chopped coriander (cilantro) stems

1 tbsp mild curry powder or spice mix on page 126

1 tsp ground turmeric

500g (1lb 2oz) haricot (navy) beans, soaked or quick soaked (see page 208)

1 x 400g (14oz) can chopped tomatoes or passata

2 tsp concentrated tamarind paste or 2 tbsp unconcentrated

Sea salt

TO SERVE

Green chillies, sliced

1 small bunch of coriander (cilantro), chopped

This is a spiced baked bean – a brunch staple in my house, first tried in Dishoom and endlessly replicated. I always make a large quantity, usually with the intention of freezing half of them, but the reality is that they are so popular they rarely make it that far.

I couldn't resist the addition of sausages in the Variations. Curry and sausage is a thing, beans and sausage is a thing, why not put them together? It works so well – the sausages soften to the texture of those normally found in a can, which I absolutely adore. If you don't, you can fry the sausages and keep them separate or just add them to the beans at the end.

Heat the oil in your pressure cooker and add the onion and carrot. Sauté on a high heat for 5 minutes until the onion has started to take on some colour, then stir in the garlic and ginger. Continue to cook on a high heat for another minute, stirring constantly, then stir in the coriander (cilantro) stems and spices.

Add the soaked/quick soaked beans to the pot with the tomatoes and tamarind paste. Pour in 600ml (21fl oz) water and season with 2 teaspoons of salt.

Close the lid, bring up to high pressure, then adjust the heat to maintain the high pressure. Cook for a further 10 minutes and then remove from the heat and allow to drop pressure naturally.

Serve with green chillies and plenty of chopped coriander.

VARIATIONS

Beans and Bacon
Add a bit of smoky flavour by adding 100g (3½oz) finely chopped smoked bacon along with the onion.

Masala Beans and Sausages
While the beans are fast soaking, fry 8 fat sausages until browned on all sides. Add to the pressure cooker when all the other ingredients have been added and cook as above.

BEANS BRAISED WITH CHORIZO AND BLACK PUDDING

SERVES 4

1 tbsp olive oil

100g (3½oz) cooking chorizo, sliced

150g (5½oz) morcilla or black pudding

1 red onion, sliced into wedges

200g (7oz) cannellini or butter (lima) beans, quick/soaked (see page 208)

100ml (3½fl oz) white wine

1 bay leaf

½ tsp chilli powder or hot paprika

1 small bunch of flat-leaf parsley, roughly chopped

100g (3½oz) your choice of greens, roughly chopped (optional)

Sea salt

There are so many types of black pudding, but as this dish uses chorizo, it makes sense to use the Spanish morcilla if you can find it.

I've deliberately made this with soaked/quick soaked beans to show how quickly a dish can be made from scratch when you still have to cook the beans. But it will work just as well with cooked beans, see Variations.

First heat the olive oil in your pressure cooker and add the chorizo. Fry quickly until brown on both sides. Add the morcilla or black pudding and brown again. Remove.

Add the onion to the cooker and fry for a couple of minutes. Add the soaked white beans and pour over the white wine. Add the bay leaf and chilli and stir to make sure the base of the pan is completely deglazed. Cover with water – just – and season with 1 teaspoon of salt. Bring up to high pressure and cook for 8 minutes. Slow release.

Return the chorizo and black pudding to the cooker and stir in, along with most of the parsley. Add any greens you like to the top. Bring up to high pressure again and release pressure immediately. Serve garnished with the remaining parsley.

VARIATIONS

To make with cooked beans, fry the chorizo, onions, and morcilla together. Add the remaining ingredients, including 500g (1lb 2oz) cooked beans, along with 100ml (3½fl oz) water or stock and bring up to high pressure. Allow to slow release.

Using bacon in place of chorizo changes the feel of the dish completely. Exchange the bay leaves for ½ teaspoon of dried sage and fry a few fresh sage leaves in a little olive oil for a garnish.

CASSOULET

SERVES 6-8

FOR THE BEANS AND HAM HOCK

600g (1lb 5oz) dry cannellini beans, or similar

1 small ham hock (optional, quick soaked if necessary, see page 84)

A bouquet garni of 1 head garlic, cut in half, crossways, 3 bay leaves, 2 cloves, 1 tsp allspice berries

1 tbsp olive oil

Sea salt

FOR THE MEAT (ALL OR A SELECTION)

6-8 garlicky sausages

2 confit duck legs (see page 130 or shop-bought can or jar)

200g (7oz) pork belly, cut into strips

TO ASSEMBLE

1 tbsp duck fat or olive oil

100g (3½oz) thick-cut bacon or salt pork lardons

1 onion, finely chopped

2 celery sticks, finely diced

1 large carrot, finely diced

Cloves from ½ head garlic, finely chopped

1 heaped tbsp tomato purée

100ml (3½fl oz) red wine

600ml (21fl oz) chicken, pork or vegetable stock or water

Bouquet garni of 2 bay leaves, 1 sprig of thyme, 1 sprig of flat-leaf parsley, a few allspice berries

TO TOP (OPTIONAL)

1 small bunch of flat-leaf parsley, finely chopped

50g (1¾oz) breadcrumbs

A quick bean and sausage dish can be a speedy evening meal – see page 221 for details – but sometimes it feels right to go all out and make the ultimate version: cassoulet. It isn't exactly special occasion food, apart from the fact that eating it is an occasion in itself, but it is definitely worth doing properly once in a while.

Try to find really garlicky sausages if you can. Toulouse sausages will work, but if you are in the UK, perhaps try for Rutland sausages, which are gloriously garlicky with just the right texture.

You can mix and match with this, including all the meat or even just the sausages. You can also take shortcuts. If you have a pile of cooked beans (you need around 1.2–1.5kg (2lb 11oz–3lb 5oz) cooked weight – the equivalent of 5–6 cans), you can ignore the initial cooking instructions. Do still pressure cook for the full 30 minutes though – the longer they cook, the creamier they will get.

First, part cook the beans and the ham hock. This is the equivalent of soaking the beans, with a little extra time added on. Put the beans and the ham hock in the pressure cooker with the bouquet garni and 1 teaspoon of salt. Cover with water and add the oil. Bring up to high pressure, cook for 5 minutes, then remove from the heat and leave to stand as it drops pressure for at least 15 minutes.

Meanwhile, fry the meat. Start with the duck confit as this will give you any fat you need to fry the rest. Fry on both sides until crisp, then remove and add the sausages and pork belly. Fry until well browned.

Drain the beans from the pressure cooker, discarding the water and the bouquet garni. If you are using the ham hock, remove the rind but leave on the bone. Set aside. Give the pressure cooker a quick wash.

Heat the fat or oil in the pressure cooker and add the bacon or salt pork and the vegetables. Fry on a high heat until the bacon has browned, then add the garlic. Cook for a further minute, then stir in the tomato purée. Pour

Cassoulet *continued*

in the red wine and bring to the boil, then add the beans and the stock or water. The liquid should just cover the beans – if it doesn't, add a little more.

Stir the belly pork into the beans if using, then tuck in the ham hock, duck legs and bouquet garni. Leave the sausages on top. Close the lid and bring up to high pressure. Cook for 30 minutes, then leave to drop pressure naturally.

The cassoulet can be served as is, with just a sprinkling of parsley, or you can make the topping by combining the breadcrumbs with the parsley. If adding the topping, transfer the cassoulet to an ovenproof dish and place under a hot grill for a few minutes.

SAUSAGE AND BEAN CASSEROLE

SERVES 4-6

FOR THE COOKED BEANS

500g (1lb 2oz) haricot (navy) beans, soaked or quick soaked (see page 208)

1 onion, left whole

5 cloves

2 bay leaves

1 tbsp neutral-tasting oil, such as groundnut, grapeseed or sunflower

Sea salt

FOR THE CASSEROLE

1 tbsp olive oil

8 sausages

100g (3½oz) smoked bacon, diced

1 onion, finely chopped

3 garlic cloves, finely chopped

1 tsp dried thyme or 1 sprig of fresh

½ tsp dried oregano

¼ tsp ground cinnamon

¼ tsp cloves

1 x 400g (14oz) can chopped tomatoes, puréed, or passata

1 tbsp black treacle (molasses) or maple syrup

1 tbsp light soft brown sugar

2 tsp Dijon mustard

A dash of Worcestershire sauce

600ml (21fl oz) chicken or vegetable stock or water

I'm sure mine isn't the only household to have some kind of sausage and bean casserole as a staple. This has fairly classic, Boston baked bean-ish type flavours, but it is so adaptable. Vary the sausages, the spicing, the type of beans (just adjust the first cooking time accordingly), add vegetables...endless possibilities.

Put the soaked or quick soaked beans in your pressure cooker. Stud the onion with the cloves and add along with the bay leaves. Cover with cold water and add the oil and 1 teaspoon of salt. Bring up to high pressure and cook for 5 minutes then allow to drop pressure naturally.

Strain the beans, discarding the onion and bay leaves. Add the olive oil to the pressure cooker and quickly brown the sausages on all sides. Remove and add the bacon and onion. Sauté until the bacon has browned, then add the garlic, herbs and spices.

Return the beans to the pressure cooker and add the tomatoes. Stir in the black treacle (molasses) or maple syrup, the sugar and mustard. Add a generous dash of Worcestershire sauce. Stir to make sure that there are no brown bits stuck to the base of the cooker. Sit the sausages on top of the beans, then pour in the stock or water. Bring up to high pressure and cook for a further 5 minutes. Allow to drop pressure naturally.

VARIATIONS

This will make a good baked bean alternative, too. Simply remove the sausage, bacon and onion from the recipe and use a well-flavoured vegetable stock, preferably with an element of smokiness to it, in place of the water.

To make with cooked beans, start the recipe with the frying of the sausages. Use 1.2kg (2lb 11oz) cooked beans and reduce the amount of liquid to 100ml (3½fl oz).

PASTA E FAGIOLI

SERVES 4

FOR THE BEANS

250g (9oz) dried borlotti beans, soaked or quick soaked (see page 208)

1 tbsp olive oil

2 sprigs of rosemary

1 large sprig of thyme

Sea salt

FOR THE PASTA

1 tbsp olive oil

1 small onion, finely chopped

1 small carrot, finely diced

1 celery stick, finely diced

3 garlic cloves, finely chopped

100g (3½oz) very ripe, sweet tomatoes, puréed

100g (3½oz) short pasta (ditalini, radiatori or a short rigatoni are best)

1 sprig of rosemary, finely chopped

1 small bunch of flat-leaf parsley, finely chopped

Such a satisfying, homely dish this one – sweet, earthy and creamy. It is wonderful on its own, but a bitter green of some sort is a great addition – try serving with the braised cime di rapa (broccoli raab) on page 250.

Put the soaked or quick soaked borlotti beans in your pressure cooker and add the olive oil and herbs. Sprinkle in 1 teaspoon of salt and add 750ml (26fl oz) water. Bring up to high pressure and cook for 9 minutes, then remove from the heat and allow to drop pressure naturally.

While the beans are cooking, heat the olive oil in a frying pan (skillet) and add the onion, carrot and celery. Sauté for a few minutes until starting to soften, then add the garlic. Cook for a further minute.

Add the vegetables to the pot of beans, along with the tomatoes, pasta and herbs. Bring up to high pressure again and cook for 4 minutes. Release pressure quickly.

VARIATIONS

This recipe uses dried beans, but if you already have a batch cooked, you can start the recipe by sautéing the vegetables and garlic in the pressure cooker, then adding around 600g (1lb 5oz) cooked beans along with 600ml (21fl oz) water or stock and the remaining ingredients.

If you have a batch of sofrito made up (see page 330), replace the oil and vegetables and simply stir 3 tablespoons of sofrito into the beans, along with the garlic and the remaining ingredients.

CHILLI BEANS WITH CHEESE AND PARSLEY

SERVES 4

2 tbsp olive oil

1 onion, finely chopped

200g (7oz) cannellini or butter (lima) beans, soaked or quick soaked (see page 208)

3 garlic cloves, finely chopped

1 tsp dried thyme

1 tbsp tomato purée

2 fresh tomatoes, finely chopped

1 tsp chilli flakes

1 tsp smoked paprika

Enough stock or water, to cover

1 small bunch of flat-leaf parsley, finely chopped

Zest of ½ lemon

75g (2½oz) Cheddar or similar hard cheese, grated

1 ball mozzarella, roughly torn

Sea salt and freshly ground black pepper

This is a vegetarian, storecupboard dish that will adapt well to the addition of smoked meat or all kinds of vegetables – I might throw in a cupful of sweetcorn from the freezer or cook greens first – for example, sprouting broccoli – and stir through before topping with the cheese. This is fast enough that it works as a weekday supper – something I find amazing considering it uses dried beans – but you can speed it up with 500g (1lb 2oz) cooked beans too if you have a batch ready to go. Just reduce the cooking time to 2 minutes.

Heat the olive oil in your pressure cooker. Add the onion and sauté for a few minutes, then stir in the beans, garlic, thyme, tomato purée, tomatoes and spices. Season with salt and pepper, then pour over just enough water or stock to cover, then bring up to high pressure. Cook for 10 minutes, then allow to drop pressure naturally.

Stir through the parsley and lemon zest, then top with the cheese. Leave, covered, on a low heat for a few minutes until the cheese has melted. Alternatively, transfer to an ovenproof dish or skillet and put under a hot grill for a few minutes. You could also brown using an air-fryer attachment if you have one.

FUL MEDAMES

SERVES 6–8 AS PART OF A MEZZE OR STARTER

250g (9oz) dried broad or fava beans

1 tsp bicarbonate of soda (baking soda), optional

3 tbsp olive oil

1 large onion, finely chopped

4 garlic cloves, finely chopped

1 tsp ground cumin

1 tsp ground coriander

½ tsp ground cinnamon

1 tbsp tomato purée

1 tbsp tahini

1 tsp pomegranate molasses (optional)

2 garlic cloves, crushed

100g (3½oz) fresh tomatoes, finely chopped

Zest and juice of 1 lemon

1 small bunch of flat-leaf parsley and/or mint, finely chopped

Sea salt and freshly ground black pepper

TO SERVE

250g (9oz) thick strained yogurt or labneh

1 tsp sumac

Pitta breads

Lemon wedges

Pickled chillies

This is a dish that took me a long time to perfect, but I persisted because I haven't managed to find a jarred or canned version I really love. It is also the only bean dish I recommend using bicarbonate of soda (baking soda) in. The reason for this is that the quality of dried fava beans is inconsistent; while the flesh will soften, the skins frequently won't without the help of the bicarb, even in a pressure cooker.

If you know your beans are fresh – well within their best before date – you can try this without the bicarb, but regardless, do try to avoid using beans that have been lurking at the back of a cupboard for a decade.

First, quick soak your beans. Put in the pressure cooker and cover generously with cold water. Add 1 teaspoon of salt and the bicarbonate of soda (baking soda), if using, and close the lid. Bring up to high pressure and cook for 5 minutes. Allow to drop pressure naturally for 5 minutes, then release the remaining pressure. Drain the beans and rinse out your pressure cooker.

Heat the olive oil in your pressure cooker and add the onion. Sauté until translucent and starting to take on some colour, then stir in the garlic, spices and tomato purée. Stir in the beans. Cover with 400ml (14fl oz) water and add 1 teaspoon of salt. Bring up to high pressure and cook for 10 minutes. Allow to drop pressure naturally. Make sure the beans are cooked – if some are still on the hard side, you can return the cooker to high pressure again for another couple of minutes.

Mash some of the beans if you like – it is up to you how you do this, I like a mixture of whole and broken up. Stir in all the remaining ingredients and season with a little more salt and pepper. Serve with yogurt sprinkled with sumac, pittas, lemon wedges and chillies.

BLACK-EYED PEAS WITH CHIPOTLE, SQUASH AND KALE

SERVES 4

1 tbsp olive oil

2 rashers of bacon, diced (optional)

1 onion, finely chopped

1 red pepper, diced

1 tsp chipotle paste

250g (9oz) black-eyed peas, soaked or quick soaked (see page 208)

200g (7oz) squash or pumpkin, peeled and cut into large chunks

1 large bunch of kale or chard, shredded (optional), or 6 cubes frozen spinach (left frozen)

4 garlic cloves, finely chopped

3 tbsp finely chopped coriander (cilantro) stems

½ tsp ground cinnamon

1 bay leaf

1 tsp dried oregano

Zest of 1 lime

1 x 400g (14oz) can chopped tomatoes

250ml (9fl oz) ham, chicken or vegetable stock or water

Sea salt and freshly ground black pepper

TO SERVE (OPTIONAL)

Chilli flakes

Lime wedges

Coriander leaves

Grated cheese

It is not always necessary to soak or quick soak black-eyed peas as they do cook very quickly without, but if you want to cook them in a one-pot like this with vegetables, a shorter cooking time is preferable as it gives you more flexibility with the vegetables you can add without the risk of them overcooking.

This is a good brunch dish as it is very quick – I will serve with eggs (see Variation) and tortillas of some sort, perhaps simple cheese quesadillas. I have included a small amount of bacon in the ingredients list as I like the smoky flavour, but as often as not will make it vegetarian. Simply omit if you wish.

Heat the olive oil in your pressure cooker. Add the bacon (if using) and onion and sauté on a medium–high heat until the bacon has crisped up and rendered out some fat and the onion has started to brown.

Add the red pepper and chipotle paste and stir for another minute, then add all the remaining ingredients. Stir to combine and season generously with salt and pepper.

Close the lid and bring up to pressure. Cook at high pressure for 5 minutes, then remove from the heat and allow to drop pressure naturally. Stir gently (you don't want the squash to collapse) and serve with as many of the serving suggestions as you wish.

VARIATIONS

Add eggs as described on page 44 as for shakshuka or fry separately.

Replace half the tomatoes with 200ml (7fl oz) coconut milk.

To make with cooked beans, add 500g (1lb 2oz) beans at the same time as you would add the black-eyed peas, cook for 2 minutes and leave to drop pressure naturally.

PARCHED CARLIN PEAS OR CHICKPEAS

SERVES 8–10 AS A BAR SNACK

250g (9oz) black carlin peas or any type of chickpea (garbanzo bean), soaked or quick soaked (see page 208)

400ml (14fl oz) water or vegetable or chicken stock

1 tbsp olive oil

Malt vinegar

Sea salt and freshly ground black pepper

This is the basic method for cooking carlin peas, which will also work with all types of chickpeas too.

Little pots of these are a popular snack in the north of England, especially around Bonfire night, where they are usually doused liberally in salt and vinegar. They are incredibly moreish and although I think salt and vinegar is hard to beat, I've included some other flavour options in the Variations.

Put the soaked or quick soaked peas in your pressure cooker with the water or stock. Add the oil and 1 teaspoon of salt. Bring up to high pressure and cook for 15–20 minutes, depending on the texture you want – 15 minutes will give you an al dente, just tender pea, another 5 minutes will give you something much softer.

Drain the peas and return to the cooker. Leave on a low heat to allow them to dry out a bit, then season generously with salt and pepper. Douse in malt vinegar and serve immediately with extra malt vinegar on the side.

VARIATIONS

Use carlin peas or chickpeas for a great bar snack or tapas. After cooking, heat 1 tablespoon of oil in a pan and add the chickpeas. Toss in lemon zest, chilli powder or finely chopped rosemary. Dress with a little lemon juice.

Use carlin peas or chickpeas and fry with a slice of butter, a little chai spice, black pepper and a either 2 teaspoons of jaggery, light soft brown sugar or honey for a slightly sweeter snack.

BEANS BRAISED WITH ANCHOVIES AND GREENS

SERVES 4

FOR THE BASIC SAUCE

2 tbsp olive oil

1 x 50g (1¾oz) can anchovies

3 large garlic cloves, crushed

Zest and juice of 1 large lemon

A generous pinch of chilli flakes

Sea salt and freshly ground black pepper

FOR A QUICK BEAN AND GREEN BRAISE

400g (14oz) cooked beans (cannellini, borlotti or butter/ lima beans work best – see page 208)

1 courgette (zucchini), sliced

1 large bunch of greens or sprouting broccoli

100g (3½oz) cherry tomatoes (optional)

TO SERVE

Chilli flakes

This anchovy sauce is one of the most useful sauces you can have in the kitchen. I make it all the time, sometimes as a dip for green vegetables (especially sprouting broccoli) or as the base for a very quick dish such as this one. It is enormously versatile. Here it is used to braise beans and greens – my idea of a perfect dinner.

PLEASE, PLEASE, PLEASE squeeze your lemon BEFORE you start cooking this dish, so you can add it all at once, otherwise the sauce will be in danger of boiling dry and burning, which you do not want to happen.

Heat the olive oil in the pressure cooker, then add the anchovies, oil and all. Break up with the back of a wooden spoon until mashed, then add the garlic. Stir for another minute, then add the lemon zest and juice. Season with plenty of pepper and a little salt. Add the chilli flakes. At this point the sauce is ready to use and you can use it as a base for cooking any greens – but make sure you don't let it reduce down. If you do let it thicken, add 50ml (1¾fl oz) water or more lemon juice.

Add the beans and give a quick stir, then layer over the courgette (zucchini) followed by the sprouting broccoli. Dot around a few cherry tomatoes, if using. Bring up to high pressure and immediately fast release. Stir everything very gently together and serve with a scattering of chilli flakes.

VARIATIONS

You can add any herbs to this – very finely chopped rosemary or savory are very good, add along with the garlic. And use any flavour you like as a garnish – basil, parsley and mint work well.

BUTTERBEAN SUCCOTASH

SERVES 4-6

2 tbsp olive or groundnut oil

1 large onion, diced

2 celery sticks, diced

1 red pepper, diced

1 green pepper, diced

200g (7oz) squash or pumpkin, left unpeeled and diced

1 large courgette (zucchini), diced

150g (5½oz) okra, trimmed and halved

3 garlic cloves, crushed

3 sprigs of tarragon

250g (9oz) ham hock, roughly torn into pieces

500g (1lb 2oz) cooked butter (lima) beans (see page 208)

200g (7oz) sweetcorn

200g (7oz) fresh or canned tomatoes, puréed (optional)

200ml (7fl oz) ham hock, chicken or vegetable stock

Sea salt and freshly ground black pepper

TO SERVE

A few sprigs of chives, wild garlic or spring onions (scallions), finely chopped

A few tarragon leaves, finely chopped

This is a favourite of mine – it is mellow and sweet and very savoury. I make it usually when I have cooked a ham hock so I can add ham hock meat and a little stock to it, but it is also good as a vegetarian dish.

Okra have a reputation for sliminess, but you can mitigate this in a couple of ways. First, make sure the okra you are using is fresh and crisp – it should be a deep, clean green and firm to touch. Second, you can soak it in vinegar after you have cut it – after a very short period of time it will start drawing out the starchy liquid and you can then rinse it and use.

Heat the oil in your pressure cooker. Add the onion, celery, peppers, squash, courgette (zucchini) and okra and sauté on a high heat until the vegetables are all starting to look soft around the edges – around 5 minutes. Stir in the garlic and tarragon and stir for another minute, then gently fold in the ham hock, beans and sweetcorn.

Pour over the tomatoes, if using, then the stock and season with salt and pepper. Close the lid and bring up to high pressure. Cook at high pressure for 2 minutes, then allow to drop pressure naturally.

Serve sprinkled with the finely chopped herbs.

HOW TO COOK LENTILS AND SPLIT PEAS

Cooking lentils is a daily occurrence in my household. Even if I'm not making a pot of lentil soup, or a dal for a quick lunch with flatbreads or cooking up some whole lentils (Puy, beluga, mung beans) to use in a salad, they get added to all kinds of things. A handful of red lentils is frequently added to pasta dishes (see page 163), soups and stews to help thicken (as they disintegrate). I will add brown, green or Puy lentils to rice and other grains, and probably most of all, use them as a meat substitute to either reduce or completely replace the meat in ragùs and other chopped meat dishes.

Apart from red lentils, which will always disintegrate when you cook them, you don't have to worry too much about ratios if cooking lentils to a useable, intact al dente. Just cover generously with water (as usual, make sure the cooker isn't more than two-thirds full), add salt and 1 tablespoon of oil, bring up to high pressure and cook according to the timings below. They should always be allowed to drop pressure naturally.

A quick tip about cooking lentils – the sort that release a lot of starch – such as red lentils, chana, toor, split mung dal, split peas – do not take kindly to being cooked at pressure more than once. The reason is that the starch will have thickened the liquid and will catch on the bottom if you try to bring it back up to pressure. So don't be tempted to do two-stage cooking with these lentils. For example, don't add greens after the initial cooking and attempt to bring back up to pressure – you should cook the greens first, then add back in to warm through once you have cooked the lentils. The exception to this is when defrosting, see page 234 for details.

Here are some quick timings for some of the more common types of lentils. As for the beans, they will cook faster in water, which is why there is a discrepancy between the simple timings here and those in most of the recipes that follow. And if you do want to cook them by absorption method and reduce the amount of liquid, generally you need to cook at a ratio of 1:2. Most of these lentils don't need to be soaked or quick soaked; the exception is whole urad dal, which does benefit from it.

Red lentils and split peas – 1–2 minutes (1 to keep shape, 2 to break down)
Green, brown and Puy lentils – 1–2 minutes for al dente
Chana dal (split chickpeas/garbanzo beans) – 2–3 minutes (2 to keep shape, 3 to break down)
Mung beans – 7 minutes
Black beluga lentils – 6 minutes
Split urad dal (white) – 5 minutes
Whole urad dal (black) – 12 minutes (5 with soaking)

A USEFUL POT OF LENTILS

SERVES 4

2 tbsp olive oil

1 large onion, finely diced

1 large carrot, finely diced

3 celery sticks, finely diced

OR 4 tbsp sofrito (see page 330)

3 garlic cloves, finely chopped

1 large sprig of thyme

2 tbsp tomato purée

200g (7oz) green or brown lentils, rinsed

100ml (3½fl oz) red or white wine

300ml (10½fl oz) vegetable or chicken stock or water

Sea salt and freshly ground black pepper

This is the sort of dish that can be used as a base for all kinds of meals. It is worth baking a double batch and freezing in small portions that you can use to eke out other leftovers or odds and ends. If I happen to have a small portion of ragù left, I might use a portion of these lentils combined to make a pasta sauce or a cottage pie. Or put a block of them, frozen, on top of some rice or pasta – they will defrost and reheat in the time it takes for the rice or pasta to cook – you just need to stir them through after releasing pressure.

You can usually cook green and brown lentils in the same way as red lentils – 1 minute at high pressure, natural release. But this doesn't work when you are adding lots of other acidic ingredients and are reducing the amount of liquid substantially, which is why the cooking time here is much longer.

Heat the olive oil in your pressure cooker. Add the onion, carrot and celery or the sofrito and sauté until starting to soften and colour around the edges. Add the garlic and thyme. Stir for another minute, then add the tomato purée. Stir until the paste starts to separate and smells very aromatic, then stir in the lentils and season with plenty of salt and pepper. Pour in the wine. Allow to come up to the boil, then pour in the stock or water. Close the lid and bring up to high pressure. Cook for 7 minutes, then allow to drop pressure naturally.

VARIATIONS

For a quick sausage and lentil casserole
Fry sausages first, then return to the pressure cooker before bringing up to high pressure. Really good with whole merguez sausages or sliced chorizo sausages. If using merguez, perhaps add ½ teaspoon of ground cinnamon too. Very good with the roast squash on page 264.

For a more substantial vegetarian meal
Add 1 diced aubergine (eggplant) and 150g (5½oz) sliced mushrooms to the other vegetables. Sauté until the aubergine is looking browned, then proceed as above. The aubergine will break down, but the overall flavour and effect will be rich, savoury and smoky.

Add greens
Frozen broad (fava) beans or spinach or robust greens, such as kale or chard, can be added before the lentils come up to high pressure, most others should be cooked first and then stirred back in at the end of the cooking.

STORECUPBOARD POTAGE

SERVES 4

1 tbsp olive oil

1 large onion, finely chopped

3 celery sticks, finely chopped

3 carrots, finely diced

A few sprigs of rosemary

1 tsp dried thyme

2 garlic cloves, finely chopped

2 tbsp tomato purée

75g (2½oz) brown lentils

50g (1¾oz) split red lentils

75g (2½oz) green or yellow split peas

75g (2½oz) pearled barley, spelt or farro

1 litre (35fl oz) vegetable or chicken stock or water

1–2 lamb bones or similar (see intro)

150g (5½oz) broad (fava) beans (frozen are fine)

200g (7oz) kale, finely shredded (optional)

This is really economical and is infinitely variable. I've given suggestions here on the types of vegetables, pulses and grains that can be used, but it really is up to you – use any leftover vegetables you have. You could also use one of those pulse/grain mixes you can buy in the supermarket.

The first time I made this I used a couple of lamb bones I had in the freezer – they imbued the whole thing with flavour and I could almost imagine I was eating a lamb hotpot. You could use instead a pork or ham bone, duck, game...or keep it vegetarian, it will all work.

There are lots of dishes in this book where I advise greens can be added after the main cooking has taken place. Do not do so with this dish as any attempt to return to high pressure will result in the base burning because of the high starch content of the pulses. Either add greens with the water or stock or cook separately as a side dish.

Heat the olive oil in your pressure cooker, then add the onion, celery and carrot. Sauté on a high heat for 5 minutes until starting to take on some colour, then add the herbs, garlic and tomato purée. Stir to combine.

Add the lentils, split peas and barley, then pour over the stock or water. Tuck in any bones you might want to add for flavour, then add the broad (fava) beans and kale. Bring up to high pressure and cook for 20 minutes. Allow to release pressure naturally.

VARIATION

To make it even more of a storecupboard/freezer dish, use 4 tablespoons of sofrito (see page 330) in place of the onion, celery and carrot.

A FEW QUICK DALS

WHITE URAD DAL

This is a creamy, white, split lentil that is best kept simple. Rinse 250g (9oz) until the water runs clear. Heat 2 teaspoons of coconut oil in your pressure cooker and sauté 1 finely chopped onion until translucent. Stir in 15g (½oz) grated ginger, 4 grated/crushed garlic cloves, 1 teaspoon of cumin seeds, the finely chopped stems from 1 small bunch of coriander (cilantro) and ½ teaspoon of ground turmeric or 1 teaspoon of curry powder, followed by the lentils and 375ml (13fl oz) water or stock (the ratio is 1:1.5). Season and bring up to high pressure. Cook for 5 minutes, then allow to drop pressure naturally. Stir in the coriander leaves and garnish with a few sliced green chillies.

WHOLE MUNG DAL WITH SPINACH

This is a really good storecupboard/freezer dal. Heat 1 tablespoon of coconut or olive oil in your pressure cooker. Add 1 finely chopped onion with 1 teaspoon of mustard seeds. When the mustard seeds pop, add 3 finely chopped garlic cloves with either 1 tablespoon of a favourite curry or spice mix OR use 1 teaspoon each of ground turmeric, cumin, coriander, fenugreek and ½ teaspoon each of ground cinnamon and chilli powder. Add 1 finely chopped tomato and 250g (9oz) mung beans. Pour over 500ml (17fl oz) water, or enough to cover the mung beans completely, and season with salt and pepper. Drop 8 cubes of frozen spinach on top. Bring up to high pressure and cook for 6 minutes. Remove from the heat and allow to drop pressure naturally. Stir the spinach into the dal (it will have stayed on top). Season with more salt and pepper and a little lemon juice. Serve with yogurt and sliced green chillies.

LENTILS BRAISED WITH DRIED LIMES

Serve this with some yogurt, rice or flatbreads and maybe a tomato and onion salad on the side. Or even just a couple of fried eggs. Heat 2 tablespoons of olive oil in your pressure cooker. Sauté 1 finely chopped onion along with 1 teaspoon of cumin seeds, ½ teaspoon each of ground cardamom, turmeric and cinnamon. Add 250g (9oz) green, brown or Puy lentils. Stir in 100g (3½oz) freshly chopped tomatoes and season. Pierce 3 dried limes (brown or black) all over with the tip of a skewer, then add to the cooker along with 1 large sprig of tarragon, then pour over 400ml (14fl oz) stock or water. Bring up to high pressure and cook for 7 minutes, then allow to drop pressure naturally. Stir in finely chopped parsley, mint, dill, tarragon, chervil...as many or as few herbs as you like and serve hot.

EVERYDAY SPICED DAL WITH VEGETABLES

This a thicker, more robust dal, using red lentils and adding vegetables to make it more of a one-pot. Heat 1 tablespoon of coconut oil in your pressure cooker. Add 1 diced onion, red pepper and sweet potato. Sauté for a few minutes, then add 4 chopped garlic cloves, 15g (½oz) chopped ginger and 2 tablespoons of chopped coriander (cilantro) stems. Stir in 1 tablespoon of mild curry powder, or any spice mix you prefer, followed by 250g (9oz) well-rinsed red lentils and 200g (7oz) chopped tomatoes. Pour over 600ml (21fl oz) water or a combination of water and coconut milk. Season, bring up to high pressure and cook for 1 minute, then allow to drop pressure naturally. Serve with sliced green chillies, coriander and lemon wedges.

DAL MAKHANI

SERVES 4

300g (10½oz) black urad lentils

2 tbsp oil

4 garlic cloves, crushed

30g (1oz) piece ginger, peeled and grated

1 large cinnamon stick

2 black cardamom pods

1 tsp ground turmeric

1 tsp ground cumin

½ tsp ground fenugreek

½–1 tsp Kashmiri chilli powder

1 tbsp tomato purée

25g (1oz) butter

50ml (1¾fl oz) double (heavy) cream

Sea salt

TO SERVE (OPTIONAL)

20g (¾oz) butter

1 onion, thinly sliced

A few sprigs of coriander (cilantro)

Green chillies, sliced

This is probably one of the most famous of celebratory dal recipes, traditionally taking hours and hours of slow cooking, rolled out on special occasions and given a luxurious feel thanks to the butter and cream. The dal to use is the black urad – it is a whole dal, do not make the mistake of buying the white, hulled urad dal instead.

Lentils don't normally need soaking – this is the exception to the rule because black urad dal do take quite a long time anyway and the tomato purée increases this. So it makes sense to part-cook them without the tomato purée first. It is still a quick recipe – hours of stirring reduced to something achievable in less than half an hour from start to finish.

Put the lentils in your pressure cooker with 1 teaspoon of salt and cover with cold water. Add 1 tablespoon of the oil. Close the lid and bring up to high pressure. Adjust the heat to maintain high pressure and cook for 5 minutes, then remove from the heat and leave to stand for 5 minutes. Release any lingering pressure.

Drain the lentils, discarding the water, and return to the pressure cooker with the garlic and ginger, the whole and ground spices and the tomato purée. Stir thoroughly and add plenty of salt. Cover with 600ml (21fl oz) cold water and add the remaining oil. Bring up to high pressure again and this time cook for 7 minutes. Allow to drop pressure naturally.

While the lentils are cooking, prepare the onion. Heat the butter in a frying pan (skillet) and add the onion. Cook on a medium–high heat stirring regularly until browned.

Crush some of the lentils either with a masher or by squashing them against the side of the cooker with wooden spoon. Set on a low heat and beat in the butter and cream, in the same way you would beat butter into a risotto. Let the liquid reduce down a little – it will thicken as it cools.

Serve with the onion, coriander (cilantro) and/or green chillies, as you wish.

SIMPLE GARLICKY DAL

SERVES 4

250g (9oz) split red lentils, split mung or toor dal

1 tbsp olive or coconut oil

2 large garlic cloves, finely chopped or grated

1 large bunch of coriander (cilantro), finely chopped

100g (3½oz) tomatoes, finely chopped

½ red onion, finely chopped

½ tsp dried mint

2 tsp red wine vinegar or lemon juice

Sea salt and freshly ground black pepper

FOR THE TAHINI AND LEMON SAUCE

3 tbsp tahini

Juice of 1 lemon

1 large garlic clove, crushed

1–2 tsp za'atar

1 tsp sumac

TO GARNISH (OPTIONAL)

Chilli flakes

Coriander (cilantro) leaves

Sliced or pickled chillies

This is a very easy, adaptable dal. It works best with the sort of dal that will break down a bit when cooked, rather than keep their shape; in particular split red or toor dal. You could also use chana dal or split peas, which will take a little longer – 2 minutes to cook through and soften, 3–5 minutes to break down.

Serve with as many of the extras as you like. Or consider serving with a big pile of sautéed greens such as cime di rapa (see page 250), or, if you have some made up, the chickpeas with lemon and chilli in the recipe on page 229 makes a really good addition.

Rinse the dal thoroughly until the water is no longer milky with starch. Put into your pressure cooker with the oil, garlic, coriander (cilantro) and 1 teaspoon of salt. Cover with 1 litre (35fl oz) of cold water. Close the lid and bring up to high pressure. Cook for 1 minute, then allow to drop pressure naturally. Stir to make sure the coriander is thoroughly mixed in – the dal will start to thicken as it cools.

Meanwhile, make the sauce by mixing together the tahini, lemon juice and garlic with enough warm water to give it the texture of double (heavy) cream. Season with salt and pepper and sprinkle over the za'atar and sumac.

Mix the tomatoes and red onion together with the mint and vinegar or lemon juice. Add plenty of salt.

Serve the dal with the sauce, salad and as many of the garnishes as you like.

VARIATION

This also makes a good soup. Just reduce the quantity of lentils to 200g (7oz). Use as many of the garnishes as you like.

BELUGA LENTILS WITH CURRY LEAVES

SERVES 4

200g (7oz) beluga lentils, well rinsed

A handful of fresh or frozen curry leaves

1 tbsp olive or coconut oil

When I first cooked these together I could not believe how the flavour of curry leaves intensified through pressure cooking. It is one more example of how pressure cooking seems to push flavour into the heart of other ingredients. These make an excellent side dish and in particular complement the fish curry on page 146. But they are especially good in the salad below.

Put the lentils in your pressure cooker with 1 teaspoon of salt and the curry leaves. Add enough cold water to cover, then pour in the oil. Bring up to high pressure and cook for 7 minutes, then leave to drop pressure naturally. Drain.

BELUGA LENTIL, CAULIFLOWER AND TOMATO SALAD

SERVES 4

1 red onion, finely sliced

Juice of 1 lime

½ portion of cooked beluga lentils (above)

1 romesco cauliflower, cooked (see page 266)

100g (3½oz) salad leaves or spinach

150g (5½oz) cherry tomatoes, halved

1 red onion, finely sliced

Sea salt and black pepper

FOR THE DRESSING

2 tbsp olive oil

2 tsp sherry vinegar

A pinch of mild curry powder

A pinch of hot chilli powder

I don't like interfering with the flavour of the lentils in this salad, which is why the dressing is very simple. It is also really good served with dollops of the mango chutney yogurt on page 47.

Put the red onion in a bowl and add ½ teaspoon of salt. Cover with the lime juice and leave to stand for 30 minutes. Leave the lentils and romesco cauliflower to stand until just warm or room temperature.

Make the salad dressing by whisking all the ingredients together, along with plenty of salt and pepper.

Arrange the lentils, cauliflower, leaves and tomatoes over a platter and garnish with the red onion. Drizzle with the salad dressing.

LENTILS AND WILD RICE BRAISED WITH LAMB AND GREENS

SERVES 4

1 tbsp coconut oil

1 onion, finely chopped

1 tsp mustard seeds

1 tsp cumin seeds

3 black cardamom pods

A few fresh curry leaves

15g (½oz) piece ginger, grated

4 garlic cloves, grated

250g (9oz) any lean cut of lamb or goat, such as leg, finely diced

100g (3½oz) chard, any type of kale or collard greens, shredded

50g (1¾oz) each of urad dal, chana dal and mung beans

75g (2½oz) brown or wild rice

2 tbsp tomato purée

150g (5½oz) coconut cream

Sea salt and freshly ground black pepper

This is another of those recipes that uses just a small amount of meat to add flavour – I am always amazed at exactly how much flavour is spread through the whole dish. It takes much longer to cook than most of the lentil dishes in this book because I've included urad dal, which should normally be soaked or quick soaked (see page 233). But it works as written because the unsoaked lentils will cook in the same time as the rice. You can adapt this way of cooking to other lentil and grain combinations. For example, brown, Puy or green lentils or chana dal will cook in the same time as basmati or long-grain rice.

Heat the coconut oil in your pressure cooker. Add the onion, spices and curry leaves. When the curry leaves start to crackle, add the ginger, garlic and lamb or goat and greens and stir to combine. Add the dal, beans and rice, then stir in the tomato purée. Pour in the coconut cream and season with salt and pepper.

Pour in 500ml (17fl oz) water and bring up to high pressure. Cook for 20 minutes, then allow to drop pressure naturally.

QUICK AND EASY PURÉES

SERVES 4

BROAD BEAN PURÉE

An Italian classic – a good alternative to mashed potato and traditionally served with caramelized endive (see page 256). Quick soak 250g (9oz) split dried broad (fava) beans according to page 208. Drain thoroughly and wash out your pressure cooker. Return the beans to the cooker with the unpeeled cloves from a whole head of garlic (reserving 1), a piece of pared lemon zest and 1 sprig of thyme. Add 2 tablespoons of olive oil, 1 teaspoon of salt and 600ml (21fl oz) water. Bring up to high pressure and cook for 10 minutes and allow to drop pressure naturally.

Remove the garlic cloves from the pot and squeeze out their flesh. Mash briefly and return to the pot, along with the reserved clove, crushed. Remove the lemon zest and thyme, then stir – you should find that the beans have broken down and will quickly form a purée. Taste for seasoning and add a generous squeeze of lemon juice before serving.

SPLIT PEA PURÉE

Really good with sliced ham – and if you have boiled the ham and have the stock, use it to cook the pea purée too. Heat 1 tablespoon of olive oil or butter in your pressure cooker. Sauté 1 finely chopped onion until translucent, then add a couple of finely chopped garlic cloves. Stir in 250g (9oz) green or yellow split peas, followed by 1 teaspoon of salt and 500ml (17fl oz) stock or water. Bring up to high pressure and cook for 3 minutes. Leave

to drop pressure naturally. Taste for seasoning and adjust as necessary. Beat in another tablespoon of butter if you like and beat to form a thick purée. It will thicken as it cools.

This also makes a superb soup. Add any finely diced vegetables you like, thyme or bay and garlic and perhaps some fresh or dried chilli. Use 1 litre (35fl oz) of stock and cook as for the broad bean purée.

MUSHY PEAS

These are so much nicer than the chip-shop version – sweeter, probably because there is absolutely no need to add bicarbonate of soda (baking soda) – the marrowfat peas soften beautifully in the pressure cooker and release enough starch to thicken the cooking liquor.

Pre-soak 250g (9oz) marrowfat peas as described on page 208. Drain and cover with 400ml (14fl oz) water. Add 1 teaspoon of salt, 1 tablespoon of olive or rapeseed (canola) oil and an optional 1 teaspoon of dried mint. Return to high pressure and cook for 6–8 minutes. Allow to drop pressure naturally. Add a large knob of butter and stir to form a thick, textured purée before serving.

VEGETABLES

Since owning my first pressure cooker I have fundamentally changed the way I cook vegetables, and they are the main reason my pressure cookers live on the hob – they are used daily, if not always for the main meal, then usually for some kind of vegetable side dish. Pressure cooking produces perfectly cooked vegetables that have a better flavour, a higher nutritional content and will have been cooked using a fraction of the time, fuel and, most of all in the case of vegetables, water. Think about how you usually cook vegetable side dishes. Most of us will boil or steam without giving a second thought to how long it takes or how much water we are using. Pressure cooking will have those vegetables cooked to al dente (or softer if you prefer) in a fraction of the time it takes for that saucepan of water to come up to boil, even if you are using water from a kettle, and using the merest splash of water, too.

I have generally found that saying this provokes a degree of scepticism and I understand why – so many people equate pressure cooking with overcooked, soggy, sludgy and sulphurous greens. The reason for this is nothing to do with the pressure cooker – it is the way in which pressure cookers have traditionally been used. Most vegetables take next-to-no time to cook in the pressure cooker with minimal amounts of liquid, but read a pressure cooker manual, or many of the recipes online and even some cookery books and you will see highly inaccurate, lengthy timings. For example, I recently saw a cauliflower recipe in which florets were cooked for 30 minutes, when they normally take no longer than the time it takes for you to bring your cooker up to pressure. This is the kind of mistake that gives pressure cookery a bad name, and will put off novice users – who wants to open their pressure cooker and be confronted with a pile of soggy grey mush?

Another issue with the way vegetables have been traditionally cooked in the pressure cooker is the insistence that pressure cookers need a minimum amount of liquid to work. Of course, without liquid in the pot, the pressure cooker cannot create steam and therefore cannot reach high pressure – however, a very small amount is needed to achieve this, particularly when cooking times are short. The smaller amount of liquid used, the faster your cooker will come up to pressure and the faster your vegetables will cook. You will see from the techniques I have developed in this chapter that the amount of liquid needed can be, for steaming, as little as the amount clinging to greens after washing, or the butter melted when braising, or the merest splash needed when roasting. Some of these recipes do require a degree of nerve – this is one area of pressure cooking when because timings are very important, you will be dealing with the speed and violence of high heat sizzling and fast released steam. It is fast and furious, but also fun and very rewarding when you get it right.

COOKING GREENS

The quickest, simplest way to cook greens in the pressure cooker is to steam them in the main body of the pot. I love this method for several reasons. Firstly, you are saving massively on water as you don't need much more than the water clinging to the washed and shaken greens. Secondly, it is very, very fast. Thirdly, you are preserving the nutritional content and colour of the greens. Fourthly, you will find the flavour is better (generally sweeter and more intense – especially noticeable with broccoli), and finally it is very adaptable for sautéing, roasting and braising. Understanding the versatility of this method was transformative for me, and I hope it will be for you too.

The quick method is very simple. Wash the greens, put in your pressure cooker with an additional 50–75ml (1¾–2½fl oz) water if you are nervous*, season, bring up to high pressure and fast release. This will work with most leafy greens, including chard, kale, kalettes, spring greens, all kinds of cabbage, all types of Chinese greens (pak choi/bok choy, kai lan, Chinese lettuce), little gem lettuces, sprout tops, mustard greens, cime di rapa, broccoli and sprouting broccoli, cauliflower florets, all types of green beans, asparagus, courgettes (zucchini) and okra.

There are only a couple of exceptions to this in terms of greens. Collard greens take much, much longer to soften, and some types of kale, such as spigarello, need a minute at high pressure if you want to cook their woodier stems. Brussels sprouts and anything with a core, such as endive or fennel, take slightly longer too, see separate recipes on pages 256 and 259.

Once you know how this works, you can play around with the timings a little. So, for example, if you want your greens very al dente, perhaps because you are going to heat them through in another dish or finish them off in another way, just bring them up to low pressure, then fast release. If you want them softer, add 30-second increments. But the general rule of thumb is that this will work, regardless of the size of your pressure cooker.

* A lot of pressure-cooker manuals give you a minimum amount of water you need to bring your cooker up to pressure, but I can honestly say that this is nonsense. I frequently cook greens in no more than the water that is clinging to them from a thorough washing.

Once you know you can cook greens in this way you will find it is easy to adapt. You will notice there are a lot of recipes in this book that involve adding greens right at the end, after the initial pressure cooking. This is possible with dishes that aren't too starchy – those with a lot of starch released into them (some beans and most dals especially), don't take kindly to coming up to pressure again after the initial cook. For these dishes it is better to include greens at the outset or cook them separately.

BUTTERED GREENS

Adding butter from the beginning means you will not need to add water and the buttery flavours will infuse through your vegetables. This is especially good with beans, asparagus and courgettes (zucchini). Simply melt 15–25g (½–1oz) butter in the pressure cooker before you add the greens, sauté until the vegetables look glossy, then bring up to high pressure and fast release.

You can use this method for root vegetables too. Carrots are particularly sweet when cooked this way and are even better with a small amount (5g/⅛oz) of grated ginger added to the butter. Leave whole or slice into wedges or batons and coat with the melted butter. Bring up to high pressure and cook for 2–3 minutes depending on how thickly cut your carrots are. Fast release.

SAUTÉED GREENS

Add 1 tablespoon of olive oil and some aromatics before adding the greens. This might include bacon, anchovy (see page 230 for a version including cooked white beans), a bit of duck confit, garlic, herbs, citrus zest, spices. The principle is the same – get the flavour into the cooker, add the greens, cook for the same amount of time. You can use the vegetables as a side dish or as a pasta sauce or with beans stirred through. Overleaf are a few examples.

GREENS SAUTÉED WITH BACON OR CHORIZO

SERVES 4

1 tbsp olive oil

100g (3½oz) bacon lardons or chorizo, chopped

1 shallot, finely sliced

2 garlic cloves, finely chopped

1 sprig of thyme

250g (9oz) greens of your choice, well washed, excess shaken off (not bone dry)

Sea salt and freshly ground black pepper

This works well with everything but is particularly good with bitter greens such as cime di rapa (broccoli raab), escarole, mustard greens, dandelion (wild or cultivated).

Heat the oil in your pressure cooker. Add the bacon and the shallot and sauté until the bacon is crisp and brown. Stir in the garlic and thyme, then add the greens. Season with salt and pepper, then close the lid and bring up to high pressure. Release pressure immediately.

GREENS SAUTÉED WITH ANCHOVY, LEMON AND CHILLI

SERVES 4

50g (1¾oz) can anchovies, with the oil (30g/1oz drained weight)

15g (½oz) butter

4 garlic cloves, grated or crushed

Zest and juice of 1 lemon

½ tsp chilli flakes or 1 red chilli, finely chopped

250g (9oz) greens of your choice

Sea salt and freshly ground black pepper

Especially good with sprout tops, sprouting broccoli, cime di rapa. A note on adding the lemon juice – for this dish it is important to have the lemon juice ready to pour into the sauce as you cook it, so don't squeeze it directly into the cooker – if you do, it will give it time to reduce down. And another note – if you prepare the sauce ahead, heat it through and decide whether you need a splash of water before adding the greens, because it will set and may well burn otherwise.

Put the anchovies and their oil in your pressure cooker with the butter. As the butter melts, break up the anchovies with a wooden spoon. Stir in the garlic, lemon zest and chilli flakes or chilli, and cook for a minute, then pour in the lemon juice all at once. Do not give the sauce time to reduce down (this is why the lemon juice must go in all at once). Add the greens and cook as above.

SAUTÉED CABBAGE

SERVES 4

1 tbsp olive oil or 15g (½oz) butter

½ onion, finely chopped

½ tsp nigella seeds

½ tsp cumin seeds

2 garlic cloves

1 small white, green or Savoy cabbage, shredded

A few sprigs of curly or flat-leaf parsley, finely chopped

Sea salt and freshly ground black pepper

And here's another version, this time using a crisp white cabbage that needs a little time to sauté before being cooked at high pressure.

Heat the olive oil or butter in your pressure cooker. Add the onion and seeds, and sauté for a couple of minutes, then add the garlic and cabbage. Season with salt and pepper. Continue to sauté for a couple of minutes until the cabbage looks glossy – it may also start developing tiny droplets of water on the surface – then add 50ml (1¾fl oz) water. Close the lid and bring up to high pressure. Fast release immediately, then stir in the parsley.

CREAMED GREENS

SERVES 4

1 tbsp olive oil or butter

1 small onion or shallot, finely chopped

2 garlic cloves, finely chopped

250g (9oz) cabbage or other greens, shredded

75ml (2½fl oz) double (heavy) cream

Sea salt and freshly ground black pepper

This is for soft and mellow greens. It works particularly well with Savoy cabbage, or shredded Brussels sprouts. Bacon is always a good addition too.

Heat the olive oil or butter in your pressure cooker and add the onion. Sauté until it is starting to take on some colour, then stir in the garlic and cabbage and season with salt and pepper. Cook for a further minute or two, then close the lid and bring up to high pressure. Release pressure immediately or after 30 seconds–1 minute, depending on what you are cooking and how soft you want it. Stir in the cream and leave to simmer for a couple of minutes.

SPICED GREENS

SERVES 4

1 tbsp coconut oil, olive oil or ghee

1 tsp mustard seeds

A few fresh curry leaves (optional)

½ tsp ground turmeric

½ tsp ground cinnamon

½ tsp ground cumin

10g (¼oz) piece ginger, grated or finely chopped

2 garlic cloves, finely chopped

100g (3½oz) carrots, julienned

200g (7oz) greens, such as green or Savoy cabbage, spring greens or kale, washed and finely shredded

100g (3½oz) green beans, trimmed

Sea salt and freshly ground black pepper

A little finely chopped coriander (cilantro), to serve

This is a bit like a thoran; a dry curry. You can adapt it to use any spices you like, obviously. And if you don't want it dry, add 100g (3½oz) tomatoes or coconut milk before cooking.

Heat the oil in your pressure cooker. Add the mustard seeds and curry leaves, if using. When they start popping and crackling, add the spices, ginger, garlic and carrots and sauté for a couple of minutes. Add the greens and beans and season with salt and pepper. Bring up to high pressure and release pressure immediately for al dente, cook for 30 seconds–1 minute longer, depending how soft you want your greens. Serve with a little finely chopped coriander (cilantro).

BRAISED BROAD BEANS

SERVES 4

2 tbsp olive oil

1 red onion, finely sliced

100g (3½oz) pancetta or similar, diced or pulled into strips

2 garlic cloves, finely chopped

50ml (1¾fl oz) dry sherry

500g (1lb 2oz) broad (fava) beans (frozen, but defrosted are fine)

1 small bunch of mint or dill or both

Sea salt and freshly ground black pepper

This will also work well with any type of green bean (reduce the cooking time to 0-1 minute depending how al dente you want them), or peas.

Heat the oil in your pressure cooker. Add the red onion and pancetta and sauté on a high heat until the meat has browned and the onions are starting to take on some colour. Add the garlic and cook for a further minute, then add the sherry. Season, then add the broad (fava) beans and stir. Close the lid, bring up to high pressure and cook for 2 minutes. Fast release. Sprinkle with a handful of mint or dill leaves or both and serve.

GREENS BRAISED WITH TOMATOES

SERVES 4

2 tbsp olive oil

2 garlic cloves, finely chopped

4 fresh tomatoes, puréed or finely chopped

250g (9oz) greens of your choice, such as green, broad or runner (string) beans, courgettes (zucchini – baby ones left whole, large ones sliced), okra (trimmed), kale or chard

½ tsp dried oregano or thyme, or a few sprigs of fresh herbs – tarragon, parsley, savory, basil

Sea salt and freshly ground black pepper

The fashion for vegetables is to keep them very green and al dente, but cooking them slightly softer can be very comforting as they will be sweeter. In terms of short and long cooking it is literally the difference of a minute in the pressure cooker. I particularly like the Italian fashion for cooking greens for longer in tomatoes. It works especially well with green beans, courgettes (zucchini) and okra. You will get a creamier finish if you use fresh tomatoes, but you can use canned or a small portion of any of the tomato sauces on pages 332 and 333.

Vary this – you can add chilli, different chilli pastes (try harissa with runner/string beans), citrus juice, some chopped kimchi (best with cabbage, spring greens, Brussels sprouts or kale), spices, a sliced onion or peppers at the beginning before the garlic...the possibilities are endless.

Heat the olive oil in your pressure cooker and add the garlic. Cook for 1 minute and add the tomatoes. Continue to cook on a high heat for 2 minutes, then add a splash of water (no more than 75ml/2½fl oz) and the greens and herbs. Season with salt and pepper and close the lid. Bring up to high pressure and instead of fast releasing, leave to drop pressure naturally. If the sauce is at all watery (this will vary, depending on the tomatoes), leave on a low heat to reduce down a little.

BRAISED LEEKS

SERVES 4

This is a very quick way of making a warm leek vinaigrette or mimosa. To cook leeks plain, ready for a gratin, see the first Variation. If you like a slight charring to your leeks, put them on a hot griddle for a minute on each side first, but don't feel this is necessary.

Cut 4 leeks of similar thickness into thirds. Heat 2 tablespoons of olive oil in your pressure cooker, then add the leeks and roll them around until they are well coated in the oil. Add 25ml (1fl oz) vermouth or white wine and 50ml (1¾fl oz) fresh orange juice and 1 sprig of thyme. Season with salt and pepper, then bring up to high pressure. Cook for 2–4 minutes, depending on thickness (an average leek will take 3 minutes), then fast release.

Mix together 1 teaspoon of Dijon mustard, 1 tablespoon of sherry vinegar and 1 teaspoon of orange zest and use to dress the leeks. Serve warm as a side dish, or turn into leeks mimosa, by sprinkling with finely chopped egg whites followed by egg yolks, a few capers and sprigs of chervil.

VARIATIONS

You can make glossy, buttery leeks with this same method. Melt 25g (1oz) butter in your pressure cooker, add the leeks and make sure they are coated in the butter, then add either 50ml (1¾fl oz) white wine, vermouth, stock or water. Season generously, then bring up to pressure and cook as above.

For buttery leeks to stir through other dishes (eg mashed potato), finely slice them and cook for just 1 minute at high pressure

This method also works with celery or chard stems: Cut a head of celery into quarters. After coating in the oil and butter, try to arrange curved side down, then cook for 5 minutes for celery, 1 minute for chard stems and fast release. Serve as a side dish or turn into a gratin: transfer the cooked celery to a gratin dish, melt 75g (2½oz) blue cheese into the remaining cooking liquid left in the base of the pressure cooker and pour over the celery. Then mix together 50g (1¾oz) breadcrumbs, 25g (1oz) pecans, ½ teaspoon of lime zest and a few finely chopped sprigs of tarragon. Sprinkle over the celery, then dot with butter. Put under a hot grill.

CARAMELIZED ENDIVE WITH CHILLI, SOY AND ORANGE JUICE

SERVES 4

1 tbsp olive oil

1 tbsp runny honey

3–4 heads of endive, cut in half lengthways (or wedges if very large)

25g (1oz) butter

1 tbsp dark soy sauce

2 tbsp orange juice

Zest of ½ orange or mandarin

½ tsp chilli flakes

A pinch of Chinese 5 spice

Leaves from 1 small sprig of thyme

This is a bit of a riff on a recipe in my *Citrus* book, which is still one of my favourite side dishes. You can also make it with other bitter leaves. Caramelizing fennel works in a similar way, but I would take out all the aromatics, and soy and use the zest and juice of a lemon instead.

Heat the olive oil in your pressure cooker. Add the honey and stir, then add the endive, cut-side down. Cook for a few minutes until they have started to caramelize, then flip over. Add the butter, soy, orange juice and sprinkle in the orange zest, chilli flakes, 5 spice and thyme. Close the lid, bring up to high pressure and cook for 2–3 minutes, depending on the size of the endive.

CARAMELIZED ENDIVE SALAD WITH ORANGE, MOZZARELLA AND LENTILS

SERVES 4

1 portion of caramelized endives (see above)

FOR THE SALAD

2 oranges

100g (3½oz) cooked green, brown or Puy lentils

2 fresh mozzarella balls or 1 large burrata, roughly torn

1 tbsp capers

FOR THE DRESSING

1 tbsp olive oil

Squeezed out orange rinds

2 tsp sherry vinegar

Cook the endive as above, replacing the soy with 1 tablespoon of sherry vinegar and omitting the Chinese 5 spice. Keep warm.

Prepare the oranges by cutting off the top and base of the skin, then cut away the rest, following the contour of the orange, and slice into rounds. Make a dressing by pouring any pan juices from the endive into a jug and whisk with the olive oil, juice from squeezed out orange peels and the sherry vinegar. Season. To assemble, arrange the caramelized endives, lentils, orange slices and mozzarella or burrata over four plates. Sprinkle over the capers and drizzle over the dressing. Garnish with a few thyme leaves.

SMOTHERED COLLARD GREENS

SERVES 4

500g (1lb 2oz) collard greens, well washed

1 tbsp olive oil or dripping

100g (3½oz) bacon lardons or any type of fatty, smoked meat

1 onion, finely chopped

3 garlic cloves, finely chopped

1 tbsp cider vinegar

100ml (3½fl oz) stock (preferably chicken or smoked ham) or water

Sea salt and freshly ground black pepper

This recipe is a bit of an anomoly as collard greens cook so differently to every other type of green. They can be cooked fast to an al dente texture, but they really come into their own when they have a much longer cooking time – and by this I don't mean adding an extra minute, but taking it up to 15 minutes. This might seem crazy, but when you consider that collard greens are frequently cooked for a couple of hours, it doesn't seem so long in comparison. This would ruin most greens – cabbage, for example, would become soggy and sulphurous – but collard greens take on a tender, silky quality without becoming waterlogged and have a wonderful flavour – slightly acidic, slightly spicy. If you do want them slightly more al dente, reduce the cooking time to 10 minutes.

For a very long time it was virtually impossible to buy collard greens in the UK – you had to grow them yourself. But that has changed recently as they are being grown commercially in Cornwall. Well worth trying.

Shred the greens, removing any really wood stems. Heat the olive oil or dripping in your pressure cooker and add the bacon lardons or similar and the onion. Fry until the bacon is crisp and has rendered out some fat, then stir in the garlic.

Add the greens to the pot, then pour in the vinegar and stock or water. Stir to combine everything, then press the greens down a bit. Season with salt and pepper. Bring up to high pressure and cook for 15 minutes, then remove from the heat and release pressure naturally.

BRUSSELS SPROUTS WITH BACON AND CRANBERRIES

SERVES 4

1 tbsp olive oil

100g (3½oz) smoked bacon lardons

400g (14oz) Brussels sprouts, trimmed and halved

50ml (1¾fl oz) sherry – a nutty one like oloroso, or Marsala or water

1 portion cranberries in oloroso (see page 343)

100g (3½oz) roast chestnuts (optional)

Sea salt and freshly ground black pepper

If you want firm but tender, green, sweet, nutty Brussels sprouts gracing your Christmas table, this is the recipe for you. To make it less seasonal, take out the cranberries and chestnuts.

Heat the olive oil in your pressure cooker. Add the bacon and sauté until much of the fat has rendered out and it is crisp. Add the Brussels sprouts, arranging them cut-side down as much as possible, and sautéing for a couple more minutes at a high heat until they have taken on some colour. Season with salt and pepper.

Pour in the sherry – it will hiss and create a lot of steam – and immediately close the lid and bring to high pressure. Cook for 1 minute for al dente Brussels sprouts, 1½ minutes for slightly more tender. Fast release, then stir in the cranberries and chestnuts, if using. Leave for a minute, then serve.

RED CABBAGE WITH CARAWAY AND DILL

SERVES 4

1 tbsp olive oil or 15g (½oz) butter

1 onion, finely chopped

1 tsp caraway seeds

1 tbsp cider vinegar

1 small red cabbage, finely shredded

1 small bunch of dill (optional)

Sea salt and freshly ground black pepper

Red cabbage is usually eaten very soft and braised, and you can do this with this dish too, just increase the cooking time from all of 1 minute to 3! This method will keep it fresh and richly coloured. You can also add grated apple, pear or quince and vary the aromatics. Red cabbage also goes very well with ginger and sesame.

Heat the oil or butter in your pressure cooker and add the onion. Sauté until starting to colour, then add the caraway seeds, cider vinegar and cabbage. Stir to combine for a couple of minutes, or until you see beads of water start to form on the cabbage. Season with salt and pepper. Close the lid and bring up to high pressure. Cook for 1–3 minutes, depending on the texture you want. Garnish with a few dill fronds.

STEAMED ARTICHOKES

Artichokes can take up to 45 minutes to steam conventionally, but pressure cooking takes on average 8 minutes. This means you can make short work of cooking a large batch if you are just after the hearts or if you are serving them whole with melted butter or a vinaigrette.

To prepare each artichoke, trim the stem to around 2cm (¾in), making sure it is perfectly perpendicular so the artichoke can stand up. Pull away the toughest, driest leaves from the base of the stem. Cut off the top centimetre of so of the artichoke, rubbing the cut area with lemon, and trim away any of the sharp spikes if you like. Add 1cm (½in) water to your pressure cooker and add the artichokes, stem-side down. It doesn't matter if they won't sit in a single layer, you can arrange more on top. Add any aromatics you like (perhaps some pared lemon zest) and close the lid. Bring up to high pressure and cook depending on size. An average-sized artichoke – around 200–250g (7–9oz) – will take 8 minutes, fast release. Very small ones will take 5 minutes, the largest 11 minutes.

ROASTING VEGETABLES

These vegetables are cooked in such a way that they have a degree of browning or charring you would expect from grilling or roasting, but remain very juicy too. There is a lot of sizzle with these roasting recipes and you do have to work fast!

ROAST CABBAGE

SERVES 4

2 tbsp olive oil

1 small hispi, white, Savoy or red cabbage, cut into wedges or steaks

Sea salt and freshly ground black pepper

The easiest way to do this – and the way that uses up space most effectively – is to cut the cabbage into wedges, but you could do it in steaks too.

Heat the oil in your pressure cooker. When it is hot, add the cabbage wedges and sear on the cut sides on a high heat – it should take 1–2 minutes to get a decent amount of colour. Make sure there is plenty of space between them, or cook in 2 batches – it takes so little time there is no hardship doing this. Season generously with salt and pepper. There should be quite a lot of steam.

Leaving the heat on high, pour in around 1–2 tablespoons of cold water, then as quickly as you can, put on the lid. There will be a lot of sizzling and steam created as soon as the water hits the base of the pressure cooker – you want to trap as much of that steam as possible. The pressure should rise very quickly. Cook for 1 minute at high pressure, then fast release. The cabbage will be al dente – a firm but knife-tender core, soft leaves and a good charring around the edges. If you want something more tender, increase the cooking time by 30 seconds.

VARIATIONS

This will also work with any vegetable you want to cut into wedges – types of endive, halved or whole Brussels sprouts, even little gems (do 0 minutes for these), as well as asparagus and sprouting broccoli.

You can also glaze the cut sides with anything you like for extra flavour. Try XO sauce, Marmite, chilli oil (perhaps mixed with a teaspoon of honey) or curry spices mixed with oil.

ROAST PUMPKIN OR SQUASH

SERVES 4

This is virtually the only way I cook pumpkin these days. Pressure-roasting like this has so many advantages – the flesh does not become waterlogged, which makes it the best option for puréeing, and it cooks best in large, unpeeled wedges so is easier to prepare, especially useful for pumpkin that has difficult-to-remove skin. Leaving the skin on helps the pumpkin keep its integrity and it can be easily removed after cooking – or, as the pressure cooker will have softened it – it will be good to eat and full of fibre either as is or blitzed into a soup.

Follow the instructions for roast cabbage on the previous page, but cook for 2–3 minutes at high pressure before fast releasing. Glazing the pumpkin or squash will also work well – anything hot and spicy will offset sweetness, so try brushing with a hot sauce. Conversely anything sweet will help intensify it into a good place, especially if it starts to caramelize, so brushing with honey or maple syrup and sprinkling with herbs, such as dried thyme or sage, will also work.

WHOLE ROAST SHALLOTS

SERVES 4

1 tbsp olive oil

500g (1lb 2oz) shallots, peeled

25g (1oz) butter

1 sprig of thyme

½ tsp sugar

75ml (2½fl oz) red wine or port

Sea salt and freshly ground black pepper

A really good side dish, these, but also very useful for adding to other dishes, such as the bourguignon variation on page 60 or the Coq au Vin on page 110.

Heat the olive oil in your pressure cooker. Add the shallots and fry on a high heat until brown in patches. Add the butter and, when it has foamed, add the thyme and sugar. Season with salt and pepper, then pour in the wine or port – it should sizzle! Close the lid. Bring up to pressure and cook for 4 minutes for small shallots, 5 for larger ones. Leave to drop pressure naturally.

ROAST CARROTS

SERVES 4

2 tbsp olive oil

500g (1lb 2oz) carrots, left whole or halved lengthways if very large

1 tsp cumin seeds

1 small bunch of mint or parsley, finely chopped

Sea salt and freshly ground black pepper

I like to use whole carrots for this, or carrots that have been sliced in half, lengthways. They look particularly attractive if you have bought a bunch and can trim at the base of their tops. You can add any whole spices to this before you cook them, such as in this example, which uses cumin. I also like drizzling with sesame oil after cooking and sprinkling with the seeds too.

Heat the olive oil in your pressure cooker. When it is getting close to smoke point, add the carrots and sauté, shaking regularly, until they take on a little colour. Add the cumin seeds and season with salt and pepper. Add a couple of tablespoons of water and quickly close the lid. Bring up to high pressure and cook for 2-3 minutes, depending on the thickness of the carrots. Fast release and sprinkle with the fresh herbs.

VARIATION

Roast Root Vegetables
Any root vegetables can be roasted in a similar way, with the exception of peeled, floury potatoes that will give out starch and are likely to stick if your pressure cooker isn't non-stick. To get round this, line the base of your pressure cooker with a round of Teflon-coated fabric. The same method/timings will work with parsnips, celeriac (celery root), turnips and skin-on new potatoes. Don't be afraid to play around with flavours – you can even add maple syrup or honey to intensify the sweetness without any issues.

ROAST CAULIFLOWER OR BROCCOLI FLORETS

SERVES 4

2 tbsp olive, coconut or neutral-tasting oil

½ tsp each mustard and cumin seeds

1 tsp ground turmeric

1 cauliflower or romanesco, broken up into florets, or the equivalent in broccoli

Juice of ½ lemon

A few chilli flakes

50g (1¾oz) hard cheese, such as Cheddar, grated (optional)

A couple of sprigs of coriander (cilantro), finely chopped

Sea salt and freshly ground black pepper

This is such a useful dish. You can spend as long as you like browning the cauliflower, and vary the spices. It can then be added to a whole host of meals – see it paired with the braised quinoa and butterbean dish on page 202. Or – and this is one of my favourite things to do – just shove it into warm pittas with loads of coriander (cilantro) and a raita or tahini dressing.

Heat the oil in your pressure cooker. When it is hot, add the mustard and cumin seeds. Stir in the turmeric when the seeds start popping, then add the cauliflower or broccoli. Turn over in the oil until it is well dappled with turmeric, then season with salt and pepper. Cook for a couple of minutes until the cauliflower starts to brown.

Working very quickly, pour in the lemon juice and immediately close the lid. There should be enough steam generated for the pressure gauge to come up to pressure pretty instantly. For very al dente cauliflower, release pressure immediately; for just tender, leave for 30 seconds; for slightly softer, leave for 1 minute. Any more, and the cauliflower will turn to mush.

If using the cheese, heat your grill and transfer the cauliflower to an ovenproof dish. Sprinkle with the chilli flakes and cheese, then grill for a couple of minutes until the cheese has melted and started to brown. Serve sprinkled with the coriander (cilantro).

ROAST PEPPERS

SERVES 4

2 tbsp olive oil

2–4 peppers, halved and deseeded

This is the method to use when you want to peel your peppers – the pressure cooker makes the cooking faster and the skins are easier to remove, too. If you want roast peppers with the skins on, fast release instead.

Heat the olive oil in your pressure cooker. When it is really hot, add the peppers, skin-side down, and cook for a couple of minutes until the skin starts to blister and char in places. Have your lid ready, then throw in 50ml (1¾fl oz) water and immediately put the lid on – you will hopefully contain all the splutter and steam. Leave the peppers to cook at high pressure for 1 minute, then leave to drop pressure naturally. By this time, the steam will have done its job and the peppers should be easy to peel.

PEPPERS AGRODOLCE

SERVES 4

4 tbsp olive oil

1 red onion, cut into slim wedges

1 large red pepper, cut into thick slices

1 green pepper, cut into thick slices

2 garlic cloves, very thinly sliced

3–4 anchovies, finely chopped

8 green olives

1 tbsp capers, rinsed

1 piece of lemon zest, finely chopped

½ tsp chilli flakes

1 tsp brown sugar

1 tbsp red wine vinegar

Sea salt and freshly ground black pepper

This takes just a few minutes to make, but it is one of those dishes that does well when allowed to settle for a while. At the very least, leave to cool to room temperature before eating, but preferably leave for at least 24 hours, and eat it at room temperature.

Good as a light lunch or supper dish, with decent bread, but I also like using it as a garnish to the lamb and lentil dish on page 244.

Heat the olive oil in your pressure cooker. When it is hot, add the red onion and sauté for a couple of minutes, then add the peppers and cook for a couple of minutes more. Stir in all the remaining ingredients, then season with salt and pepper.

Close the lid and bring up to high pressure. Cook for 1 minute only and fast release.

WAYS TO COOK POTATOES

Here are a few useful cooking methods and timings for potatoes.

How to Bake Potatoes and Sweet Potatoes

This was one I was very sceptical about – I love the skin on a baked potato and couldn't imagine that I could get anything close to it in the pressure cooker. I was wrong about that – the interior texture of the potato is exactly what you would want – dry and fluffy, and the skin will also be dry enough to be palatable. You can also crisp it up under a hot grill for 2–3 minutes, turning regularly.

This is also the ideal way to cook potatoes for mashing, especially if you are using them to make gnocchi – the flesh will stay very dry and that means you won't end up with a gluey texture. It is especially important for the brandade recipe on page 155.

Put 2cm (¾in) water in the base of your pressure cooker. Pierce your potatoes (white or sweet) all over with a skewer – make sure you push it in right to the middle. This will help them cook but will also stop the skins splitting, important because as they cook and the moisture in the potatoes turns to steam, it will want to escape.

Cook at high pressure as follows:

Smallish (100–150g/3½–5½oz) potatoes – 10 minutes

200–250g (7–9oz) potatoes – up to 15 minutes

Anything larger – 20 minutes

Allow to drop pressure naturally. Your potatoes are ready to use.

Mashed Potatoes

For the driest mashed potatoes, I use the baking method above, but for normal everyday mash, I use one of these methods, depending on how much time I have.

Method 1: For ultra-quick mashed potatoes, simply coat the base of your pressure cooker with water – no more than 5mm – then add the peeled potatoes, cut into chunks. Season with salt. Bring up to high pressure, cook for 3 minutes, then fast release. Strain off any liquid. You will find that the potatoes right on the base of the cooker will have cooked more than those above, almost to the point of disintegration, but that doesn't really matter so much here. Mash directly in the pan or push through a ricer, adding butter and milk as you wish.

Method 2: This will give you more evenly cooked, drier potatoes. Put 1cm (½in) water in the base of your pressure cooker. Arrange chunks of peeled potatoes in your steamer basket and season with salt. Bring up to high pressure and cook for 5 minutes, then fast release. Serve as is or mash as you like.

To make a mash using potatoes and any other type of root vegetable, cut the root vegetables into slightly smaller chunks and sit below the potatoes. Cook for the same length of time. Separate the potatoes from other root vegetables before mashing as other root vegetables – especially celeriac (celery root) and swede (rutabaga) – have a higher water content and less starch. Once you have mashed them, put them on a gentle heat so some of the liquid steams off before mixing with the potato.

To make a garlic mash: Drop ½ head of garlic, unpeeled, into the water before adding the steamer basket of potatoes. After cooking, squeeze out the garlic flesh and beat into the mashed potato along with plenty of butter.

To make skordalia: Cook garlic potatoes as above, but reserve 1 garlic clove and crush it. Add this raw, and beat in 50ml (1¾fl oz) olive oil and 1 tablespoon of red wine vinegar. This is often done in a blender, but I prefer to use a potato ricer and beat in the olive oil and vinegar by hand.

To make colcannon: Make the mashed potatoes as above. Heat 25g (1oz) butter in your pressure cooker and add 100g (3½oz) diced bacon. Fry until browned, then stir in 250g (9oz) shredded green or Savoy cabbage and a few sliced spring onions (scallions). Bring up to high pressure and release immediately, then stir in the mashed potato along with 100ml (3½fl oz) double (heavy) cream and another 25g (1oz) butter.

Crushed potatoes: This is a favourite thing in my house. Cut unpeeled floury or waxy potatoes into 2cm (¾in) dice. Steam as above for 3 minutes. Heat 25g (1oz) butter in a frying pan (skillet) and add the potatoes. Leave for several minutes before stirring, so some browning occurs, then press lightly with the back of a wooden spoon to break them up, continuing to stir and cook for a few more minutes.

Par-boiled Potatoes for Roasting

Pressure cooking will give you quite fragile potatoes – and parsnips for that matter – so par-boiling should be kept to a minimum. Follow the instructions for steaming above, but cook for just 1 minute at high pressure and fast release. This will cook the potatoes just long enough to allow for the skins to fluff up while they finish cooking in the oven.

Steamed New or Salad Potatoes

For really quick potatoes, cook in a splash of water in the base of your pressure cooker for 3 minutes, or in the steamer basket for 5–6 minutes. Add aromatics for flavour – a few sprigs of mint for example– and douse in plenty of butter. If I'm using them for potato salad, I will steam and cook for an extra minute – I really like it when the flesh starts to crack and can take on more dressing.

Sautéed New or Salad Potatoes

Heat 2 tablespoons of olive oil in your pressure cooker. When the oil is very hot, add 500g (1lb 2oz) potatoes (left whole) and sauté on a high heat until starting to take on some colour. Stir in 1 teaspoon of dried herbs, 1 teaspoon of lemon zest and a few unpeeled garlic cloves. Season with salt and pepper, splash in 2–3 tablespoons of water, immediately close the lid and bring up to high pressure. Cook for 3 minutes, then fast release, keeping the poached garlic to use in other dishes. Any potatoes that need to be cut up for size are likely to stick. Adding the water will help release them, but you can also sauté using Teflon-coated fabric as described in the Variation on page 265.

VEGETABLE GRATINS

Vegetable-based gratins can take an extremely long time to bake in the oven, and that's even when you have par-boiled some of the vegetables first. So I was determined to make them work in the pressure cooker and have come up with two methods. I have included both as there are advantages and disadvantages to each.

Either way, the pressure cooker method compresses 2 stages of cooking into one – there is no need to par-cook the vegetables first. The recipe for gratin dauphinois describes both methods in detail and gives lots of ideas on how to vary it, which will hopefully help you convert your own favourite recipes.

GRATIN DAUPHINOIS

SERVES 4

15g (½oz) butter

1 garlic clove, cut in half

500g (1lb 2oz) potatoes of your choice, finely sliced

Nutmeg, for grating

1 tsp plain (all-purpose) flour

150ml (5fl oz) whipping cream

Sea salt

With this, it is up to you what type of potato you use – I use this recipe interchangeably with both floury and waxy. The floury potatoes will release more starch and give you a denser finish. It is also up to you whether you peel the potatoes or not. I tend not to, because I want the nutrition from the potato skins, but it won't affect the finished dish in any way if you don't.

I have given two methods here. The first involves arranging the potatoes in an ovenproof dish, the second cooks the potatoes directly in the main body of the pressure cooker, which shaves off quite a bit of time. There are pros and cons for each method – the first takes longer and you won't be able to cook quite as much, but you can easily put it under the grill to brown and it will look good on the table. The second method is faster and you can make a larger batch – but unless you are using the sauté-pan-sized pressure cooker, it won't fit under the grill and is more awkward for serving at the table. It also works better if you use Teflon-coated fabric.

Method 1: Rub a little of the butter over an ovenproof dish – the dimensions don't matter, as long as it will fit into your pressure cooker. Rub the garlic halves over the butter. Arrange the slices of potato in the dish, seasoning with salt and an occasional rasp of nutmeg as you go. Gently whisk the flour into the whipping cream, then add 2 tablespoons of water and pour over the potatoes.

Cut a round of baking paper to fit just inside the baking dish. Scrunch it up to stop it rolling so it will lie flat. Dot the top of the potatoes with the remaining butter, then lay the baking paper on top.

Put 2cm (¾in) water in the base of your pressure cooker and add a trivet. Place the dish on top of the trivet. Close the lid and bring up to high pressure. Cook for 8 minutes, then remove from the heat and leave to drop pressure naturally. Put under a hot grill to brown the top layer of potatoes if you like.

Method 2: This method can easily double the quantity on the previous page. Melt the butter in the base of your pressure cooker, add the garlic and sauté for 1 minute. Remove from the heat and arrange the slices of potato over the butter, seasoning with salt and an occasional rasp of nutmeg as you go and pouring over the cream mixture as before. Cut a round of baking paper to fit inside the pressure cooker and butter one side of it. Place this, butter-side down, on top of the potatoes.

Close the lid and bring up to high pressure. Cook for 3 minutes, then remove from the heat. Fast release if you like, but it will be better if you leave to stand for a few minutes before releasing any remaining pressure. If you are using the sauté pressure cooker, you can triple wrap the handles with foil and put under a hot grill to brown, if you like.

VARIATIONS

These variations – most of which I would happily eat as a main meal – can be made using either of the methods.

Vary the vegetables: Replace some or all of the potato with any root vegetables, firm-fleshed pumpkin or squash. Celeriac (celery root), parsnips, Jerusalem artichokes and thinly sliced beetroot work especially well.

Layer with other vegetables: Most non-root vegetables give out a lot of water, so it is best to cook them first to stop them flooding your gratin. You can do this conventionally or using the pressure cooker, just making sure you strain them off or squeeze any liquid out of any greens. Try a combination of fresh and dried mushrooms, sautéed in butter or oil until collapsed and dry, the caramelized onions on page 331, the buttered leeks on page 255 or any quickly steamed greens (see page 248).

Introduce fish or meat: Quickly sautéed smoked meat, slices of corned beef or shredded smoked fish, such as smoked mackerel or trout, sprinkled through work really well. So would finely chopped anchovies.

Turn into a crumble: Either finish under the grill or sauté the topping as for pangrattato.

Use butter: You can make a really good pommes Anna by melting around 75g (2½oz) butter and using it to brush each layer of potatoes. Or try with other root vegetables – one of my favourites is a version that infuses grated ginger in the butter and is used to brush over carrot, firm-fleshed pumpkin and christophine (chayote) when I can get it.

Make it vegan: Use 1 tablespoon of oil in place of the butter and coconut milk in place of the cream and milk – especially good with some heat.

QUICK KORMA

SERVES 4

1 onion, roughly chopped

4 garlic cloves, peeled

15g (½oz) piece ginger, peeled

1 tbsp coconut oil

1 tbsp mild curry powder or
½ tsp each ground cinnamon,
cardamom, coriander, turmeric,
fenugreek, plus a pinch of cloves

1 bay leaf

1 small tomato, puréed

100g (3½oz) ground almonds

1 red pepper, cut into thick strips

250g (9oz) cooked chickpeas
(garbanzo beans) or butter
(lima) beans

200g (7oz) squash or pumpkin,
or aubergine (eggplant), peeled
and cut into large chunks

½ white or romanesco
cauliflower, broken into florets

100g (3½oz) green beans
(optional)

100ml (3½fl oz) double (heavy)
cream or yogurt

Sea salt and freshly ground
black pepper

TO GARNISH

Coriander (cilantro)

Green chillies, sliced

This is one you can easily take shortcuts with. You don't have to purée the onion, garlic and ginger if you don't want to, you can just fry in the oil or use 4 tablespoons of the onion, garlic and ginger purée on page 329 instead. You can also vary the vegetables, just making sure you take into account their normal cooking times when you decide at what point to add them.

First, put the onion, garlic and ginger into a small food processor with a splash of water and blitz to a smooth paste. Heat the oil in your pressure cooker and add the paste. Fry for a couple of minutes until intensely aromatic, then add the curry powder or spices, the bay leaf and tomato. Fry for another minute or two.

Stir in the ground almonds and season with plenty of salt and pepper. Add the red pepper, chickpeas (garbanzo beans) or butter (lima) beans and squash, pumpkin or aubergine (eggplant) and pour in 150ml (5fl oz) water. Close the lid and bring up to high pressure. Cook for 2 minutes, then fast release.

Add the cauliflower and green beans, if using. Bring up to high pressure again and fast release after just 30 seconds. Stir in the double (heavy) cream or yogurt and leave to simmer very gently for a few minutes. Garnish with coriander (cilantro) sprigs and finely sliced green chillies.

BRIAM

SERVES 4

4 tbsp olive oil

1 onion, sliced into wedges

1 red pepper, diced

1 green pepper, diced

600g (1lb 5oz) waxy potatoes, thinly sliced

100g (3½oz) fresh tomatoes, finely diced

1 tsp dried or fresh oregano

2 garlic cloves, finely chopped

2 tsp red wine vinegar

12 green olives, pitted

1 large courgette (zucchini), sliced

Sea salt and freshly ground black pepper

This is a favourite Greek classic, often served with grilled meat or a baked fish. It is usually oven baked, but oil-rich, and works really well in the pressure cooker in a fraction of the time. As the cooking time is so short, you could turn it into a fish dish with a little adjustment, see Variation for details.

Heat the olive oil in your pressure cooker. When hot, add the onion and peppers. Fry for a couple of minutes, just to get started, then add the potatoes. Cook, stirring regularly, for around 5 minutes.

Add the tomatoes, oregano, garlic, red wine vinegar and olives. Season with salt and pepper and stir. Add the courgette (zucchini) and stir to coat, but then try to make sure all the courgette slices sit on top of everything else.

Close the lid and bring up to high pressure. Cook for 1 minute if you want the courgette still quite al dente; 2 minutes for slightly softer. Fast release.

VARIATION

To turn into a one-pot fish meal, take 4 thick fish fillets or steaks, season well and place on top of the courgettes (zucchini). Cook for 3 minutes at low pressure and fast release, but gently.

ALOO GOBI

SERVES 4

1 tbsp coconut oil

1 large onion, finely sliced

1 tsp mustard seeds

1 tsp nigella seeds

5 garlic cloves, crushed to a paste

1 tsp garam masala

1 tbsp tomato purée

500g (1lb 2oz) new potatoes, halved if large

1 small or ½ large cauliflower, broken into florets

2 tbsp coriander (cilantro) stems, finely chopped

Sea salt and freshly ground black pepper

Easily adaptable this, as the cauliflower cooks in the same time as any greens, so you could turn it into saag or palak aloo.

Heat the oil in your pressure cooker, then add the onion. Fry on a medium–high heat until starting to brown around the edges. Add the mustard and nigella seeds. When they start popping, add the garlic, garam masala and tomato purée along with plenty of salt and pepper. Stir for a couple of minutes until the tomato purée starts to separate, then add 150ml (5fl oz) water. Stir thoroughly.

Add the potatoes and stir to coat with the liquid. Close the lid and bring up to high pressure. Adjust the heat and cook for 5 minutes, then fast release. Stir in the cauliflower and coriander (cilantro), making sure the cauliflower is well coated in the sauce. Bring up to high pressure again and then immediately fast release.

AUBERGINE AND TOMATO BRAISE

SERVES 4

3 tbsp olive oil

2 aubergines (eggplants), thickly sliced or cut into chunks and salted if time

1 large onion, finely chopped

3 garlic cloves, finely chopped

1 large sprig of thyme or 1 tsp dried oregano

1 hot red chilli, finely chopped, or ½ tsp chilli flakes

100ml (3½fl oz) red or white wine

400g (14oz) canned or fresh tomatoes, chopped

Sea salt and freshly ground black pepper

How I approach the flavour of this braise often depends on the time of year. In the later summer months, when sweet tomatoes are ripe and abundant, I prefer to make it with fresh tomatoes and white wine – the result is lighter. Canned tomatoes and red wine are better suited to the winter months.

Heat half the olive oil in your pressure cooker. Add the aubergines (eggplants) and fry briskly until lightly browned on all sides. Remove from the cooker and add the onion. Sauté for a few minutes until starting to look translucent. Stir in the garlic, herbs and chilli or chilli flakes, then return the aubergines to the cooker. Pour in the wine and allow to bubble up and reduce down, then add the tomatoes. Season with salt and pepper.

Close the lid and bring up to high pressure. Cook for 5 minutes. Leave to drop pressure naturally.

VARIATIONS

Stir through 500g (1lb 2oz) white beans and add plenty of chopped herbs. Add cheese as below.

Cook with 400g (14oz) new potatoes and replace one of the aubergines (eggplants) with thickly sliced mushrooms or courgettes (zucchini). Serve with a green salad.

To turn into an all-in-one pasta dish
Follow the recipe above. After you have allowed the wine to reduce, stir in 400g (14oz) dry pasta. Add enough water to cover the pasta and season with salt and pepper. Pour the tomatoes over the top. Bring up to high pressure, then cook for 5 minutes. Fast release. Top with cheese and replace the lid without sealing, just to melt it through, or transfer to an ovenproof dish and put under a hot grill.

ROAST AUBERGINES WITH MISO AND HONEY

SERVES 2 AS A MAIN OR 4 AS PART OF A MULTI-DISH MEAL

2 aubergines (eggplants), trimmed

2 tbsp miso paste

2 tbsp honey or ginger syrup

1 tsp sesame oil

A generous pinch of chilli flakes or mild chilli powder

2 tbsp olive oil

TO SERVE

Sesame seeds

3 spring onions (scallions), shredded

If you have time to salt your aubergines (eggplants), you will really notice a difference in texture as it will help remove excess water. Simply prepare as stated in the recipe, sprinkle with salt and weigh down in a colander for at least 30 minutes.

Cut the aubergines (eggplants) in half lengthways and cut a crosshatch pattern in the flesh, making sure you cut just short of the skin. Salt if you have time, then pat dry.

Mix the miso, honey, sesame oil and chilli flakes or powder together. Brush this over the cut sides of the aubergines, pushing it into the cuts.

Heat the olive oil in your pressure cooker. Add the aubergines, cut-side down, and fry for at least a couple of minutes until they start to smell caramelized and are browning around the edges. Flip over and cook for a further minute. Add 50ml (1¾fl oz) water if using a shallow pressure cooker, 75ml (2½fl oz) if using a larger one.

Close the lid and bring up to high pressure. Cook for 1–2 minutes depending on size, then remove from the heat. Allow to drop pressure naturally. Serve garnished with sesame seeds and shredded spring onions (scallions).

VARIATIONS
You can use exactly the same method with different flavours.

Pomegranate Molasses
Mix 2 tablespoons of pomegranate molasses with 2 crushed garlic cloves in place of the miso and honey and garnish with chilli or Aleppo pepper flakes. Serve with ricotta, labneh or feta sprinkled with finely chopped preserved lemon (see page 336), a little za'atar, lots of fresh mint and perhaps a garnish of pomegranate seeds. And to make it a little more substantial, toss 250g (9oz) cooked chickpeas (garbanzo beans) in the pressure cooker when you have removed the aubergines (eggplants), just to warm through, then dress with a little olive oil.

Roast with Curry Leaves
Brush the aubergines (eggplants) with olive oil and sprinkle with salt. When you have browned them, throw in a few fresh curry leaves and 1 teaspoon of mustard seeds. When the seeds start to pop, add the liquid and proceed as above. This is absolutely delicious turned into a dip. Purée and mix with 200ml (7fl oz) thick yogurt, chilli flakes and lots of chopped mint. Sprinkle with a little sumac, if you like.

SALAD OLIVIER

SERVES 4

200g (7oz) waxy or salad potatoes, diced

100g (3½oz) carrots, diced

100g (3½oz) celeriac (celery root) or turnip, diced

50g (1¾oz) frozen peas

50g (1¾oz) green beans, cut into small rounds

2 tbsp mayonnaise

1 large gherkin (around 50g/1¾oz), finely chopped

1 tbsp capers, finely chopped

1 tsp mustard, preferably tarragon (optional)

1 small bunch of dill, finely chopped

OPTIONAL EXTRAS

50g (1¾oz) chopped cooked chicken or ham

¼ white onion or 1 shallot, very finely chopped

A few florets of cauliflower, blanched at 0 minute HP, chopped

2 hard-boiled eggs (see page 38), whites and yolks finely chopped separately

This is such a staple in so many cuisines; I avoided it for years because the one we were forced to eat at school was very unpalatable, made with packets of dehydrated vegetables. But thanks to Italian food writer Stefano Arturi, who persuaded me to try his 'Insalata Russa', I now understand how good it can be.

Put the potatoes, carrots and the celeriac (celery root) or turnip in a steamer basket. Arrange the green beans on top. Put the peas in the bottom of your pressure cooker and add the trivet and steamer basket. Bring up to high pressure and cook for 1 minute. Fast release. Remove the basket from the pressure cooker and strain the peas, adding to the other vegetables.

Put the mayonnaise in a bowl with the gherkin and capers and the add mustard, if using. Add the still warm vegetables, the dill and any of the optional extras, then gently stir everything together. Conventional wisdom says this is best left to chill in the fridge and the flavours are good this way – however, it is still wonderful just warm or at room temperature.

CHICKPEAS, RED PEPPERS, KALE AND SQUASH IN A PEANUT SAUCE

SERVES 4

1 tbsp olive or groundnut oil

1 onion, cut into wedges

1 red pepper, diced

200g (7oz) squash or pumpkin, peeled and diced

1 tsp garlic powder or 2 garlic cloves, finely chopped

1–3 tsp hot sauce or 1 Scotch bonnet or similar, finely chopped

1 bay leaf

200g (7oz) canned chopped tomatoes

250g (9oz) cooked chickpeas (garbanzo beans)

150g (5½oz) kale, roughly torn

100g (3½oz) smooth or crunchy peanut butter

Juice of ½ lime

Sea salt and freshly ground black pepper

TO SERVE

Coriander (cilantro)

Hot sauce

Lime wedges

This is a very quick storecupboard meal that can be varied according to what vegetables and cooked beans or pulses you have to hand. I have deliberately made it using non-perishable aromatics, but you can use fresh if you have it. I have used chickpeas (garbanzo beans) here, but I also really like butter (lima) beans in this dish.

Heat the oil in your pressure cooker. When hot, add the onion and red pepper. Cook on a high heat for 2–3 minutes, just until the onion starts to crisp round the edges, then stir in the squash, garlic and hot sauce or chilli. Add the bay leaf, tomatoes and chickpeas and season with salt and pepper. Add 75ml (2½fl oz) water and stir through the kale leaves.

Bring up to high pressure and cook for 3 minutes, then fast release. Mix the peanut butter with 100ml (3½fl oz) water and stir until smooth and pourable. Add a little more water if necessary – the texture and thickness of peanut butter varies enormously. Pour around the vegetables, stirring to combine, but really keeping it to an absolute minimum. Simmer for 2–3 minutes, then taste for seasoning. Add the lime juice a little at a time until you are satisfied with the flavour.

Serve garnished with coriander (cilantro) and with hot sauce and lime wedges at the table.

VARIATIONS

This can be turned into a meat dish and works best with chicken, lamb or goat. If adding diced chicken, you can keep the cooking times exactly as above, just adding the chicken along with the onion and making sure it is browned on all sides. To add diced lamb or goat, brown with the onions (not the peppers) and cook at high pressure for 15 minutes. Then add in everything else and proceed as above.

Once the peanut butter has been added to this dish it is advisable not to attempt to bring it up to high pressure again – it will thicken very quickly and if using a stovetop cooker it will burn on the bottom before you reach high pressure, and will set off the burn alarm on an electric version. So if you want to add any more fragile vegetables to this, for example, cauliflower, broccoli or less robust greens, you should cook those first, then add back to the cooker to warm through with the peanut sauce.

BAKED CAMEMBERT WITH POTATOES AND MUSHROOMS

SERVES 4 AS A STARTER

1 Camembert or similar

1 garlic clove, finely sliced

A few sprigs of thyme or rosemary

A few drops of truffle oil, plus extra to serve

2–3 tbsp white wine, vermouth or dry sherry

250g (9oz) new potatoes

150g (5½oz) small chestnut mushrooms

Sea salt and freshly ground black pepper

TO SERVE (OPTIONAL)

Breakfast radishes

Wedges of fennel and endive

Cherry tomatoes

Cornichons

Caper berries

Thanks to the speed of this recipe, a baked cheese has become a regular weekend lunch in my house. The potatoes and mushrooms are steamed together in the same pot as the cheese but if you prefer, you can cook them in the bottom of the pressure cooker with the cheese sitting on top in the steamer basket – the cooking time is the same.

First prepare the cheese. Remove it from its packaging and place on a piece of baking paper. Put in a round, ovenproof ceramic dish – you can get special cheese 'bakers' or similar. Cut slits in the top and push in the garlic slices and herbs. Drizzle over a little truffle oil and spoon over the white wine, vermouth or dry sherry. Fold the baking paper over the cheese – scrunching it a little should keep it in place.

Arrange the potatoes and mushrooms on the base of a steamer insert and season with salt and pepper. Balance the cheese dish on top. Put 2cm (¾in) water in the base of your pressure cooker, add a trivet, and place the steamer on top. Close the lid and bring up to high pressure. Cook for 4–6 minutes, depending on the size and ripeness of your cheese. Allow to drop pressure naturally.

Remove from the cooker and drizzle over a little more oil. Serve at the table with the potatoes, mushrooms and any or all of the suggested crudités.

STUFFED RED PEPPERS

SERVES 4

4 red peppers

1 tbsp olive oil

1 large red onion, finely chopped

1 courgette (zucchini), finely diced or coarsely grated

3 garlic cloves, finely chopped

50g (1¾oz) pine nuts

75g (2½oz) hard cheese, such as manchego, grated

100g (3½oz) couscous

Zest of 1 lemon

1 small bunch of basil or mint leaves, finely chopped

TO TOP

2 balls mozzarella

This is the sort of retro meal I never used to do when it meant switching on the oven, but now happens quite regularly when I can stuff a pepper with a few odds and sods from the fridge and cobble together a quick meal. These make a great receptacle for leftovers, especially grains, cooked meat, lentils.

First prepare the red peppers. Cut the top 1cm (½in) off each one and trim the core underneath the stem. Tip out any seeds and trim any excessive white membrane. Set aside.

Heat the olive oil in a small frying pan (skillet) and add the onion and courgette (zucchini). Fry on a medium–high heat just until the courgettes have started to collapse, then add the garlic and cook for a minute or two. Leave to cool, then stir in the remaining ingredients. Pack into the red peppers, piling them up quite high as they will reduce a little during the cooking time.

Put 2cm (¾in) water in your pressure cooker. Arrange the peppers in a ceramic dish or in a steamer basket and leave uncovered. Put on the pepper 'caps'. Bring up to pressure and cook for 5 minutes, then fast release. Remove the pepper 'caps', tear the mozzarella over the top and either leave on a low heat for the mozzarella to gently melt, or put under a hot grill for a few minutes to brown.

VARIATIONS

You can also stuff and bake other vegetables, such as pumpkins and courgettes (zucchini).

2 small pumpkins or squash, cut in half, will take the same volume of filling as above, as will 4 round courgettes (zucchini). Small pumpkins will take 4 minutes, fast release, courgettes will take 3 minutes.

1 whole pumpkin (around 1kg/2lb 4oz is the ideal size to fit into a 6-litre/210fl oz pressure cooker) will take 8–10 minutes.

DESSERTS
AND BAKING

The majority of the recipes in this section are very dependent on what electric-pressure-cooker users call the 'Pot in Pot' method – this means you essentially use the pressure cooker as a bain-marie, or as a steam oven. This is much more versatile than it sounds and will produce all the sorts of puddings you would expect to make in this way – crème caramels, cheesecakes and baked fruits – but will also do an excellent job of making sponge puddings and cakes that still brown beautifully without risk of drying out.

I have to admit that making cakes in the pressure cooker is a relatively recent thing for me, but I am in favour of anything that helps me keep the oven off and I've been truly astounded by the results.

PRESSURE-COOKED FRUIT

There are several ways to use your pressure cooker when it comes to fruit. Firstly, to make very fast compotes and purées for use in jams (jellies) the method is simple. Put fruit (left whole if small, or diced/sliced) in the base of your pressure cooker, add a little sugar, perhaps some butter and any spices you like. Add the bare minimum of water – around 50–100ml (1¾–3½fl oz) only as the fruit will be giving out liquid as it cooks – then bring up to high pressure. For ripe fruit, regardless of what it is, I find that just about everything works in 0-3 minutes; even firm fruits such as quince. This is a faster method than baking and will result in fruit that will, for the most part, soften and break down to a compote.

For firmer textured fruit, see the recipes for roasting fruit, which work especially well with pears, quinces, firm apples and mangoes and pineapples.

You can also use the pressure cooker to skin fruit, which works very well with peaches, nectarines, firm plums and damsons. Simply score a cross on the base, pile into the steamer basket and bring up to low pressure. Fast release. The skins should drop right off. This even works with chestnuts, but you should bring up to high pressure, cook for 1 minute and leave to drop pressure naturally.

SAFFRON AND BAY POACHED PEARS

SERVES 4

Juice of ½ lemon

4 firm but ripe pears

2 bay leaves

A large pinch of saffron

250ml (9fl oz) white wine

200g (7oz) caster (superfine) sugar

This is a recipe that very much brings me joy – not just because it is sunshine in a bowl, but because it will transform the woodiest of pears into something worth eating. I specify ripe pears here – if you have unripe pears you need to use, just add another minute or two to the cooking time.

This is a recipe I will usually make ahead – preferably overnight – as the colour of the pears intensifies as they are left to infuse.

Fill a bowl with water and add the lemon juice. Peel the pears, leaving the stems intact if possible. Drop into the acidulated water until you are ready to cook them. Put in the pressure cooker and add the bay leaves, saffron and wine. Pour in the sugar, then add just enough water to cover.

Bring up to high pressure and cook for 3 minutes. Remove from the heat and leave to drop pressure naturally. Leave to cool in the poaching liquid, rolling around every so often until cool. Serve on their own or take half the liquid and reduce to a syrup and serve poured over the top.

BAKED FIGS

SERVES 4

6 figs

A pinch of ground cinnamon or cardamom

2 tbsp port or orange juice

1 tbsp honey

A couple of bay leaves (optional)

TO SERVE

Crème fraîche or strained yogurt

A drizzle of honey (optional)

A few drops of orange blossom water (optional)

2 tbsp flaked (slivered) almonds or pistachios, lightly toasted (optional)

This is a really useful way of cooking figs – when it is the time of year when they are plentiful, it is good to keep a couple of batches in the fridge to pair with yogurt for quick breakfasts or lunchbox desserts, sometimes with a sprinkling of granola over the top in place of the nuts.

Cut a cross in the figs from the tip all the way down to the base, but making sure they are still intact. Push the figs gently in the middle so the tips open out a little. Place in a baking dish – it is best if they are a snug fit, but it doesn't matter too much if they aren't.

Sprinkle with the spice, pour over the port or orange juice, then drizzle over the honey. Scrunch up the bay leaves a little, then tuck them in between the figs. Put a piece of foil over the baking dish.

Put a couple of centimetres of water in the pressure cooker and balance the baking dish on your trivet. Bring up to high pressure and cook for 6 minutes for small figs, up to 8 minutes for large ones. Fast release. You can serve just with the syrup from the baking dish and a spoonful of crème fraîche or yogurt, but it is really good with flavoured cream – simply stir in honey and a few drops of orange blossom water. Sprinkle with toasted nuts, if you like.

ROAST QUINCE

SERVES 4

1 tbsp olive oil

1 large quince, peeled, cored and cut into wedges or diced

15g (½oz) butter

2 tsp honey

This is the best way to cook quince before adding to sweet or savoury dishes.

Heat the olive oil in your pressure cooker. When it is hot, add the quince wedges and sear on both sides. Add the butter and drizzle over the honey. When the butter and honey have melted and some steam has generated, close the lid. Bring up to high pressure and cook for 2 minutes only. Fast release. The quince should be just tender throughout but still firm enough to keep its shape. It is now good for adding to other recipes (see Variation on page 73).

For a sweeter, more tender quince, suitable for desserts, double the amount of honey and increase the cooking time by 1 minute, or leave to drop pressure naturally.

BAKED RHUBARB

SERVES 4

15g (½oz) butter, plus extra for greasing

250g (9oz) rhubarb, cut into 3–4cm (1¼–1½in) lengths

Zest and juice of 1 mandarin or ½ orange

25g (1oz) caster (superfine) sugar

This cooking method will preserve the shape of the rhubarb – try it over ice cream or alongside the Cardamom Rice Pudding on page 298.

Take a ceramic dish that will comfortably fit into your pressure cooker and butter it. Add the rhubarb and citrus zest, tossing them together so the zest is evenly distributed, then pour in the juice. Sprinkle over the sugar and dot with butter.

Cover the dish with foil and place on top of the trivet in your pressure cooker. Close the lid and bring up to high pressure. Cook for 5 minutes and fast release. The rhubarb should have kept its shape and be knife tender and any juices in the dish should be syrupy.

STUFFED APPLES

SERVES 4

4 apples

2 tbsp light soft brown sugar

1 tbsp maple syrup

25g (1oz) butter

½ tsp ground cinnamon

A pinch of cloves

A rasp of nutmeg

50g (1¾oz) raisins or sultanas
(golden raisins)

1 tbsp bourbon or rum

25g (1oz) chopped pecans

Sea salt

This works best with smallish eating apples, particularly the firm-fleshed sort that don't easily collapse into a purée when you cook them. However, you can make them successfully with Bramleys, you just have to be very careful about the cooking times to prevent them from bursting. You can bake them cored and whole, or cut them in half and sprinkle the filling over them, both will work in the same time. It is important not to overcook them as if they start to steam internally they can easily burst – they will still taste wonderful but may need a bit of judicious camouflaging with cream or ice cream.

First, core the apples and pierce lightly all over with a skewer – this will help reduce the risk of bursting. Alternatively, cut in half and cut out the cores. Arrange in a round ceramic dish or in a lined steamer basket.

Mix the sugar, maple syrup, butter, spices and dried fruit together and add a pinch of salt. Stuff into or on the apples, then drizzle with the bourbon or rum. Sprinkle over the nuts.

Put 2cm (¾in) water in the base of your pressure cooker and add the trivet. Place the steamer basket or dish on top. Close the lid and bring up to high pressure. Cook for 5 minutes, then leave to drop pressure naturally.

CARDAMOM RICE PUDDING

SERVES 4

150g (5½oz) pudding or short-grain rice

900ml (31fl oz) whole milk

75g (2½oz) caster (superfine) sugar

40g (1½oz) butter

6 cardamom pods, lightly crushed

Sea salt

TO SERVE

1 portion Baked Rhubarb (see page 296)

If you take out the cardamom, this gives you a blueprint for any type of rice pudding you want to try. There are some suggestions in the Variations.

Put all the ingredients for the pudding into the pressure cooker and add a pinch of salt. Close the lid and bring up to high pressure. Cook for 15 minutes, then remove from the heat and allow to drop pressure naturally.

Set the cooker on a low heat and stir the pudding for a minute or two until it looks thick and creamy.

VARIATIONS

Replace the caster (superfine) sugar with dark muscovado sugar, and the cardamom pod with a split vanilla pod. Serve with the Marsala raisins on page 343.

Add herbs to flavour the rice: 1 fig leaf, 2 bay leaves or a handful of lemon verbena work beautifully.

Stir in 3 squares of dark chocolate at the end and serve with a quick cherry compote (put 250g/9oz pitted cherries in your pressure cooker and sprinkle with 2 tablespoons of sugar. Stir on a low heat until the sugar has dissolved, then add 50ml (1¾fl oz) water and the juice of ½ lemon. Bring up to high pressure, cook for 2 minutes, then leave to drop pressure naturally).

RASPBERRY AND LEMONGRASS JELLIES

SERVES 4

2 lemongrass stems, roughly bruised then sliced

500g (1lb 2oz) raspberries

Filtered or spring water

75g (2½oz) caster (superfine) sugar

Juice of ½ lemon

5 gelatine leaves, soaked in water

This uses the juice extraction method as described on page 344 for making jellies. It gives an intensely flavoured yet crystal-clear juice that does not have to be strained before using.

First, prepare your pressure cooker. Put 3cm (1¼in) water in the base and top with a folded up piece of fabric or a trivet. Put a steamer basket inside a bowl that will fit inside your pressure cooker and line with muslin (cheesecloth). Put the lemongrass stems in the bottom of the steamer basket and top with the raspberries (the raspberry juice will drip through the lemongrass taking on flavour as it drops into the bowl).

Cover the bowl with clingfilm (plastic wrap) and put in your pressure cooker. Bring up to high pressure and cook for 5 minutes, then allow to drop pressure naturally. The bowl should contain lemongrass-infused raspberry juice.

Measure the juice and add enough filtered or spring water to make it up to 500ml (17fl oz). Put in a saucepan with the sugar and lemon juice. Stir on a low heat until the sugar has dissolved. Drain the gelatine leaves and add to the saucepan. Stir until the gelatine has dissolved, then strain into a jug. Divide between 4 glasses and leave to set for several hours.

VARIATIONS

This is also good if you add 50ml (2fl oz) vodka – increase the gelatine to 6 leaves not 5. Or dispense with the lemongrass and replace 100ml (3½fl oz) of the water with a fairly sweet white wine.

CHOCOLATE LAVA PUDDINGS

SERVES 4

Melted butter or cake release spray, for greasing

125g (4½oz) dark chocolate (70% cocoa solids)

100g (3½oz) butter

2 tbsp dark or golden rum

2 eggs and 2 egg yolks

55g (2oz) golden caster (superfine) sugar

35g (1¼oz) plain (all-purpose) flour

TO SERVE

Cream or ice cream

These are dense, fudgy cakes with a liquid centre and are best served immediately as the centre will set over time. However, reheated and served with copious amounts of cream, they are still very good.

It is important to note with this particular pudding that your choice of cooking vessel will impact on how fast it cooks. Ramekins and individual aluminium pudding basins will take 6 minutes, anything thinner will shave it off to 5 minutes.

Brush 4 small ramekins with melted butter or use cake release spray.

Melt the chocolate, butter and rum together in a bowl, then stir until smooth. Beat the eggs, egg yolks and sugar together until mousse-like. Pour the chocolate mixture around the edge of the egg mixture, and sprinkle the flour on top. Fold together, as gently as you can, until the batter is a rich, dark brown.

Divide the mixture between the ramekins and place on the steamer basket. Pour a cup of just-boiled water into the pressure cooker, then balance the steamer basket on top of the trivet.

Close the lid and bring to high pressure. Cook for 6 minutes, then fast release. Turn the puddings out on to individual plates and serve immediately with cream or ice cream.

VARIATIONS

There are some wonderful ways to vary this. A simple way is to add a different flavoured centre. Try pushing 2–3 boozy cherries or 1 teaspoon of peanut butter into each individual ramekin, making sure they are completely covered by the chocolate batter.

CRÈME CARAMEL

MAKES 6 SMALL CARAMELS

Butter, for greasing

FOR THE CRÈME

500ml (17fl oz) whole milk

1 vanilla pod or ½ tsp vanilla extract

2 eggs and 4 egg yolks

100g (3½oz) caster (superfine) sugar

FOR THE CARAMEL

200g (7oz) granulated sugar

100ml (3½fl oz) water

The most important thing about a crème caramel is that smooth, slippery texture, which is much more achievable with small individual puddings rather than one big one.

First, butter 6 small ramekins. Put the milk into a saucepan with the vanilla and bring almost to the boil. Remove from the heat and leave to infuse.

Put the sugar and water for the caramel into a saucepan and dissolve slowly, brushing down from the sides with a dampened brush. When all the sugar has dissolved, turn up the heat and boil until the sugar has turned a a rich, fairly dark brown, being careful not to let it burn. Err on the side of caution, knowing that it will continue to cook for a short while after you remove it from the heat. Divide the caramel between the ramekins, swirling it round to coat the sides as well as the base. But be careful – the ramekins will quickly heat up from the caramel. Set aside.

To make the crème, reheat the milk to blood temperature, then strain. Whisk the eggs, yolks and sugar together until combined – the aim isn't for froth or mousse-like texture here. Pour the milk onto the eggs, stirring constantly, then strain through a sieve into a jug and leave to stand for a few minutes. If there are any air bubbles on the top, skim them off (or disperse if they are large), then divide the mixture between the ramekins.

Cover the ramekins with foil, then arrange in your pressure cooker – the easiest way to do this is to upturn a shallow steamer basket to give you a firm base. Make sure the water sits below the top of the basket, then add the ramekins, stacking them on top of one another if necessary. If you have a small pressure cooker, you might need to do this in two batches.

Bring up to high pressure and cook for 5 minutes for small ramekins, 4 minutes if you are cooking in metal basins. Remove from the heat and allow to drop pressure naturally, then check for doneness. A toothpick should come out clean. Cool down, then chill in the fridge for at least 3 hours – these are best served ice-cold.

CHOCOLATE AND VANILLA CHEESECAKE

SERVES 6-8

FOR THE BASE

125g (4½oz) biscuits (digestive/ Graham Crackers, shortbread, choc chip)

50g (1¾oz) butter

FOR THE FILLING

2 tbsp plain (all-purpose) flour or cornflour (cornstarch) (optional)

100g (3½oz) light soft brown sugar

425g (15oz) cream cheese

2 eggs

100ml (3½fl oz) sour cream

1 tsp vanilla extract

100g (3½oz) dark or milk chocolate, melted

Sea salt

TO SERVE

200g (7oz) cherry compote (shop-bought or see recipe on page 298)

I always make my cheesecakes in the pressure cooker these days, not just because of the time saved but because they never crack. Once you have cooked the cheesecake, it is really important to chill it overnight – this will allow it to relax and drop into that dense texture we expect from a baked cheesecake.

This is a simple, unsophisticated vanilla and chocolate version that is very popular in my household, especially if I serve it with cherry compote (see page 298). You could stir a couple of tablespoons through the cheesecake as well if you want to.

You can adapt any cheesecake recipe to work in the pressure cooker; I've given you another couple of options in the Variations, opposite. I have also given the option of adding a little flour to the recipe as it will make a denser, New-York-style cheesecake.

First, make the base. Wrap a 20cm (8in) loose-bottomed cake tin in foil – not to cover, just to make sure the base and sides are watertight. Then line the tin with clingfilm (plastic wrap) or just the base with Teflon-coated fabric. Crush the biscuits in a food processor or the old-fashioned way, using a bag and a rolling pin. Melt the butter in a saucepan and stir in the crumbs. Press into the lined tin and put in the fridge to chill.

To make the filling, an hour or so before starting, remove any filling ingredients from the fridge – the texture will be better if they are at room temperature when you start mixing them. If using, mix the plain (all-purpose) flour or cornflour (cornstarch) with the sugar and add a generous pinch of salt. Beat the cream cheese until smooth, then add in the sugar (or sugar/flour mixture if using), followed by the eggs and finally the sour cream and vanilla. The texture will be better if you do this by hand – you don't want to incorporate too much air. When your mixture is thick, smooth and lump free, take around one third of it and put into a separate bowl. Pour the melted chocolate into the smaller amount of mix, then stir until completely combined. Pour half of the plain mix on top of your prepared base, followed by all the chocolate mix and then the remaining plain mix. Very gently stir a couple of times to get a marbling effect. Do not do this too much as it is easy to overdo it and find you have pretty much combined it. Put around 2cm (¾in) water in your pressure cooker and put the trivet on top – make sure the trivet sits above the water level. Place the cake tin on a foil handle (see page 11) and fold down the sides, making sure they don't touch the cheesecake.

Bring up to high pressure and cook for 15 minutes. Remove from the heat and allow to drop pressure naturally. Open the lid – you will find that water will have collected on top of the cheesecake. Soak this up with a piece of kitchen towel. Leave to cool to room temperature, then transfer to the fridge to chill overnight.

VARIATIONS

Lemon, Raisin and Marsala Cheesecake
The New-York-style cheesecake works especially well with some grated lemon zest in the filling; serve with the raisins on page 343, using Marsala or oloroso in place of rum or tea.

Mandarin and Blueberry Cheesecake
Add the zest and juice of 1 mandarin to the filling. After pouring the filling over the base, dot with 150g (5½oz) tart blueberries. Some of these will burst during the cooking and bleed purple into the filling. Don't worry about the amount of liquid you will have to blot from the cheesecake after cooking – it will not affect the texture of the cheesecake once it has been chilled.

Coconut Dulce de Leche and Rum Cheesecake
Add 25g (1oz) toasted desiccated (shredded) coconut to the biscuit base. Add a few optional drops of coconut extract to the filling. Add 200g (7oz) canned dulce de leche (see page 334) to the filling and reduce the sugar to 50g (1¾oz). Cook as in the main recipe. Loosen the rest of the dulce de leche with 2 tablespoons dark or spiced rum and spread over the cooked cheesecake and sprinkle with toasted coconut. Chill as above.

CHOCOLATE LIME PUDDING

SERVES 4

50g (1¾oz) butter, softened, plus extra for greasing

100g (3½oz) caster (superfine) sugar

Zest and juice of 2 limes

2 eggs, separated

25g (1oz) cocoa powder

25g (1oz) self-raising (self-rising) flour

200ml (7fl oz) whole milk

25g (1oz) chopped dark chocolate or dark chocolate chips

Sea salt

TO SERVE

Whipped cream or ice cream

This is based on the miracle that is a self-saucing pudding. It reminds me of those chocolate lime sweets I used to love when I was a child, only it is much better. The time spent here is in the prep as the cooking time is also pretty miraculous.

Butter an 18cm (7in) round ovenproof dish – Pyrex or ceramic is ideal.

Beat the butter, caster (superfine) sugar and lime zest together until very soft and aerated – it will probably also be a bright green from the lime zest. Beat in the egg yolks. Mix the cocoa and self-raising (self-rising) flour together with a generous pinch of salt. Add the lime juice to the milk – it will curdle just as if you were making buttermilk with lemon juice.

Beat the flour mixture and milk and lime mixture into the batter. Whisk the egg whites until stiff, then gently fold through the batter until completely incorporated. Stir in the chocolate shards or chips – this will really intensify the chocolate hit.

Scrape into your prepared dish and cover with baking paper. Add 2–3cm (¾–1¼in) water to your pressure cooker and add a trivet. Place the dish on the trivet, using the foil handles (see page 11) if necessary. Close the lid and bring up to high pressure. Cook for 5 minutes, then remove from the heat to drop pressure naturally.

Serve with a large dollop of whipped cream or ice cream.

SPICED PLUM COBBLER

SERVES 4

Butter, for greasing and to serve

4–6 plums, pitted and cut into chunks

2 tbsp light soft brown sugar, plus extra to serve

¼ tsp each ground cinnamon, cardamom and star anise

FOR THE COBBLER TOPPING

75g (2½oz) self-raising (self-rising) flour

½ tsp baking powder

¼ tsp ground cardamom

¼ tsp ground cinnamon

25g (1oz) chilled butter, diced

1 tbsp light soft brown sugar

30ml (1fl oz) buttermilk

Sea salt

You can make cobblers, crisps and crumbles in the pressure cooker. Not in vast quantities I grant you, but that isn't always a bad thing, and this is quick enough to make midweek if everyone is desperate for a homely dessert. I've deliberately made this more fruit than topping as I think it works better, but you could double the quantities of cobbler for something much more substantial.

Generously butter an 18–20cm (7–8in) round ovenproof dish. Toss the plums in the sugar and spices and put in the base of the dish. Make the cobbler mixture – put the flour into a bowl with the baking powder, spices and a generous pinch of salt. Rub in the butter until resembling very fine breadcrumbs, then stir in the sugar. Mix in the buttermilk, keeping the stirring to an absolute minimum. Drop heaped spoonfuls over the plums.

Put 2cm (¾in) water in the base of your pressure cooker and add the trivet. Place the dish on top. Bring up to high pressure and cook for 15 minutes. Leave to drop pressure naturally. Remove from the heat and leave to stand for a few minutes just to let the cobbler topping soak up some of the plum juices. Dot with butter and brown sugar and put under the grill to crisp and brown, if you like.

VARIATIONS

Make this with any type of fruit, treating them in the same way as the plums.

Turn into a crumble
Rub 50g (1¾oz) chilled butter into 75g (2½oz) plain (all-purpose) flour and mix with 25g (1oz) oats, 25g (1oz) flaked (slivered) almonds, and 2 tablespoons of demerara sugar. Sprinkle over the fruit and dot with more butter. Cook as above including the optional grilling.

STEAMED SPONGE PUDDINGS

MAKES A 750ML/1-LITRE (26FL OZ/35FL OZ) PUDDING

FOR THE SPONGE

175g (6oz) butter, softened, plus extra for greasing

175g (6oz) light soft brown sugar

1 tsp vanilla extract

175g (6oz) self-raising (self-rising) flour

3 eggs

1 tbsp milk

FOR THE TOPPING

4 tbsp jam (jelly), marmalade, curd or golden (corn) syrup

TO SERVE

Custard and/or cream

The traditional steamed pudding, whether made with suet (see page 312) or butter, is a winter mainstay in our house. This recipe gives you the basics with variations below – hopefully this will give you everything you need to convert your favourite steamed pudding recipes.

Take a 750ml (26fl oz) or 1-litre (35fl oz) pudding basin and coat the inside with a generous layer of softened butter. Put the jam, curd or golden syrup in the base and set aside.

To make the sponge, cream the butter and sugar together until very soft and aerated, then add the vanilla, flour and eggs. Mix together and check the consistency – add just enough milk to give it a dropping consistency.

Pile on top of the jam or golden syrup and spread evenly. Fold a pleat into a piece of foil and secure around the pudding with a sturdy elastic band or string. Put 5cm (2in) water in the base of the pressure cooker. Either put the pudding on a piece of folded fabric (I use an old table napkin) or place on the trivet. You can use a foil handle for easier removal if you like (see page 11). Loosely put the lid on top of the pressure cooker without sealing it down. Bring the water up to the boil and steam without pressure for 15 minutes. Close the lid and bring up to high pressure and cook for 35 minutes. Allow to drop pressure naturally. Check the pudding is done – a skewer inserted into the centre of the pudding should come out clean.

Serve with custard (see page 334) or cream or both.

VARIATIONS

Lime and Cardamom Steamed Pudding
Add the zest of 1 lime and 1 tablespoon of well-flavoured honey to the butter and sugar when creaming together. Add 1 teaspoon of ground cardamom to the flour. Put 2 tablespoons of honey on top of the sugar in the base of the basin, then thinly slice 1 lime into rounds and arrange in a single layer over the base. Increase the steam time to 45 minutes.

Pear and Ginger Steamed Pudding
Add 1 tablespoon of treacle or molasses and 50g (1¾oz) finely chopped stem ginger to the butter and cream. Add 1 tablespoon of ground ginger and 1 teaspoon of mixed spice to the flour. For the topping, peel, core and dice 2 fairly firm pears. Put 3 tablespoons of light soft brown sugar into a bowl with 1 teaspoon of ground ginger and a pinch of mixed spice. Mix together, then toss with the pears. Pile into the pudding basin and top with the sponge. Steam as for the basic recipe.

Other Fruits

Try any orchard fruits. Make sure that they are not overripe.

Rhubarb works very well with ginger and orange, so add orange zest to the sponge. Bake the rhubarb first as per page 296 so it doesn't make the sponge soggy.

Berries – either on their own or mixed with orchard fruits. Apple and blackberry is of course a winner. Freezer packs of berries are really useful for this kind of pudding.

Dried fruit can be just stirred through the sponge, along with any spices.

Upside Down Cakes

You can make any upside down cake using the same sponge mixture but using a cake tin instead of a pudding basin. Use an 18–20cm (7–8in) cake tin and line it with baking paper if it is loose-bottomed. Butter generously. For a pineapple upside down cake, drizzle 3 tablespoons of golden (corn) syrup over the battered base of your cake tin and arrange pineapple slices over. Spoon over the sponge batter, cover, and cook for 30 minutes at high pressure, natural release. Leave to cool in the tin for at least 5 minutes before turning out.

BUTTERSCOTCH APPLE STEAMED SUET PUDDING

SERVES 4

FOR THE BASIN

25g (1oz) butter, for greasing

75g (2½oz) light or dark soft brown sugar

FOR THE CRUST

200g (7oz) self-raising (self-rising) flour

25g (1oz) chilled butter, cubed

75g (2½oz) suet

25g (1oz) light soft brown sugar

Sea salt

FOR THE FILLING

5–6 eating apples, peeled, cored and diced

1 tbsp lemon juice

50g (1¾oz) butter

50g (1¾oz) light soft brown sugar

½ tsp ground cinnamon

Pinch of ground cloves

Pinch of allspice

TO SERVE

Custard or cream

Steamed suet puddings are a British classic that, personally, I don't think can be bettered but are in danger of being overlooked. When I was writing this book, they cropped up as a technical challenge on *The Great British Bake Off* and, without exception, the contestants were completely thrown by the idea of a suet crust in general and Sussex Pond Pudding in particular (see Variations, opposite).

The sweet crust can also be used to make savoury puddings (see page 60) – just make sure you omit the sugar from the crust and the basin lining.

First, butter a 750ml (26fl oz) or 1-litre (35fl oz) pudding basin. Sprinkle over the sugar, making sure any excess ends up in the base.

Make the crust. Put the flour in a bowl and add a generous pinch of salt. Rub in the butter, then stir in the suet and sugar. Add just enough water to create a firm, fairly dry dough – you don't want tackiness. Cut off around a quarter of the dough for the lid, then roll out the rest and use it to line the basin.

To make the filling, toss the apples in the lemon juice. Melt the butter in your pressure cooker, then stir in the sugar, apples and spices. Close the lid and bring up to high pressure. Cook for 1 minute only and fast release. Spoon the filling into the lined basin.

Roll the remaining pastry into a round and place it on top. Pinch the edges together, making sure it is completely sealed.

Fold a pleat into a piece of foil and fix over the pudding. Put 5cm (2in) just-boiled water in the base of the pressure cooker. Place the pudding either on a piece of folded up fabric as above, or on the trivet. Use the foil handle if necessary. Put the lid on without sealing and when plenty of steam has been generated, steam without pressure for 15 minutes. Close the lid, bring up to high pressure and cook for at least 30 minutes. Allow to drop pressure naturally.

Carefully work round the sides of the pudding with a palette knife, before turning out on to a serving plate. Serve with custard or cream.

VARIATIONS

You can fill this type of pudding with all kinds of fruit. There is no need to cook them first, but you will want to prepare them for cooking by peeling, coring, pitting and chopping as appropriate. You will need between 600–750g (1lb 5oz–1lb 10oz) prepared fruit to fill a lined 750ml (26fl oz) or 1-litre (35fl oz) pudding basin.

Sussex Pond Pudding
Cut deep incisions through the skin of 1 large lemon or orange or a couple of limes. Mix together 100g (3½oz) each butter and light soft brown sugar and an optional ½ teaspoon of ground cinnamon. Put half of this in your lined basin, add the lemon and top with the rest of the mixture. Seal the lid and proceed as above, cooking at high pressure for 1 hour 15 minutes.

Apple and Berry Pudding
Use 500g (1lb 2oz) eating apples and 200–250g (7–9oz) any type of berry or currant. Toss in 50g (1¾oz) caster (superfine) sugar.

Quince, Raisin and Ginger Pudding
Slice 2 large quince, toss with 100g (3½oz) raisins, 2 pieces of finely chopped stem ginger and 75g (2½oz) light soft brown sugar.

Apple Charlotte
Use slices of buttered bread in place of the suet crust and cook for the same length of time. I find that the bread crust varies in terms of how well it browns, so sometimes I might crisp it up under the grill for a couple of minutes, but usually it doesn't need it.

JAM ROLY-POLY

SERVES 4

1 portion of suet pastry with optional zest of 1 lemon or orange added to it (see page 312)

Butter, for greasing

FOR THE FILLING

150g (5½oz) jam (jelly), marmalade, curd or mincemeat

When I was growing up a lot of desserts were centred on jam (jelly) because so much of it was made in the summer months for the rest of the year. This makes very good use of it although depending on how sweet your tooth is, you might prefer to use marmalade or curd instead. You can also add other ingredients. For example, a handful of chocolate chips over orange curd or marmalade works really well.

Roll the pastry out on a floured work surface to a rectangle of around 30 x 20cm (12 x 8in). Spread with your choice of filling, leaving a 1cm (½in) border on three of the sides, but spreading to the edge of one of the shortest sides. Brush the border with water, then roll up from the borderless side and pinch the edges together.

Butter a large piece of foil and put the pudding in the centre of it. Bring up the longest sides, folding a pleat in the centre, then fold in the shortest sides.

Put 5cm (2in) water in the base of your pressure cooker. Put the pudding in the steamer basket or directly on to the trivet and steam without pressure for 15 minutes. Close the lid and steam at high pressure for 30 minutes, then allow to drop pressure naturally.

VARIATION

For a less sweet pudding, sprinkle the rolled out pastry with brown sugar, your choice of spice and citrus zest. Take around 100g (3½oz) dried fruit – raisins, sultanas (golden raisins), currants or finely chopped figs or apricots – and sprinkle over the pastry. Press down lightly so the fruit doesn't fall off as you start to roll it. Proceed as above.

CHRISTMAS PUDDING

SERVES 4

500g (1lb 2oz) dried fruit (raisins, sultanas/golden raisins, currants, chopped prunes, pears, dried blueberries, glacé cherries)

175ml (5¾fl oz) rum or brandy

75g (2½oz) candied peel, finely chopped (I buy or make large pieces and finely chop; the flavour is much better)

125g (4½oz) self-raising (self-rising) flour

1 tsp ground cinnamon

½ tsp allspice

¼ tsp each ground cloves, ground mace, ground cardamom

150g (5½oz) fresh breadcrumbs

175g (6oz) shredded suet

175g (6oz) dark muscovado sugar

4 eggs

150g (5½oz) grated quince or apple

Zest of 1 orange

Sea salt

TO SERVE

50ml (1¾fl oz) vodka

You can use any recipe you like for Christmas pudding – they all steam in the same way. You could also use these timings for classics such as cloutie dumplings.

This recipe is enough to fill 2 x 750ml (26fl oz) basins, 1 x large 1.5-litre (52fl oz) basins or 8–10 mini basins, but it will halve easily. You need at least a 6-litre (210fl oz) pressure cooker for the largest size pudding.

Either soak your dried fruit in the rum overnight or quick soak in the pressure cooker (see page 343) using just 150ml (5fl oz) of the rum and adding the remaining 25ml (1fl oz) when you remove the lid.

Mix all the remaining ingredients together with a generous pinch of salt, then add the fruit. Pile into pudding basins, making sure you have pushed the mixture down well to reduce the risk of air pockets.

Fold a pleat into foil or baking paper and secure around the top of the basin – you can tie with string, making a handle at the same time, or just fix into place with an elastic band. Make a foil handle according to page 11 and place the pudding in the centre of it. Lift into the pressure cooker. You can either place the pudding on a trivet or on to a folded up piece of cloth – it is not necessary for the basin to be suspended above the water. Add around 5cm (2in) water to the base of the cooker.

Bring up to the boil and steam for 15 minutes, then fix the lid in place. Bring up to high pressure. For mini puddings, steam for 40 minutes; for a medium pudding, steam for 1–1½ hours, depending how dark you like it; and for a large pudding, steam for 2 hours. Allow to drop pressure naturally, cool and leave somewhere cool and dark until you are ready to eat it. To reheat on Christmas day, the small puddings will just need 10 minutes at high pressure, the medium and large will need 30 minutes.

To serve traditionally, take a sprig of holly, wrap the base of the stem in foil and stick it in the top of the pudding. Heat the vodka in a small saucepan, then set it alight and pour over the pudding. It should flame for a good while.

OLD-FASHIONED BREAD PUDDING

SERVES 4

Butter, for greasing

250g (9oz) bread of your choice, torn

1 tsp baking powder

75g (2½oz) dark soft brown or muscovado sugar

250ml (9fl oz) whole milk

1 egg

1 tsp vanilla extract

50g (1¾oz) butter, melted, plus 15g (½oz) for topping

2 tbsp demerara sugar

FOR THE FLAVOURING

150g (5½oz) dried fruit

Zest of 1 lemon

½ tsp ground cinnamon

½ tsp mixed spice

OR

100g (3½oz) chopped chocolate of your choice

100g (3½oz) chopped nuts (pecans are good)

25g (1oz) candied orange peel or the zest of 1 orange

½ tsp ground cardamom

This isn't the bread pudding in the sense of the American version of bread and butter pudding, but the version that is more like a dense cake, good hot with custard but usually cooled and served in squares. It is comfortingly stodgy. I am offering two versions here. The first is much more traditional, with the dried fruit and the lemon zest; the second is a rich, almost decadent version with chocolate.

Butter and line an 18–20cm (7–8in) round tin. Put the bread in a large bowl and add the baking powder and sugar. Whisk the milk, egg, vanilla and butter together and pour this over the top. Mix thoroughly, squishing together with your hands if necessary – the idea is to break up the bread as much as possible – there will still be tougher bits of crust that don't succumb easily, that's just how it should be.

Mix in your choice of flavourings, then press into the prepared tin. Cover the top with foil. Put 2–3cm (¾–1¼in) water in the base of your pressure cooker. Add a trivet and place the cake tin on top. Bring up to high pressure and cook for 30 minutes. Allow to release pressure naturally.

Heat your grill to a medium setting. Dot the pudding with butter and sprinkle with the demerara sugar. Put under the grill for just a couple of minutes to crisp it up a little.

FRUIT CAKE

SERVES 8–10

500g (1lb 2oz) dried fruit – any mix you like, but including finely chopped citrus peel for flavour

Zest of 1 orange

50ml (1¾fl oz) rum, brandy or whisky

125g (4½oz) butter, softened

125g (4½oz) dark soft brown sugar

250g (9oz) plain (all-purpose) flour

1 tsp ground cinnamon

¼ tsp each allspice and ground cardamom

Pinch of ground cloves

Pinch of grated nutmeg

2 eggs

Sea salt

Dense cakes such as fruit cakes do really well in the pressure cooker – not least because they traditionally take a very long, slow cooking time in the oven so it is hard to keep the top and edges from over-browning before they are completely cooked through in the middle. Cooked in the pressure cooker, they don't dry out, but still form a proper crumb and crust.

You can substitute your favourite fruit cake recipe here of course. A halved recipe will work well in a 15–16cm (6–6¼in) round tin and will take just 35 minutes to cook.

Put the fruit and orange zest into a bowl and cover with the alcohol. Leave to stand while you make the batter.

Beat the butter and sugar together until very soft and aerated. Mix the flour with the spices and a generous pinch of salt. Beat the eggs and flour mix into the butter and sugar, then add the fruit, including the liquid. Stir thoroughly and scrape into a lined 18cm (7in) round tin. Cover with a piece of baking paper or foil and seal with string or a strong elastic band.

Put 2cm (¾in) water in the pressure cooker. Place a trivet in the cooker and arrange the cake tin on top of a foil handle. Lower the cake on to the trivet. Close the lid and bring up to high pressure. Cook for 1 hour. Leave to drop pressure naturally. Remove the foil and leave to cool in the tin. Wrap up well and leave for a couple of days, if possible, before eating.

ORANGE SEPHARDIC CAKE

SERVES 8–10

1 orange

3 eggs

110g (3¾oz) caster (superfine) sugar

125g (4½oz) ground almonds

1 tsp baking powder

1 tsp orange blossom water (optional)

Butter, for greasing

Sea salt

TO SERVE

Caster (superfine) sugar

2 tbsp toasted almonds

Strips of orange zest

Whipped cream

This cake is based on the classic recipe found in Claudia Roden's *A Book of Middle Eastern Cooking*. It traditionally takes quite a while to make because the oranges have to be boiled until soft, so the benefit of using the pressure cooker is twofold; you can cook the oranges in a fraction of the time and then cook the cake in the pressure cooker too.

First, put the orange in your pressure cooker and add 500ml (17fl oz) water. Close the lid and bring up to high pressure. Cook for 10 minutes and then remove from the heat. Leave to drop pressure naturally. When the orange is cool enough to handle, break up and remove any pips, then put into a food processor and blitz until quite smooth. Leave to cool.

Break the eggs into a bowl and whisk until well broken up and frothy. Beat in the sugar, followed by the almonds, baking powder, a generous pinch of salt and the orange blossom water, if using. Finally, stir in the puréed orange.

Take an 18cm (7in) round cake tin and butter it. Pour in the cake batter. Cover the tin with baking paper or foil, and seal with string or a large elastic band. Put 5cm (2in) just-boiled water in the base of your pressure cooker and add the trivet. Place the cake tin on the trivet. Loosely cover with the lid and allow to steam for 15 minutes without pressure, then bring up to high pressure and cook for 20 minutes at high pressure. Allow to drop pressure naturally for at least 5 minutes. Check for doneness – a skewer inserted in the centre should come out fairly clean, with perhaps the odd dry crumb clinging to it.

Leave to cool in the tin for 15 minutes, then turn out on to a cooling rack. Dust with the sugar, toasted almonds and orange zest and serve with whipped cream.

BLUEBERRY BUNDT CAKE

SERVES 6–8

Cake release spray (optional)

75g (2½oz) butter, softened, plus extra for greasing (optional)

100g (3½oz) caster (superfine) or light soft brown sugar

Zest of 1 lemon

100g (3½oz) plain (all-purpose) flour, plus extra for dusting (optional)

½ tsp baking powder

1 egg

75g (2½oz) sour cream or yogurt

75g (2½oz) blueberries

FOR THE ICING (OPTIONAL)

1 tbsp blueberries

1 tbsp lemon juice

150g (5½oz) icing (confectioners') sugar

This can be served warm as a pudding or cold as a cake and I've given an icing option accordingly. The quantities of this recipe are for a 16–17cm (6¼–6½in) Bundt tin; you can also use it to make 6 little steamed puddings in ramekins or pudding basins instead.

Coat the inside of your Bundt tin with cake release spray or butter and flour, tapping off any excess flour.

Cream the butter, sugar and lemon zest together until very soft and aerated. Add the flour, baking powder, egg and sour cream or yogurt and combine. Fold the blueberries into the cake batter, then scrape into the prepared tin. Cover the tin with baking paper or foil and seal with string or a large elastic band.

Put 2cm (¾in) water in the pressure cooker and balance the Bundt tin on a trivet or steamer insert. Close the lid and bring up to high pressure. Cook for 35 minutes, then allow to drop pressure naturally. Alternatively, for a very slightly lighter cake, steam for 15 minutes at no pressure, then at 30 minutes high pressure, natural release. Turn out on to a wire rack to cool.

For the icing, put the blueberries into a saucepan with the lemon juice and heat until the berries burst. Push through a sieve, then add the liquid a teaspoon at a time to the icing (confectioners') sugar until you have the right consistency. Drop spoonfuls of icing on top of the cooled sponge, allowing them to glide down the side.

VARIATIONS

For a Lemon and Raisin Rum Syrup version, swap the blueberries out for 100g (3½oz) raisins. Put these in your pressure cooker with 100ml (3½fl oz) golden rum. Bring up to high pressure and remove from the heat to drop pressure naturally. Leave to cool and add in place of the blueberries. Make the icing by mixing the icing (confectioners') sugar with 1 teaspoon of lemon zest, 1 teaspoon of rum with a few drops of warm water.

For an Orange/Mandarin and Cranberry version, replace the lemon zest and juice with orange or mandarin and add the dried cranberries in oloroso (see page 343).

BASICS

This is a chapter filled with building-block, first-principle recipes that help make life just that little bit easier, as well as generally tasting better. These recipes are designed with planning ahead in mind. By this I don't mean that you need to plan your meals in advance – I am going to hold my hands up right now and admit that I am rubbish at this. No, the recipes here are designed to give you more flexibility in the kitchen when you are particularly time-pressed. The key here is batch cooking and being able to freeze small portions. Batch cooking for me encompasses cooking large amounts of beans, lentils or grains at a time as well as complete meals such as chillies, curries and casseroles. But it also extends to stock making. Of course, I will often make a chicken stock with one carcass and a few vegetable scraps – but I am just as likely to make a large batch and portion it up for the freezer. I will do the same with basic tomato sauces, which can be endlessly adapted and will give your dishes more depth of flavour than just using canned tomatoes. Having cubes of different sofritos, caramelized onions, ginger, garlic and onion for curries are also all immensely useful.

Let me give you an example. Most mornings I use the pressure cooker to make lunch for my children's Thermoses. Sometimes this is pasta that is cooked fresh that morning, or a quick rice dish or dal. But often it is a composite meal from the freezer. A portion of black beans, some frozen sweetcorn or spinach and coriander (cilantro) stems, a couple of cubes of pepper sofrito, a portion of tomato sauce. All put in the pressure cooker at the same time with a splash of water and any extra flavour (I might fry any vegetables briefly with a bit of cumin, for example, or add a bit of leftover meat). Then it is literally a case of bringing up to high pressure, removing from the heat and leaving to drop pressure naturally.

You can freeze in any amount, but it makes sense to do this in multiples of quite small quantities as well as large. This gives you greater flexibility and is more economical as you will be less likely to waste anything. Ice-cube trays that hold 1–2 tablespoons per cube are ideal for tomato sauces and sofritos and for very-well-reduced stock. You can then turn them out into bags or larger containers. Light stocks are best stored in multiples of 100ml (3½fl oz), 500ml (17fl oz) and litre (35fl oz) quantities. And to save space, try storing flat in reusable bags.

STOCKS AND SAUCES

One of the best things about pressure cooking is that it really helps you make the most of the ingredients you have, particularly when it comes to using by-products and leftovers. Many of us are well-intentioned, meaning to make stock with the chicken carcass left over from Sunday's lunch, but few of us manage to find the time. With a pressure cooker to hand, making stock on a regular basis becomes much more feasible – you could even have it on the hob and cooked by the time you've finished clearing up the kitchen after Sunday lunch.

This has always been the case, but the modern pressure cookers – the sort that won't hiss and spit at you as they cook – make the process even more efficient; they work at high pressure as a completely sealed vessel, letting out little or no steam. This means that all the flavour particles and liquid stay in the cooker – anything that evaporates to steam will condense back down again as soon as you remove it from the heat and leave it to drop pressure naturally. The depth of flavour is already superb because of the high cooking temperature – this ensures that you don't lose any of it. It also means you won't lose liquid to evaporation.

A note on storage – I freeze a lot of stock once I have skimmed it, but if you need to save space, you can reduce stock by simmering uncovered for as long as you like. You can do this just to concentrate the flavours or to reduce to a jus, the latter being especially useful if you want to freeze cubes to enrich sauces and gravies.

How to Make a Basic Stock

THE PROCESS

First decide if you need to brown off or roast any of the carcasses, bones, shells, scraps of meat. This isn't strictly necessary as the temperature reached under pressure will help with caramelization. However, it will give you a slightly darker stock and it is something I will always do with shellfish because it will definitely give more depth of flavour. You can brown in the pressure cooker, just make sure you deglaze the base thoroughly afterwards.

Put any carcasses, bones, shells, scraps of meat into your pressure cooker with any vegetables and aromatics you like and cover with cold water. For the best-flavoured stock, make sure everything is well broken up and that the liquid is quite tightly packed with solids. For example, do not cover a single chicken carcass with 3 litres (105fl oz) water. The ideal ratio is double the amount of liquid to solid matter. Make sure that the contents do not go over the two-thirds mark of your pressure cooker.

Bring up to high pressure and cook as follows:

> Chicken and poultry: 30–45 minutes
>
> Red meat: 45 minutes–1 hour
>
> Fish and shellfish: 5 minutes
>
> Vegetables: 5 minutes

Leave to drop pressure naturally. You can then either leave to cool before straining (the stock will continue to infuse) or strain right away (recommended if the stock is particularly fatty). Pour through a colander first, then line a sieve with muslin (cheesecloth) or kitchen towel and strain again.

Leave to stand and allow any fat to collect on top. Skim this off and store for use for frying and roasting. If you chill the stock first, the fat will be easier to remove.

Store in the fridge for up to a week or in the freezer for 3–6 months.

(Note: I used to recommend skimming before bringing up to high pressure but have come to realize this doesn't make any difference to clarity.)

The Ingredients

POULTRY STOCK

This is the stock most people will make most frequently using mainly chicken, but any other type of poultry will work. You can make a good one with a carcass left over from a roast chicken, but for extra flavour, you can also add a few chicken wings. If you are able to obtain trays of chicken backs/carcasses that are usually sold for pence, if not given away, these make excellent stock and here is a tip: depending on how they have been butchered, they may contain a fair amount of meat – I have one supplier in my farmers' market who even leaves the chicken oysters attached. When there is enough meat, I will often remove it first. The simplest way to do this is to proceed as on page 324 but bring up to high pressure and immediately remove from the heat and leave to drop pressure naturally. You will find that the meat will slide very easily off the carcass(es) and will be enough to add to a risotto or pasta dish or to be combined with other ingredients for a sandwich filling. Then return the carcass(es) to the pressure cooker, add the vegetables and aromatics you like, then bring up to high pressure again. Cook for 30 minutes for cooked carcasses or 45 minutes for raw.

My ideal is to use either cooked or raw carcasses, and a couple of extra chicken wings. If the chicken is good quality, even the lightest of stocks will set to a loose jelly (jello) – a sure indication that it is rich in collagen.

RED MEAT STOCKS

Do not be tempted to just use bones for these stocks – the flavour will be unpleasantly thin. Marrow bones are excellent for texture but they need meat for flavour. This need not be an expensive undertaking, you can ask for bones that are more likely to have meat attached – for example ribs – or you can also ask for trimmings, which will often be a mixture of meat and fat. This is good – the fat will help flavour the stock and then can be used for cooking when skimmed off. You will therefore be making stock and rendering fat for dripping and lard at the same time. I will also keep a freezer bag of meat trimmings. Or will use a small quantity of a cheap cut with plenty of connective tissue – a 100g (3½oz) piece of shin, diced, is ample. Brown this first before using in the stock and make sure you deglaze well as this will all add flavour.

FISH AND SHELLFISH STOCKS AND COURT BOUILLONS

Use bones, skin, fish heads of white fish if you can – oily fish is too strongly flavoured for stock. And if you have time, wash your trimmings first – I put a kettle of boiling water over them to remove the worst of the blood. For shellfish, whole prawns (shrimp), langoustines and/or lobster are preferable because they are generally cheaper than buying them peeled and you will get so much flavour from the heads and shells. Fry off in a little oil first, then deglaze the pan with alcohol. They will give out a rich, ochre-coloured oil, the droplets of which will enhance all your seafood dishes with an appetizing beauty and flavour.

Wine and vermouth both add good flavour to fish stocks – you can use as much as half wine and half water, but I will usually stick to around 100ml (3½fl oz). Seafood stocks benefit from alcohol, especially when paired with tomatoes.

VEGETABLES FOR STOCK

The basic vegetables to add are onion (skin on for the colour), carrot and celery. You can add virtually anything else with the exception of potatoes and other very starchy root vegetables, most brassicas, because they become unpleasantly sulphurous after lengthy cooking, and vegetables such as okra, which will not help the texture. Use whole vegetables and dice them before using – this will give a much better flavour than leaving them whole or just roughly chopping – or keep a bag of scraps in your fridge or freezer for anything you might want to use. Peelings, fibres and rind from pumpkins and squashes, trimmings from mushrooms and asparagus, pea pods, tomato and garlic skins. I save the tiny garlic cloves found in the middle of the head for stock. Think about what you are going to use the stock for. A mixture of fresh mushroom trimmings, dried mushrooms and Jerusalem artichoke peelings will give you a really intense, umami-rich stock, whether vegetarian or enhancing any meat, especially if you add tomato skins or tomato purée. Asparagus and peas will give you a light summery stock.

AROMATICS FOR STOCK

What you add here depends on the ultimate use for your stock. If you have nothing particular in mind, but you just want to use up a store of bones, keep the flavours fairly neutral. So, for example for a chicken stock I might just add bay, parsley, thyme, garlic and black peppercorns. Unless you want any particular flavour to dominate, use quite sparingly, because the pressure cooker does a very good job of pushing flavour into the liquid. Use whole spices or very lightly crushed spices judiciously (be especially careful of cinnamon and clove, which love to dominate). For citrus flavours, use lightly Microplaned zest as opposed to pared zest as any pith can become unpleasantly bitter when cooked for too long.

Certain aromatics are best added at a later stage – sometimes because their flavour is just too intense and dominant (eg chilli) or because the flavour can become muted over time (eg rosemary). Here you can follow the method used to infuse stock found on page 174, but to recap, simply make your stock and when it has dropped pressure, add in the stronger aromatics, bring up to high pressure again, immediately remove from the heat, then leave to drop pressure again before straining. This will infuse the existing stock with brighter, fresh flavour.

CHEESE RINDS AND CHEESE STOCK

If you keep rinds from hard cheeses such as Parmesan in your freezer for making minestrone, you will know how much flavour they can give out; when you pressure cooker them, this is intensified. It is worth saving them up, along with any other edible cheese rinds and making a very simple stock with them. This will make superb soups (see page 35), and can be used in pasta and rice dishes.

You can keep this completely plain and simply just pressure cook around 200–250g (7–9oz) rinds with 1 litre (35fl oz) of water for 30 minutes. You will find that a lot of the cheese will have disintegrated into the liquid. When you strain the stock, solids will rise to the top and set to a fat, which you can remove easily once it has been chilled. This is well worth keeping for enhancing and enriching all kinds of dishes, especially anything cream based. You can also add any vegetables as for vegetable stock (opposite) or use vegetable stock as a base. Try just an onion, carrot, celery and perhaps some garlic.

BASE STOCK FOR RAMEN

MAKES 2 LITRES (70FL OZ)

2kg (4lb 8oz) raw pork bones

1 pig's trotter, preferably split

500g (1lb 2oz) chicken bones

250g (9oz) chicken wings

1 head garlic, cut in half

15g (½oz) piece ginger, thickly sliced

1 bunch of spring onions (scallions), roughly chopped

This is the stock I use when I'm attempting to make a proper ramen. It is a really good multipurpose stock too – it is very collagen rich so will have a very wobbly, slightly tacky texture to it, which adds an extra dimension to broths. It is quite labour intensive, but worth it. I should say that this won't give you the milky-coloured stock you might expect from ramen but the flavour and texture is there, I promise.

If possible, soak the bones in cold water overnight – this will help remove impuritites that can make the broth darker than you want it. Put the pork bones, trotter and chicken bones and wings in the pressure cooker and cover with water. Bring up to high pressure, then allow to drop pressure naturally. Drain, discarding the water, then wash everything thoroughly – the pressure cooker and the bones – making sure you get rid of any starchy residue that will have formed.

Return the pork bones and trotter to the pressure cooker (reserve the chicken for later) and cover with 2 litres (70fl oz) of water. Bring up to high pressure and cook for 1½ hours. Leave to drop pressure naturally. Open the lid, add the reserved chicken, the garlic, ginger and spring onions (scallions). Return to high pressure and this time cook for 45 minutes.

Strain and leave to cool. You will find a thick layer of fat on the top of the stock – reserve this for cooking, but also set some aside to add to your ramen – the fat will help the end result texture.

DASHI STOCK

MAKES 1 LITRE (35FL OZ)

1 piece kombu

10g (¼oz) bonito flakes or 15g (½oz) dried shiitake mushrooms

Put the kombu in the pressure cooker and cover with 1 litre (35fl oz) of cold water. Add the bonito flakes or for a vegetarian dashi, shiitake mushrooms. Bring up to high pressure and cook for 1 minute. Remove from the heat and leave to drop pressure naturally. Strain and use.

ONION, GARLIC AND GINGER BASE

MAKES AROUND 300G (10½OZ)

2 tbsp vegetable or coconut oil or ghee

4 large onions, finely chopped

2 heads of garlic, peeled

100g (3½oz) ginger, peeled and roughly chopped

Sea salt

This is very useful if you make a lot of curries. The best way to store portions if you are planning on keeping it for more than a week is to freeze it in ice-cube trays. Once frozen, decant into a freezerproof bag or tub. The flavour intensifies with freezing, which means that you will need less than normal for your curries.

Heat the oil in your pressure cooker. Add the onion and 1 teaspoon of salt, then stir until giving off plenty of steam. Close the lid and bring up to high pressure. Cook for 3 minutes, then fast release. Strain off the liquid in the cooker and use this to supplement stock in sauces.

Put the garlic and ginger in a food processor with a couple of tablespoons of the onion liquid and blitz until well broken down – exactly how smooth you take it is up to you. Stir into the onions, return to high pressure and cook for another minute. Fast release. Cool, then either store in the fridge in a sterilized jar, or freeze as described above.

You can use this from frozen and add straight into the pressure cooker just before cooking in any of the curries in this book that use the onion/ginger/garlic combination. It isn't necessary to defrost first.

SOFRITO

MAKES AROUND 500G (1LB 2OZ)

50ml (1¾fl oz) olive oil

2 large onions, finely chopped

3 carrots, finely diced

3 celery sticks, finely diced

3 garlic cloves, crushed or grated

Any herbs you like (optional)

Sea salt

A 'holy trinity' of soft, lightly caramelized vegetables is a really useful thing to keep in the fridge, especially if you are cooking a lot of dishes that only need a minute or two of high pressure cooking. This will pack a decent flavour punch and means you can skip the need to chop and sauté an onion for virtually every meal.

I don't tend to add herbs, as the sofrito is more versatile without, but that is up to you. The oil content will help preserve it and it will usually be fine for up to 2 weeks in the fridge. Alternatively, spoon into ice-cube trays, freeze and then turn out into freezer bags or tubs.

Heat the olive oil in your pressure cooker and add all the remaining ingredients. Season with 1 teaspoon of salt. Stir until the vegetables are hot enough to start creating steam, then make sure they are all pushed down the sides and bring up to high pressure. Cook for 5 minutes, then fast release. Boil off any excess liquid just for a couple of minutes. If you have used any woody herbs, such as bay or thyme sprigs, remove before using in sauces.

VARIATIONS

Replace the carrots with 2 green peppers or 1 green and 1 red pepper, finely chopped. You could use lard, dripping or butter in place of the olive oil.

Add 1 finely chopped fennel in place of one of the onions.

CARAMELIZED ONIONS

MAKES AROUND 600G (1LB 5OZ)

1 tbsp olive oil

1 kg (2lb 4oz) onions, sliced

15g (½oz) butter

¼ tsp bicarbonate of soda (baking soda)

1 tsp demerara sugar (optional)

Sea salt

One of the biggest cons in the recipe writing world concerns the length of time it takes to caramelize onions properly. It is a very, very lengthy process, should never be short of an hour and can take much longer. I almost gave up on a pressure-cooker version; the difficulty was figuring out how to get them to caramelize when under pressure as they will soften and give out a lot of water. This method solves the problem.

The sugar is optional as onions can vary in terms of sweetness levels.

Heat the olive oil in your pressure cooker. Add all the onions and 1 teaspoon of salt and cook on a high heat, stirring, until they start giving off steam. Close the lid and bring up to high pressure. Cook for 3 minutes and fast release – at this point the onions will be softened, but won't have collapsed, and will have released most of their liquid.

Strain the onions, reserving the liquor (you should expect around 200ml/7fl oz) for another use. Heat the butter in the pressure cooker. Return the onions to the pressure cooker and add the bicarbonate of soda (baking soda) and sugar, if using. Season with salt. Return to high pressure and cook for a further 3 minutes. Fast release again. This time you should be left with soft, golden brown onions and very little liquid in the pot.

The onions are now ready to be used for soup and gravy, but if you want a sticky, rather than a soft texture, you can keep going and cook the onions on a high heat for a few more minutes. The way to do this is to leave them for a minute at a time before stirring so the sugar crystals start to form underneath. These will be perfect for dishes such as pissaladière.

VARIATION

You might want to flavour the onions – add aromatics at the start of the process, such as a couple of bay leaves or a star anise.

QUICK TOMATO SAUCE

MAKES AROUND 900ML/71FL OZ (UNREDUCED)

3 tbsp olive oil

1 onion, finely chopped, or 4 tbsp sofrito (see page 330)

3 garlic cloves, finely chopped

1 tsp dried oregano

1 sprig of thyme or rosemary

2 x 400g (14oz) cans chopped tomatoes or fresh equivalent

Pinch of ground cinnamon

Pinch of sugar

1 sprig of basil

Sea salt and freshly ground black pepper

Tomatoes have a reputation for trickiness, thanks to their ability to trigger burn warnings on electric pressure cookers, and can on occasion scorch in a stovetop pressure cooker. However, there are a couple of things you can do to avoid this happening. First of all, if you are using an electric pressure cooker, consider using the ceramic insert. Secondly, use oil and onion as a barrier between the base of the cooker and the tomatoes. Thirdly, important if using a stovetop version – get the pressure cooker up to pressure as fast as possible – the longer it takes, the higher the chance of burning.

I used to always peel and deseed tomatoes to make tomato sauce, but these days I don't bother – there is so much flavour and fibre in skin and the jelly (jello) around the seeds, I prefer to leave them in. The pressure cooker will soften the tomato skins very well. And these days most blenders and food processors are powerful enough to make short work of them.

Heat the olive oil in your pressure cooker and add the onion or sofrito. Sauté the onion for several minutes if you have time – it will still soften and develop flavour if you don't, but will give out more liquid when cooked at high pressure. Add the garlic and herbs, then pour in the tomatoes. Don't stir. Add the cinnamon and sugar and season with salt and pepper. Lay the sprig of basil on top. Bring up to high pressure and cook for 5 minutes. Leave to drop pressure naturally. Remove the basil. Roughly purée the sauce if necessary – it should be a good texture for a pasta sauce base and can be reduced down as you like.

NO PREP TOMATO SAUCE

MAKES AROUND 800ML/28FL OZ (UNREDUCED) WITHOUT VEGETABLES OR 1 LITRE (35FL OZ) WITH VEGETABLES

2 tbsp olive oil

15g (½oz) butter

2 x 400g (14oz) cans chopped tomatoes or fresh equivalent

1 onion, peeled

1 carrot, left whole

3 garlic cloves

A pinch of sugar

1 tsp dried oregano

1 sprig of thyme or rosemary or 1 bay leaf

1 sprig of basil

Sea salt and freshly ground black pepper

This is based on a Marcella Hazan sauce, which is beautifully buttery and rich.

Heat the olive oil and butter in your pressure cooker. Pour in the tomatoes, then all the remaining ingredients and season with salt and pepper. Bring up to high pressure and cook for 10 minutes, then allow to drop pressure naturally.

Remove the sprigs of herbs and vegetables. The vegetables make an excellent chef's perk as they will be sweet and tender, or you can purée with the tomatoes to add extra sweetness to the sauce.

VARIATIONS

Using either tomato sauce
If you want to make a richer, wine-based sauce, you won't need to add much – 100ml (3½fl oz) red or white wine is plenty. Add with the tomatoes, or for more depth, add the wine along with 1-2 tablespoons of tomato or pepper purée and stir thoroughly before adding the tomatoes.

To make a vodka sauce (which is lovely, it really helps bring out the flavour of the tomatoes), add a scant 25ml (1fl oz) vodka after the natural release cooking time or just before you are going to serve. Simmer for a few minutes. Add 50ml (1¾fl oz) single (light) cream and chilli flakes, if you like. Especially good with seafood.

DULCE DE LECHE

MAKES 397G (14OZ)

TO ADD FLAVOUR

Decant a 397g (14oz) can of condensed milk into an ovenproof dish. Add any flavour you like – whole spices, vanilla, lime, desiccated (shredded) coconut, sea salt – and cover tightly with foil. Cook for the same amount of time. When you remove the bowl from the pressure cooker, beat well, then transfer to a jar.

This is a great shortcut – boiling a 397g (14oz) can of condensed milk to get dulce de leche can take 2–4 hours conventionally, plus there is the additional hassle of having to keep an eye on it to make sure it doesn't boil dry.

To pressure cook, simply put a folded up piece of tea towel or similar in your pressure cooker and put the condensed milk can on top. Add 2cm (¾in) water. Close the lid and bring up to high pressure, then cook for 20 minutes for a very light caramel; up to 30 minutes for a much darker colour. Allow to drop pressure naturally, then leave the can to cool down before opening.

PROPER CUSTARD

MAKES 400ML (14FL OZ)

4 egg yolks

2 tbsp caster (superfine) or light soft brown sugar

300ml (10½fl oz) whole milk

1 vanilla pod, split

1 coffee bean (optional)

No standing over a hot stove, stirring, which is especially a boon in the middle of summer if you want to make a custard base for ice cream – just use this same method. The coffee bean doesn't add coffee flavour, just depth.

Prepare your pressure cooker by adding enough water to come 2cm (¾in) up the sides, then putting in the trivet or a folded piece of fabric. Put the egg yolks and sugar into a bowl small enough to fit into your pressure cooker and stir to combine. Add the milk, vanilla pod and coffee bean, if using, then cover with baking paper.

Put the bowl on the trivet or fabric, then close the lid and bring up to high pressure. Cook for 5 minutes, then fast release. Whisk briefly to bring everything together – it will immediately take on a smooth, slightly thickened texture. Strain into a jug and serve immediately or chill.

QUICK PRESERVED LEMONS

MAKES 680G (1LB 8OZ)

4 lemons

1 tsp salt

Preserved lemons are usually either expensive to buy, often with a slight whiff of mustiness about them, or take at least 6 weeks to cure when homemade. This version is instant so can be used immediately, and will also keep indefinitely in the fridge if stored in a sterilized jar. The syrupy lemon juice the zest sits in is very useful in all kinds of ways, including salad dressings. This method also works very well with other types of citrus fruit – try with Seville or blood oranges when they are in season.

Pare the zest off the lemons in thick strips, then scrape off any thick pieces of pith from the zest. Put into the pressure cooker, then juice the lemons and add the juice to the cooker along with the salt. Bring up to high pressure and cook for 2 minutes, then leave to drop pressure naturally.

Transfer to a sterilized jar and cool. Store in the fridge indefinitely.

MARMALADE

MAKES 4 x 300G (10½OZ) JARS

500g (1lb 2oz) Seville oranges

Juice of 1 lemon

1kg (2lb 4oz) preserving or granulated sugar

There are two main ways of making marmalade that are vastly aided by the use of a pressure cooker – the method you choose depends on how much clarity you want in your finished marmalade stacked up against how much chopping you want to do. I give both methods here so you can take your pick. Both of these are for Seville orange marmalade, but you can adapt for other types of citrus too, using the same quantities.

METHOD 1

This makes a bright, clear marmalade with long strands of peel suspended in a light orange jelly (jello).

Wash the oranges thoroughly, then cut in half and juice. Scrape out all the remaining membrane and pulp – you will be left with the orange shells with a clean white interior. Put the membrane and pulp and any seeds from the juicer on to a square of muslin (cheesecloth) and tie into a bundle.

Cut the orange shells in half and shred into long strips. Put these in a bowl with the juice and muslin. Add 600ml (21fl oz) water and leave to stand overnight.

When you are ready to make the marmalade, put the contents of the bowl in your pressure cooker and close the lid. Bring up to high pressure and cook for 10 minutes. Allow to drop pressure naturally. Check the peel – you should be able to break a piece of it in two by squeezing it between your fingers. Remove the bundle of seeds and membrane and squeeze it gently over the cooker to extract any juice before discarding.

Add the lemon juice and sugar to the pressure cooker and stir on a low heat until the sugar has dissolved. Bring to the boil and keep it at a rolling boil until setting point is reached. This will take anything from 20–30 minutes, but start testing at 15 minutes. When setting point has been reached (see page 345), remove from the heat and leave to stand for 15 minutes, then stir to make sure the peel has been evenly distributed. Transfer to sterilized jars and seal.

500g (1lb 2oz) Seville oranges

1kg (2lb 4oz) preserving or granulated sugar

METHOD 2

This is a chunkier, darker marmalade. You can make it more so by using a combination of light and dark sugars. It is also particularly good for adding other aromatics to – whisky, rum, finely chopped stem ginger, for example.

As before, wash the fruit thoroughly. Put in the pressure cooker with 600ml (21fl oz) water. Close the lid, bring up to high pressure and cook for 10 minutes. Remove from the heat and allow to drop pressure naturally. Test that it is done – you should be able to pierce the skin of the fruit easily with the handle end of a wooden spoon.

Remove the fruit from the pressure cooker, but do not discard the liquid. When they are cool enough to handle, cut the oranges in half and scoop out the membrane and seeds. Push through a sieve to extract as much liquid as possible and add back to the pressure cooker. Tie the remains into a muslin (cheesecloth) parcel and drop into the pressure cooker.

Shred or dice the orange skin with a sharp knife. Add to the strained liquid along with the sugar. Heat gently, stirring until the sugar has dissolved, then proceed as opposite.

VARIATION

My favourite flavour for this can be found in my *Citrus* book – Dark and Stormy marmalade. Replace half the sugar with dark muscovado sugar, add the zest and juice of 2 limes, 100g (3½oz) finely chopped stem ginger and finish by stirring in a couple of measures of rum and a dash of Angostura bitters.

PASSION FRUIT CURD

MAKES AROUND 350G (12OZ)

2 eggs

225g (8oz) caster (superfine) sugar

Contents of 4 passion fruit, around 200g (7oz)

40g (1½oz) butter

Discovering exactly how quickly and easily curds can be made in the pressure cooker was such a game-changer for me – I still can't believe quite how well it works. And this recipe feels even more miraculous in terms of time saved. I was always put off by the need to sieve passion fruit before making curd with them – it is really difficult to get all the pulp from around the seeds as it can be stringy and slippery and just doesn't want to shift. But then it struck me that as curd needs sieving after cooking anyway, why not just do it all at the end? Once the passion fruit have been cooked in the pressure cooker, the pulp comes straight off – much less wastage, much less hassle, much, much quicker.

This is quite a small amount and you can increase as much as you like, but you can also reduce by half if you want some curd very quickly, as a topping. The beauty of a recipe like this is that the short time makes doing even a tiny amount worthwhile.

Put the eggs and sugar in a heatproof bowl and beat together to combine. Scoop the contents of the passion fruit into the bowl along with the butter. Cover the bowl with baking paper or foil.

Put 3cm (1¼in) water in the base of your pressure cooker, then add a trivet. Balance the bowl on top, using the foil handles (see page 11) if it is a tight fit and you think it might be tricky to remove. Close the lid and bring up to high pressure.

Cook for 10 minutes at high pressure, then remove from the heat and allow to drop pressure naturally. Remove the bowl from the cooker, then push the contents through a sieve. Leave to cool or immediately transfer to a sterilized jar. It will keep in the fridge for several weeks.

VARIATIONS

For citrus curd, use around 75ml (2½fl oz) citrus juice, plus the zest of 1 fruit for the quantities of eggs, sugar and butter above.

For berries (blackberries, blackcurrants, raspberries work best), you will need 200g (7oz) fruit, plus the juice of ½ lemon or lime.

MANGO CHUTNEY

MAKES 1.3KG (3LB)

1.2kg (2lb 11oz) semi-ripe or ripe mangoes, skinned and diced

200g (7oz) sultanas (golden raisins) or raisins (optional)

1 onion, diced

1 red pepper, diced

1 Scotch bonnet, very finely chopped (seeds optional)

4 garlic cloves, finely chopped

25g (1oz) piece ginger, very finely chopped or grated

1 large sprig of thyme

2 bay leaves

300ml (10½fl oz) cider vinegar

1 tsp salt

1 tsp finely ground white pepper

½ tsp ground allspice

1 tsp nigella seeds

500g (1lb 2oz) light soft brown sugar

A good example of how a pressure cooker can speed up the process of chutney making, as it will soften everything in a fraction of the time, before you get down to the business of stirring and reducing. Use the same method for making any type of chutney.

This is closer to a Caribbean-style chutney than an Indian one and will also work if you replace some of the mango with pineapple.

Put all the fruit, vegetables, chilli, garlic, ginger and herbs in your pressure cooker and cover with the cider vinegar. Add the salt and spices. Close the lid and bring up to high pressure. Adjust the heat to maintain high pressure and cook at high pressure for 5 minutes. Fast release.

Add the sugar and stir on a low heat until the sugar has dissolved. Simmer slowly, stirring regularly, until the chutney has reduced and thickened – a good indication of readiness is if you can clear a path along the base of the cooker with your wooden spoon.

Leave to cool for 15 minutes and then give it another stir. Ladle into sterilized jars and seal down when completely cool. Leave somewhere cool and dark for at least 6 weeks to allow the flavours to mellow. Keep refrigerated once opened.

PRESSURE-SOAKED DRIED FRUIT

This is a very useful method for any time you need to soak fruit. I rarely bother to soak anything overnight any more, I just put the fruit in the pressure cooker with an equal weight of liquid – alcohol, tea, juice, even water – bring up to pressure, remove from the heat and leave to drop pressure naturally. It is simple as that and you will find that the fruit will be plump, glossy and will have absorbed most, if not all, of the liquid. Use it for your Christmas pudding, for cakes or add sugar and more liquid and use as a topping for everything from rice pudding to yogurt or ice cream.

The simple rule to follow is use equal amounts of fruit to liquid – this will mean that most of the liquid will be absorbed.

HERE ARE A FEW EXAMPLES

Cranberries or Raisins with Oloroso or Marsala – Really good with the Brussels sprouts on page 259 or added to the cake on page 320.

Dried Fruit with Tea – Useful for any kind of tea bread such as Bara Brith. It works best with currants, sultanas, raisins and prunes. Vary the type of tea as much as you like – Earl Grey is lovely for anything you might want to add citrus zest to. Either brew the tea first or put teabags/wrapped loose-leaf tea in the pressure cooker with water.

Raisins with Spices and Rum – Add 1 vanilla pod, cinnamon stick, allspice berries and mace in a bouqet garni or stir in dried spices. Stir in 25g (1oz) dark soft brown sugar for every 100g (3½oz) raisins after cooking, along with an extra tablespoon of rum.

Prunes in Armagnac – Use equal amounts of strong tea and Armagnac or any other brandy and add a little more Armagnac after cooking.

Figs in Port and Orange Juice – Use double the amount of port to figs and add 2 tablespoons of honey and the juice of 1 orange – this will give you a syrup around the figs.

PREPARING JUICE FOR PRESERVES

The pressure cooker can really help up your game when making preserves – the high-pressure steaming seems to intensify flavour as well as help break down the fruit to extract as much flavour as possible. To make any kind of jam (jelly), simply replace the initial simmering of fruit with a quick blast at high pressure instead. Berries will often burst in the time it takes to get up to pressure, most diced orchard fruits will soften in 1 minute, depending on how ripe they are.

If you want to extract juice from fruit to make jellies, cordials, syrups and liqueurs, there are several options – see the different methods on the following pages.

METHOD 1

This gives a diluted juice, in useful quantities for making jellies and some cordials... It takes no time at all in terms of cooking and prep, but longer in terms of straining.

Weigh your fruit. For very ripe fruit, add half the amount of liquid again, for unripe fruit, use equal quantities. Prepare the fruit – berries can be left whole, orchard fruits roughly chopped, unpeeled and cored. Firmer-fleshed fruits, including pineapple, cucumber and squashes, are better roughly puréed.

Put in the pressure cooker with the water and any aromatics, then bring up to high pressure. Do zero minute, natural release for very ripe berries; up to 5 minutes for fairly firm apples, pears and quinces. Firm, whole rosehips will take 10 minutes and will need mashing after cooking.

Strain through a scalded jelly (jello) bag or a sieve lined with muslin (cheesecloth) and use in your recipe.

THYME AND CHILLI JELLY

This is a quick example of a savoury jelly (jello) that you can adapt for any aromatic or flavour. Add bouquet garnis and spices when you pressure cook and stir in finely chopped herbs at the end. Take 1kg (2lb 4oz) Bramley apples and roughly chop – peel, core and all. Add to the pressure cooker with 1 large sprig of thyme, a few allspice berries and 1 Scotch bonnet chilli you have pierced all over with a knife tip. Add 1 litre (35fl oz) of water. Cook and strain as described above. Measure the amount of liquid and use 450g (1lb) sugar for every 600ml (21fl oz) liquid. Put in a saucepan and stir until the sugar has dissolved, then boil rapidly until setting point is reached (a temperature of 105°C/221°F), or the saucer test – chill a saucer, drop a little of the boiled liquid on to it; if it wrinkles and sets as it cools, it is ready. Leave to stand and stir to disperse any foam that may have formed on the top, then add finely chopped thyme and Scotch bonnet. Decant into jars. Stir regularly while cooling to make sure the thyme and chilli are evenly dispersed.

METHOD 2

This is a gentler method that still needs straining but gives you clearer, undiluted juice. Put your fruit in a bowl that will fit in your pressure cooker. Cover with clingfilm (plastic wrap). Put the bowl on a trivet or on a folded up piece of fabric and add 250ml (9fl oz) water. Bring up to high pressure and cook for 5 minutes for ripe berries; up to 15 minutes for orchard fruits. Leave to drop pressure naturally. The juice will have seeped out of the fruit and can be strained as on page 344. If you want to avoid straining, you can put the fruit in a percolated insert or line a bowl with muslin (cheesecloth) so it can be lifted straight out after cooking.

BLACKBERRY AND LIME CORDIAL

Add the Microplaned zest of 1 lime to 1kg (2lb 4oz) blackberries. Cook and strain the liquid as described above. Measure the liquid and transfer to a saucepan. Use 350g (12oz) granulated sugar for every 500ml (17fl oz) liquid. Stir on a low heat until the sugar has dissolved, then add the juice of 1 lime and and optional 1 tablespoon of citric acid to help preserve it. Decant into sterilized bottles. Store in the fridge for several weeks once opened and serve with iced and/or sparkling water.

TEAS AND OTHER INFUSIONS

This is another one that I was sceptical about, but actually there are sound reasons for infusing under pressure rather than simmering or steeping. Firstly, time – long infusions are done in the time it takes for your cooker to come up to pressure and naturally release. Secondly, cost – putting aside the time and fuel spent simmering vs pressure cooking, pressure cookers extract flavour more efficiently, so your ingredients will go further. Finally, the finished result – which will be close to a cold infusion rather than steeped tea, mainly because there will be more clarity and flavour but less tannic bitterness. This is what sold it for me. For example, I will make a large batch of iced tea and will only need 1 teabag for 2 litres (70fl oz) of water, along with the zest of a lemon and a chopped up peach if I have it. This will work with all kinds of other aromatics too – add mint for Moroccan mint tea. Plus as the tannins are not so pronounced, I find I need less sweetener too.

CHAI

MAKES 1.5 LITRES (52FL OZ)

2 cloves

1 blade mace

1 tsp cardamom pods

1 tsp black peppercorns

10g (¼oz) piece ginger, sliced

2 cinnamon sticks

1 tonka bean (optional)

1–2 teabags or 1 tbsp loose leaf tea

50g (1¾oz) light soft brown sugar

500ml (17fl oz) whole milk

This would normally take 30 minutes of simmering, plus a couple of hours infusing – so quite time consuming when your family can go through a batch daily as mine can. Instead, you will only need to infuse for as long as it takes for the pressure cooker to drop pressure, making it more or less instant.

Put the spices and tea into your pressure cooker and add 1 litre (35fl oz) of water. Close the lid and bring up to pressure, then allow to drop pressure naturally. Stir in the sugar and milk, then return to high pressure. Again, leave to drop pressure naturally. Strain into a clean jug or saucepan and serve.

CARIBBEAN SORREL OR HIBISCUS DRINK

MAKES AROUND 1 LITRE (35FL OZ)

75g (2½oz) dried hibiscus, sorrel or dried rosehips

1 cinnamon stick, lightly crushed

1 tsp allspice berries, lightly crushed

3 cloves

25g (1oz) piece ginger, thinly sliced (optional)

300g (10½oz) granulated or caster (superfine) sugar

Zest and juice of 1 lime

1 tsp citric acid (optional)

This is an example of how you can use dried ingredients to make cordials or liquid for jellies (jellos) and sorbets. It is known as a Christmas drink throughout much of the Caribbean as that is when the sorrel plant flowers, but you can buy it dried here, usually as hibiscus. It is as tart as cranberries, so does need added sweetness.

Put the hibiscus, sorrel or rosehips into the pressure cooker with all the spices and lime zest. Pour over 750ml (26fl oz) water. Close the lid and bring up to pressure. Cook for 2 minutes and leave to drop pressure naturally. Strain through a sieve, pushing through as much liquid as you can and transfer to a saucepan. Add the sugar, lime juice and citric acid, if using, and stir until the sugar has dissolved. Decant into sterilized bottles. Once opened, store in the fridge for several weeks.

LEMON BARLEY WATER

MAKES AROUND 750ML (26FL OZ)

100g (3½oz) barley

Zest of 1 lemon, lime or orange or few slices of ginger or a pandan leaf

Pinch of salt

Juice of 1 lemon (optional)

Sugar or honey, to taste

I often make this before I cook barley for other dishes as it is literally a drink and a dish for the price of one.

Take the barley and rinse it thoroughly. Put in your pressure cooker with 1 litre (35fl oz) of water, then bring up to high pressure. Cook for 2 minutes. Allow to drop pressure naturally for 5 minutes, then release any remaining pressure and strain. Put the liquid back in the pressure cooker, add the citrus zest, ginger or pandan leaf and salt. Bring up to high pressure again, then immediately remove from the heat and leave to drop pressure naturally. Strain and add the lemon juice, if you like, and sweeten with sugar or honey to taste. Cook the barley in salted water for just 15 minutes and use in any savoury recipes.

INDEX

ACKNOWLEDGEMENTS

This book has been a labour of love and one I have wanted to write for a very long time. It was made possible by wonderful Sarah Lavelle – thank you, Sarah, for understanding why I believed a second pressure cooker book was necessary. Thank you to everyone else who worked on it – Katherine Keeble and Emma Marijewycz at Quadrille, all the hardworking and talented people on the photoshoot – Andrew Hayes-Watkins who not only has a brilliant eye but is a joy to work with, Lola Milne, Sonali Shah and Hattie Arnold who stepped in and got to grips with pressure cooking very quickly and I have to also mention Marina Filippelli who was very much there in spirit. And thank you to Vicky Orchard for keeping the editing process (on my side at least), relatively stress-free.

Since my first book on pressure cooking was published, I have been grateful for the number of vocal and enthusiastic people who have embraced and recommended it – it has been an amazing word-of-mouth experience. The same people have offered encouragement, support and a healthy dose of inquisitiveness during the writing process of this book, which has been a huge boost, especially during the endless lockdowns when I felt it would never be finished. So many thanks to Bee Wilson, Thane Prince, Hattie Ellis (thanks for all the chats around sustainability and recipe feedback), Deborah Robertson, Annie Gray, John Hassay, Melanie Jappy, Stefano Arturi, Lesley Mackley, Ella McSweeney, Sheila Dillon, Xanthe Clay, Christine McFadden, Melissa Cole, Maria Elia, Grant Hawthorne, Alastair Instone, Carl Legge, Mark Diacono, Nicola Miller and Linda Duffin, Julia Pal, Jennifer Middleton, Isobel and Fiona Kirkpatrick, Naomi Knill (for great feedback on recipes too), Jenni Nichols, Gina Navato, Jonathan and Alison Redding of Norfolk Gin, Alom Shaha, Annie Levy and Joanna Cary. Sarah Pettegree and Jane Stewart both deserve particular thanks for bringing me back to Norfolk to demo (thanks for giving up your kitchen, Jane!), for recipe feedback and, in Sarah's case, for indefatigable promotion of my pressure cooker writing. Thank you to you all and to absolutely everyone else who has ever asked me a pressure cooking question – your curiosity has really helped me test the boundaries of what is possible and so really informed this book.

A special thanks to Maria Bravo, electric pressure cooker expert (please check out her Feisty Tapas website and her Facebook pages, they are excellent), who has recommended my recipes far and wide as well as being an excellent sounding board when talking electric pressure cookers.

Thanks to Jenny Linford and Jinny Johnson – the two people I feel I can always call and who always give me good advice. The process of writing a cookery book would be much lonelier without you both. And the same applies to the best of agents, Clare Hulton. Thanks also to Diana Henry for general food writing advice.

Finally, thanks to my family – my sister-in-law Andreia for opening my eyes to the genius of pressure cooking all those years ago, my parents for plugging my books all round the Mani and (in the case of my mother) doing some recipe testing too, and Shariq, Adam and Lilly for always being hungry – all the inspiration I need to create good food, fast.

Managing Director: Sarah Lavelle
Editor: Vicky Orchard
Senior Designer: Katherine Keeble
Typesetter: Seagull Design
Photographer: Andrew Hayes-Watkins
Food Stylist: Lola Milne
Food Stylist Assistants: Sonali Shah and Hattie Arnold
Prop Stylist: Rebecca Newport
Head of Production: Stephen Lang
Senior Production Controller: Nikolaus Ginelli

Published in 2022 by Quadrille, an imprint of Hardie Grant Publishing

Quadrille
52–54 Southwark Street
London SE1 1UN
quadrille.com

Cataloguing in Publication Data: a catalogue record for this book is available from the British Library.

Text © Catherine Phipps 2022
Design © Quadrille 2022
Photography © Andrew Hayes-Watkins 2022

ISBN 978 1 78713 532 1

Printed in China

FSC
www.fsc.org
MIX
Paper from responsible sources
FSC™ C020056